TABLE OF CONTENTS

INTRODUCTION 9
Fridays, Fish sandwiches, Welcome Mats and Dandelions

CHAPTER 1 19
Setting the Table—What Is (And Isn't) Hospitality

CHAPTER 2 29
Las Posadas—A Place of Welcome

CHAPTER 3 39
"You Prepare a Table Before Me..."
—The God of Relational Hospitality—Part 1

CHAPTER 4 57
A Woman, A Well and A Holy Welcome

CHAPTER 5 71
"Bearing With One Another..."—
The God of Relational Hospitality—Part 2

CHAPTER 6 85
A Good Neighbor and a Godly Welcome

CHAPTER 7 101
Entertaining Angels—Welcome as Worship

CHAPTER 8 119
"And You Welcomed Me..."—Whatever My Need

CHAPTER 9 .... **129**
"When Peace Like a River…"
–Welcoming Adversity When Life Hurts

CHAPTER 10 .... **151**
Putting Out the Welcome Mat–Hospitality and Households of Faith

CHAPTER 11 .... **167**
Welcoming Those Who Are Late to the Party

CHAPTER 12 .... **181**
The Hospitable Host and The Welcome Guest

CHAPTER 13 .... **193**
Welcome, Barriers and Boundaries

CHAPTER 14 .... **211**
Welcome Refreshment

CHAPTER 15 .... **233**
A Welcome Opportunity

CHAPTER 16 .... **249**
Welcoming Ties That Bind

CHAPTER 17 .... **263**
The Uncomfortable "Yes"–When Welcome Is a Challenge

CHAPTER 18 .... **281**
The Welcome Discipline of a "Two-Question" God

CHAPTER 19 .... **297**
God's Warm Welcome–To His People, Through His People

CHAPTER 20 .... **311**
God's Welcoming Embrace

CONCLUSION **323**
Welcome Home

NOTES **337**
Discussion Starters

ENDNOTES **345**

> With love and appreciation to my parents, Don and Lynette, who were the first people to model for me the love of God in Christ, and regularly extended hospitality to others. With deepest affection to my children, Addisyn, Chloe, Brett, and Tressa, who sacrificed much time away from me, so I could dive into God's Word and develop this project to its fullest potential. They continue to model for me what the love and support of Jesus looks like to His people, never failing to encourage me with the words, "How do we eat an elephant? One bite at a time." And most of all to my wife, Leslie, without whose love, sacrifice, encouragement, determination and Christlikeness, I would never have completed this project. I do not deserve the sacrificial love she lavishes upon me. She shows me Christ's hospitality every day. "Many women have done excellently, but you surpass them all."
> —**Proverbs 31:29**

> Put on then, as God's chosen ones, holy and beloved, compassionate hearts, kindness, humility, meekness, and patience, bearing with one another and, if one has a complaint against another, forgiving each other; as the Lord has forgiven you, so you also must forgive. And above all these put on love, which binds everything together in perfect harmony.
> —**Colossians 3:12–14**
>
> Therefore welcome one another as Christ has welcomed you, for the glory of God.
> —**Romans 15:7**
>
> Do not neglect to show hospitality to strangers, for thereby some have entertained angels unawares.
> — **Hebrews 13:2**
>
> I planted, Apollos watered, but God gave the increase.
> —**1 Corinthians 3:6**
>
> We do not draw people to Christ by loudly discrediting what they believe, by telling them how wrong they are and how right we are, but by showing them a light that is so lovely that they want with all their hearts to know the source of it.
> —**Madeleine L'Engle,**
> *Walking on Water: Reflections on Faith and Art*

INTRODUCTION
Fridays, Fish sandwiches, Welcome Mats and Dandelions

veryone has powerful childhood memories that have shaped them into the person they are today. For me, one of my most formative memories happened when I was ten years old. I was working for my father as a 'gopher' at the time, (you know - 'go for this', 'go for that') in his electrical contracting business. Ours was a family owned operation, right down to its employees: my brother and I were the gophers, my sister answered the phones, my mother was the accountant, bill collector and all-around glue that held the business together, and Dad was the CEO (Chief Electrical One-man-band).

Our family business work fleet consisted of one F-250 truck that had been modified to serve as our mobile office/electrical supply store/break room/toolbox when we were on the road. It was also ground zero where Dad's business was run: be it repairing water wells in the field, making house calls to fix a shorted out electrical plug, fixing a wiring harness in a slaughterhouse or wiring in a new home. Dad made sure that he made the most of every single moment of his workday – right down to whether he sat or stood at a work site (spoiler alert: Dad *never* sat on the job).

Dad was, and still is, the hardest working man I've ever known. He lost his left foot in a freak construction accident when he was a child, which shaped the rest of his life in learning how to adapt to the world around him. It absolutely impacted his will to work harder than anyone else, to prove he was just as capable as anyone. If Dad caught my brother or I finding an empty paint bucket, turning it upside down and using it as a makeshift chair to take a load off, he would march up to us and say, "Son, if I can work standing up on *one* leg, you're *not* sitting down with *two*!" He was very proud of what he had accomplished in his life, telling us on more than one occasion, "If someone were to ask me, 'What did you do today?', I can say, 'Get in the truck, and I'll show you.'" I'm forever grateful for his work ethic and it deeply shaped my own.

Even though his love for electrical contracting ultimately didn't rub off on me (my brother would prove to be blessed with that skill – I still worry about burning down the house, like most of you, when I play with electricity), I wouldn't take for the 'gopher time' spent with my Dad. Because, while I had no desire to do electrical work, almost daily I got to have exclusive, one-on-one access to my father; whether it was driving from one job to another or working side by side, we did it as father and son.

I learned about his joys and sorrows, his family history and who impacted his life. I got to hear regular renditions of his quirky pearls of wisdom, later dubbed by the family as 'Dad-isms'. A favorite of his was, "Can't never could do nothin' and beat couldn't till he could." If you can decipher that one for me, let me know. But the only reason he shared that Dad-ism more than others, was due to the impact his grandfather had on him – who, as it turns out, coined that 'Dad-ism' before Dad did. Most of all, I witnessed the tremendous heart my father had for sharing hospitality.

Which brings us to *Fridays – Fish sandwiches –* and *Miss Mable*. Three things that I'll forever associate with the heart of my father.

Miss Mable was African American and in her late-80s. She lived in the part of town that was commonly referred to as 'The Flats' – a derogatory term that symbolized the invisible racial boundary of 9th Street, where white people lived on one side of it and the majority of Hispanics and African-Americans in our town lived on the other.

Miss Mable's daily routine would be to walk from her house to visit her older brother, who lived in our town's sole nursing home, to take him a home cooked lunch, feed it to him and discuss the soap opera, *Days of Our Lives.* You could often find her walking Division Street, a main artery in my town, whether it was rain or shine, hot or cold, dressed in a dark modest skirt, blazer, beret and dress shoes. A true Southern Belle, marching with purpose, head down against the traffic and the ever-present West Texas wind; typically carrying a crock pot and plastic Wal-Mart bag with utensils and napkins inside.

While one had to admire her determination, the effort to do this every day was daunting: her brother's nursing home was clear on the other side of town – easily a three-mile walk one way, so even if you were young and in good shape it would have been a good stretch of the legs. No doubt this daily hike was an excruciating ordeal for someone in their 80s, hunched over with osteoarthritis, worn down by the passage of time and a life that had been mostly unforgiving. But love has a way of overcoming pain and inconvenience.

Miss Mable's routine was fairly well known in my hometown of roughly six thousand souls. And yet, countless cars would drive past her on Division Street without so much as a pump of the brakes to acknowledge the elderly lady's presence. The combination of caution by the drivers and an all-too-present awareness of Miss Mable's skin color meant that she spent many three-mile walks carrying her crockpot and plastic bag.

Unless my Dad happened to be driving down Division Street.

If Dad saw the little Southern Belle walking along the highway, he turned on his caution blinkers and pulled to the shoulder. He would roll down the window and say, "Afternoon, Miss Mable! Need a ride?" Miss Mable would gladly accept and that was my unspoken que to get out, hold the truck door open for her and help her with her bags. She'd sit in the middle as Dad drove, talking about the oppressive West Texas heat or freezing wind chill, depending on the time of year - her tiny frame barely touching either of us in the confines of the cab. Dad would pull into the nursing home, we'd help her with her bags and Miss Mable would express her thanks in her lovely Southern belle accent, while Dad gave her a hug.

We'd go about our normal work routine for about an hour, where the unspoken rule among us was to swing by the nursing home to pick up Miss Mable. The same pattern of loading her up in the truck would repeat itself and then we'd make our way to Sonic to get Miss Mable a drink. But if it was a Friday, that was the best day of all for Miss Mable. Because that meant something special was available at Sonic that wasn't ordinarily on the menu. A fish sandwich.

Now, I have no love for fish sandwiches. My days spent as a Roman Catholic had burned me out on eating fish on Fridays or any other day. But for Miss Mable, she *lived* for them. And Dad knew it by getting to know her as they rode together in his truck. So, he would ask for the fish sandwich special and an unsweet iced tea, hand them to the little old lady in the middle of our cab and we'd be on our way to her house. They'd be chatting and enjoying each other's company the whole way, until we offloaded her at her home. Then we went about our workday, again.

Dad did all this and more: whether it was taking time out of his day to drop off items at our church for the Christmas program, helping a random teenage girl whose car wouldn't start, or buying an extra BBQ sandwich for an old high school friend who was down on his luck. I regularly saw him going to one elderly widow's home, who was convinced that her oven was broken. Dad knew it was just a circuit breaker that had tripped, so he'd reset the breaker, smile at her, and say, 'No charge.' They went through the usual routine of the widow insisting to pay Dad and he insisting it was no trouble. Then she'd laugh, give him a hug and we'd be on our way to the next job. A lesser man would have billed her for his time, because our world teaches that 'time is money.' But my father was *not* a lesser man. For him, *all* people were worth his time.

And I was watching... listening... learning.

If you were to bring up these stories to my Dad, today, I doubt he'd remember all of them. That's because, when you're giving of yourself every day – your heart isn't keeping score.

To this day, I couldn't tell you how long it took to pick Miss Mable up, drop her off, pick her up again, take her to Sonic and drop her back at home. But I can tell you the things I learned from my Dad along the way: that real men take care of the weaker among us, that people are called to make time for people, that God sees all skin colors as the beautiful kaleidoscope of His design, and that making time for someone is never an inconvenience – it's a *calling*. My father modeled a man who answered the call and took the time to welcome people into his world. And I was a richer son and a better man by getting a literal 'front row seat' in the cab of his truck, to witness hospitality in action on a daily basis.

WELCOME MATS AND DANDELIONS

My mother once spent weeks looking for the perfect welcome mat for our home – and to Dad's shock, she settled on a mat that had two huge smiling frogs on it with the words, "Welcome to Our Pad" in bright yellow letters across the top. She told our family that the bright letters on the mat would get peoples' attention. Dad thought the big smiling frogs would have done the trick. Like that welcome mat - there was *nothing* subtle about Mom. Ever the extrovert and social butterfly, she loved the color yellow, a color that reflected her bright soul that illuminated the lives she touched. Mom's infectious smile, joyful laughter and 'sunny-side-up' perspective on life drew you in and warmed your heart. If you met my mother - you weren't a stranger to her for long.

I was blessed with a mother that lived hospitality. I recall each December my mother asking me and my siblings to pack up our gently used toys to gift them to needy children. And she went through the bags to make sure we were giving away good toys. I remember her offering aide to a blind boy who had gotten lost in a park on a hot summer in July. She made sure he got home but not before giving him a big glass of her signature 'grape flavored slushie-Kool-Aid.'

I loved books as a child, so Mom's practice was to take me to bookstores when I'd saved up enough money. At one bookstore, a kind man who worked there patiently helped me find Tarzan books – an obsession for me when I was little. When he kneeled down to get at my eye level and show me a book, Mom happened to notice that he had a hole in his shoe. It was obvious he was struggling to make ends meet but did his best to look professional. When we went to the counter to pay, Mom gave him a fifty dollar 'tip' to thank him for his kindness to me. We were not a wealthy family by any means, and this was fifty dollars in '1980s money.' Only later, when I became a man, did I fully appreciate the sacrifices Mom made to show kindness to other people.

Mom graciously welcomed the random friends I'd bring by for dinner – once housing and feeding my entire college youth group for a weekend. She would take time to bake a pie without notice to deliver to a social event at the church. She regularly went to the nursing home in town to visit friends and family – just because they had no one to talk to.

Since Mom loved the color yellow, I wanted to make sure she had that color around her. Some of my earliest childhood memories were of me going into our backyard or across the street to the vacant lot and picking the yellow dandelions that grew there in the spring and summertime. Of course, when you're six years old, you don't think about the delicate process of pulling the stem along *with* the flower, so I'd often come home with handfuls of yellow dandelion heads. If I happened to put some forethought in to it that day, I'd bring with me a little white Corning ware bowl with painted blue flowers on the side of it, to hold the dandelions I'd discovered on my excursions.

Every time – *every* time – that I showed up with my decapitated yellow wildflowers, either in hand or in my little bowl, Mom would get so excited and say, "Oh, how *beautiful*! I know just the place for them." She would set them either in the bay window above the sink so she could "Look at them while she washed dishes" or set them on the dinner table as "The perfect place setting." Which, of course, made me want to find even *more* dandelions. I've been a sucker for praise, ever since.

In fact, my efforts were often rewarded by Mom making my dandelions a center-stage place setting when people came over. Mom would point to the little Corning ware bowl with the painted blue flowers on the side and with a flourish of her arm, say, "Look at what Rance picked for me, today! Aren't they *beautiful*!" Mom showed me that my little gestures were *never* little, to her. She gave me one of my first tastes of the immeasurable worth that a thoughtful gesture of the heart could make to people.

Both my parents were regular hosts on most weekends for family gatherings, Thanksgiving and Christmas gatherings, leading Christmas caroling at the nursing home and at the homes of shut-ins, hosting games of Shanghai on Friday nights with friends and family – their card game of choice. It was routine to have the occasional random person stop by our driveway - be it to visit, to drop something off, pick something up or just pull up in their cars and say hello. I'll forever be grateful for the lavish hospitality I witnessed from my parents, in a home that wasn't perfect, but a home that was graced by God; filled with struggles and joys, sacrifice and service, laughter and love – which extended beyond our home and permeated our everyday lives.

We live in a world today that sadly doesn't have 'Shanghai on Friday nights.' And I don't mean *card games* - I'm talking about *connection.* We live in a world that is more connected than ever with social media, FaceTime, blog posts and countless other Internet interactions. Smart watches give us instant notifications on just about everything. It's a fascinating modern world we live in and I look forward to what innovations our children will enjoy, one day. But this innovation has a dark side. The problem is we are also the most *disconnected* people in history. Studies show that depression is at an all-time high among those aged ten to twenty-nine years old. Anxiety has become one of the greatest mental health issues – for *toddlers*.

While there are several root causes to these issues, one common denominator, no matter the generation, is that while most people have plenty of experience using FaceTime, they haven't had much 'face-to-face time'. In those moments of face-to-face connection, people learn how to talk to people and how to share their life with others. They learn how to cope – with the challenges, sorrows and struggles of life, and learn they are not alone – by interacting with others. Without this vital interaction being met, we have a new generation of people who have no social skills to deal with hardship, pain and loss. No wonder we're prescribing antidepressants to pre-teens at rates unheard of just *ten years ago*. Today's world suffers from a 'poverty of relationships.' It is time for us to reclaim the connections we've lost - and the s*acredness* that takes place when I *really* know you - and you know *me*.

A WARM WELCOME

Maybe you have some great memories of your family growing up. Warm moments of welcome and extending kindness to others that continue to live in your heart. Those moments have shaped you into the person you are today, when you think of welcoming others. Perhaps you had the opposite childhood, where tension, rejection or worse dominated your early formative years. No doubt those trying times shaped you into the person you are, as well, when it comes to opening your door – and your heart, to other people.

Whether your early memories are happy or sad – open or closed off to others – people from all walks of life struggle with sharing – and receiving - hospitality. Just because you had a happy childhood with an 'open door policy' to people doesn't guarantee that you're a people-person, either. Sometimes, we're just built a certain way towards welcoming others. Maybe you know someone who seems to be a total 'Rockstar' when it comes to hosting a party and you think, "There is no way I could *ever* do that. I break out in cold sweats just thinking about *attending* those parties." So, that perception has led to you not entertaining the notion of 'entertaining'.

Let me say from the start that, wherever you're at in your life and whatever your thoughts are about welcoming others, I don't have a secret agenda, here. I'm not going to try to use our time together to make you be someone you're not. Everyone has to make their own way in relating to others in this world. But if you stick with me, you may find that what you thought was hospitality – *never was.* And that changes everything, in all the ways that truly matter in this life.

This book is a one-stop-shop kind of book – no extra study guide or video series to purchase. All the discussion starters and discussion questions are right here – including a Notes section at the end for your personal thoughts. That way, whether you're reading this book on your own devotionally or gathering in a small group, you'll be able to participate however you like. I'd suggest taking a notebook with you, though, for deeper note taking or discussion thoughts.

My prayer (because I've been praying for you and putting these words together for you long before you opened this book) is that you'll consider taking this journey with me. I believe you will find a refreshing view of God's Word that will broaden your perspective when it comes to extending welcome in your life – maybe even lightening your load a little. I'm convinced our struggles with hospitality begin with a misunderstanding of what hospitality was meant to be. Opening the door of your heart to welcome people doesn't require a fresh set of paint, new cabinets and flatware—it only takes a fresh *perspective*—and that happens when we see what God has to say about welcoming people, using His eyes to be aware of what He is doing in our world and then, trusting the Holy Spirit's leading to contemplate what that might look like in your life.

That's it. No agendas, no special place settings, no 'one more thing' to do. Who knows? Maybe all it takes is a Friday and a fish sandwich?

So, consider joining me at my table for a while and seeing where God leads. You don't need to bring a thing – just yourself (and maybe this book – otherwise the conversation will be a bit one-sided). Pull up a chair and I'll put on the coffee, as we explore God's welcome, together. Sugar and creamer are by the coffee pot, if you need it. There's plenty of room at the table for you. I look forward to our conversation…of getting to *really* know you… and you knowing *me*… as we seek to know the heart of God together, and His open, waiting arms. So, welcome home! And welcome to the journey.

> Be present at our table, Lord;
> Be here and ev'rywhere adored;
> Thy creatures bless, and grant that we
> May feast in paradise with Thee.
>
> **—Lutheran Service Book**
> *775, public domain*

CHAPTER 1
Setting the Table -
What Is (And Isn't) Hospitality

Matthew 25:35
'For I was hungry and you gave me food,
I was thirsty and you gave me drink,
I was a stranger and you welcomed me...'

SETTING THE TABLE

Olive Garden's advertising catchphrase for years was, 'When you're here - you're family.' The implied result from their slogan was that, if you went to Olive Garden, you would have a great dining experience - because you would *feel welcome.*

If you've ever eaten at Olive Garden, you certainly get the feeling of being welcomed. Before you get to the front door of the restaurant, an attendant is holding open the door for you, inviting you inside. The attire of the servers is semi-formal, with vests and ties, visually conveying you are about to experience something special. Once you are inside, a second attendant welcomes you and takes down your table requests and the number of guests eating with you. Another attendant welcomes you and leads you to your seat. You are made to feel special – and the result is a feeling of welcome. For the American consumer, this is the definition of hospitality – and that is no accident.

Creating an atmosphere where people feel welcome is big business. The United States Hotel Industry alone generated a revenue of 208 billion dollars in 2017[1]. And creating a place of welcome has generated interest on the home front, as well. This is best shown in the rapidly growing home entertainment industry. Martha Stewart led the charge in this field in the early 1980s, eventually being labeled a 'Lifestyle Guru' via her television shows, websites and her self-titled magazine, *Martha Stewart Home*[2]. Stewart's website currently has an entire section dedicated to teaching people to make their homes a reflection of the best that the service industry has to offer in terms of hospitality[3].

While the business model of hospitality makes a person feel welcome, it avoids deep connection and relationships. So, what we see play out in society is not necessarily the art of hospitality, so much as the secular art of 'entertaining'. We see the business world's core motivations to entertaining being transparently expressed in the advice dispensed by so-called 'experts' towards the average person desiring to host others in their home. Martha Stewart, famous for her views on entertaining, is quoted as saying:

"Entertaining, like cooking, is a little selfish, because it really involves pleasing yourself, with a guest list that will coalesce into your ideal of harmony, with a menu orchestrated to your home and taste and budget, with decorations subject to your own eye. Given these considerations, it has to be pleasureful."[4]

It's clear our world has many preconceived notions of what hospitality is. Our personal preconceived notions and experiences shape our views on this topic as well. These views impact how we live out hospitality in the home – or whether we engage other people at all.

In this chapter, we'll take a look at how we may have misunderstood the definition of hospitality as Christians and how we might reclaim the biblical definition again to become a more authentic community of faith.

Prayer: *Lord, as we begin this study of hospitality together, open our minds and hearts to Your truth, remembering that You are the Author of true hospitality. Amen*

TABLE TALK

Take a moment to discuss the following together:

1) When I hear the word 'hospitality,' I think it means:

2) What experiences shaped your view of hospitality?

3) What things do you hope your home will be for the ones who come over to visit?

4) What things do you hope your home will be for the people who live there?

5) Think of a time when you were the stranger or outsider – what things did someone do to make you feel welcome?

AT THE TABLE

1) **Briefly skim over Genesis 1.** How does God display acts of hospitality in creation?

2) **Briefly skim over Genesis 2.** How does God's actions display His hospitable nature?

3) **Read Genesis 2:18.** How were Adam and Eve created for community?

REFLECTION

At the very beginning of all things, the Creator and Sustainer, the Alpha and Omega, offers the first act of hospitality as He welcomed us in His first week of creation. God creates all things, in an incredibly intricate tapestry of sun, moon, stars, all manner of vegetation and living creatures. He does all this to point toward His glory, power, and majesty – but He also demonstrates His hospitable nature as He welcomed humanity into His world to live in the Garden of Eden with Him – and He provides all they need to support this body and life[5].

Adam and Eve and the Lord are a 'tri-unity' - communing together in a home built by God's own hand, living in harmony, enjoying the Creator's hospitality—truly *relational hospitality*. A holy expression of the community that existed between man and God, echoed within the Holy Trinity itself.

For God, hospitality is not about *entertaining* – hospitality is a state of *being*. It is relational hospitality. Fellowship with Him leads to fellowship with His People, which draws us into fellowship with others in our world. Relational hospitality is God opening the door of our hearts to welcome others into our lives. Instead of Olive Garden working to make people *feel welcome* – God calls us to *welcome people*.

When Jesus begins His ministry as the Son of God come to save the world, He uses hospitality and community as a means to begin His mission on earth.

4) **Read Luke 10:1-12.** What instructions does Jesus give to His disciples?

5) What does Jesus instruct the disciples to do if someone refuses to extend hospitality to them?

REFLECTION

When the disciples are going two by two in ministry, Jesus sends them to be guests in peoples' homes for several reasons:

(1) Jesus wants His disciples to depend upon hosts, even those who

are not aware of Jesus' ministry.

(2) They should be grateful to their hosts and content with what they have been provided; and

(3) The message of the Gospel and Jesus as the Christ – *not* the disciples' social standing – will be the focus in the hospitality relationships the disciples make.

How is this different from the world's view of hospitality today? What can we learn from Jesus' instructions?

6) **Read 1 Peter 2:9-10** How are Christians addressed at the very beginning of this passage? What does this say about St. Peter's understanding of the Christian community?

7) How do you respond to the truth that as a Christian, you are part of a chosen race, a royal priesthood, a holy nation?

8) What does St. Peter say the Christian community is called to do?

9) How are Christians made in to "God's own people"?

BRINGING IT HOME

Take a moment to read **Matthew 25:31-46.**

This passage of Scripture usually causes some confusion among Christians, when it comes to understanding what it means to extend Christian hospitality to others. Verse 40 calls one particular group, 'the least of these.' Most of us assume the least of these refer to the poor and the outcast of society, which is why this verse is often interpreted to mean that the best way for Christians to 'show Jesus' in the world is to care for the poor and the outcast. To be sure, the poor and outcast do need the mercy and grace of those who follow Jesus.

But is caring for the poor and outcast the *main point* of this Scripture passage?

A better way to understand the text is to first understand who are 'the least of these'.

Some people interpret this text to mean that verse 32 ties 'all the nations' to the phrase, the 'least of these'. The argument goes that Jesus is referring to His kin, the Jews, and therefore is telling us how we should treat the nation of Israel. This argument is often used to mean that our salvation depends on how we treat the modern state of Israel in our foreign policy. But Jesus nowhere refers to the Jews as His 'brothers'. Nowhere does Scripture require caring for one people group over another to be a requirement for salvation. So that interpretation doesn't work with this text.

The more common explanation of 'the least of these' in this text is that this phrase refers to the poor, the outcast and the needy. After all, who better matches the definition of the 'least of these' than the hungry, thirsty, homeless, naked, sick and imprisoned? Proponents of social justice readily grab on to this viewpoint.

The problem with this viewpoint is that it doesn't match the phrase, "the least of these *my brothers…*" While it is important that we care for the poor and all the rest, God's Word does not teach that this is a requirement for salvation. So, is there a better way to understand what 'the least of these' means?

A wise professor once told me that the best way to understand the *text* is to look at the *context*. If one passage of Scripture is unclear, then look at the surrounding text that is clearer, then look at the chapter, followed by the book. Since we're in St. Matthew's Gospel, we need to look at who else he describes in his Gospel as hungry, thirsty, homeless, naked, sick and imprisoned.

Let's take a look at **Matthew 10:1-42.**

In Matthew 10:9-10, this Gospel tell us that the disciples had no *money,* no *bag for food*, no *drink* and no *extra clothes*. In 10:11-14 it tells us the disciples had *no home* to stay in. In 10:17-20 it tells us the disciples would be *arrested* and *put in prison*. Even the order of events the disciples will face in Matthew 10:1-42 almost exactly matches the order of needs from Matthew 25:31-46.

So, it sounds like the *disciples* are the people described as 'the least of these'.

Matthew 10:40 and 42 drive home this connection, "Whoever receives you receives me, and whoever receives me receives him who sent me." "And whoever gives one of these little ones even a cup of cold water because he is a disciple, truly, I say to you, he will by no means lose his reward."

This makes a strong case that the "least of these, *my brothers...*", are the *disciples.* In fact, any time Jesus uses the term "brothers" in St. Matthew's Gospel, it is always referring to the *disciples* (see Matthew 12:48-50; 28:10).

Therefore, it becomes clear that our salvation doesn't hinge on how well we care for the poor, though caring for the poor and outcast are part of what it means to be a Christian.

Our salvation hinges on our response to the Gospel. *Belief* or *unbelief.*

The response of belief in the Gospel then impacts the welcome we extend to our brothers and sisters in Christ—*His disciples,* today. The commitment we have as God's people is to the Gospel, first, followed by our commitment to welcome one another as the Body of Christ. Extending hospitality to 'the least of these', Jesus' disciples, today.

Therefore, we are humbly called to care for one another in Christ, first, then called out from our faith communities into the community God has placed us.

Our salvation isn't the *cause* for caring for the poor and needy. It is the *result.*

This is significant, because it helps us understand the order of hospitality and welcoming as Christians.

Our first mission field is to our brothers and sisters in Christ. We often forget that part.

And just as importantly, within that mission field, are the brothers and sisters in Christ we encounter on a day-to-day basis.

THOSE PEOPLE WE CALL "FAMILY"

We are 'the least of these', who need the hospitality and welcome of our God—and by His Grace we receive it through the forgiveness of Jesus. As His forgiven people, we are then called out to welcome others with His Grace. And that calling out is first to our *families,* followed by our *church families,* and then to our *world.* This is the heart of God's welcome - *by* His people and *to* His people.

1) What difference does it make to start our discussion of the Christian community and hospitality by seeing it as a gift of God's grace?

2) Why do Christians need one another? What is the goal of all Christian community? Of Christian hospitality?

3) What do we mean when we say we belong to one another as brothers and sisters in Christ?

4) How does God making us His community change our views on hospitality? How does this shape your 'community' at home?

5) Since God is the author of hospitality and community, how does that change what hospitality and community looks like for His people?

Savior, like a shepherd lead us;
Much we need Your tender care.
In Your pleasant pastures feed us,
For our use Your fold prepare.
Blessed Jesus, blessed Jesus,
You have bought us; we are Yours.
Blessed Jesus, blessed Jesus,
You have bought us; we are Yours.

We are Yours; in love befriend us,
Be the guardian of our way;
Keep Your flock, from sin defend us,
Seek us when we go astray.
Blessed Jesus, blessed Jesus,
Hear us children when we pray.
Blessed Jesus, blessed Jesus,
Hear us children when we pray.

You have promised to receive us,
Poor and sinful though we be;
You have mercy to relieve us,
Grace to cleanse, and pow'r to free.
Blessed Jesus, blessed Jesus,
Early let us turn to You.
Blessed Jesus, blessed Jesus,
Early let us turn to You.

Early let us seek Your favor,

Early let us do Your will;
Blessed Lord and only Savior,
With Your love our spirits fill.
Blessed Jesus, blessed Jesus,
You have loved us, love us still.
Blessed Jesus, blessed Jesus,
You have loved us, love us still.

—Lutheran Service Book
711, public domain

Closing Prayer: *Lord, through Your Son, Jesus, You have made us into a people called to live as Your forgiven sons and daughters. Help us to think Your thoughts as we journey together and rediscover Your plan to welcome others as You have welcomed us. In Jesus' Name. Amen.*

CHAPTER 2
Las Posadas – A Place of Welcome

John 1:1-3, 10-12
"In the beginning was the Word,
and the Word was with God, and the Word was God.
He was with God in the beginning.
Through him all things were made;
without him nothing was made that has been made.
He was in the world, and though the world
was made through him, the world did not recognize him.
He came to that which was his own,
but his own did not receive him.
Yet to all who received him, to those who
believed in his name,
he gave the right to become children of God."

SETTING THE TABLE

Merry Christmas, everybody! Now, I know what you're thinking: "Did I just skip a chapter or something? Why are we starting a chapter on Christmas?" Maybe by the time you're reading this chapter, Christmas Day has come and gone for you. Or maybe it's on its way. Or maybe, you're taking a break from the

Christmas rush and pausing to read this book. Or maybe you're in the middle of a hot July, which is about as far from Christmas as you can get. Regardless of where you're at on the calendar, there's something magical about Christmas and the feelings that go with it,.

Mel Tormé certainly thought so. Tormé was in the middle of one of those blistering hot July days in the early 1940s, at a time when air conditioning was non-existent. Since he was a song writer, Tormé thought he'd stay cool by *thinking* cool – and what better way to cool off than to think about a cold Christmas day? So, Mel put pen to paper, and wrote down the words, "Chestnuts roasting…Jack Frost nipping…Yuletide carols… Folks dressed up like Eskimos." In forty minutes, Tormé filled in the blanks to compose one of the most played Christmas songs of all time – *The Christmas Song*. That's what happens when a cold Christmas day and great memories live in your heart.

But what about those of us who believe that the birth of the Christ-child is *more* than just a date on the calendar? How might we continue to celebrate Christmas, long after the world has said goodbye to it? I think *part* of the answer lies in the meaning behind a unique celebration that I once participated in, called: "Las Posadas".

Prayer: *Lord, as we call to mind the season of Christmas, help it to call to mind that very first Christmas, when You entered our world to welcome us to You. Amen.*

TABLE TALK

Take a moment to discuss the following together:

1) What childhood memories do you have about Christmas?

2) What experiences from Christmas have shaped your view—for good or bad—about celebrating Christmas?

3) Call to mind your most favorite Christmas of all—be it from

your childhood or when you were an adult. What made it so special?

AT THE TABLE
1) **Read Luke 2:1-20**. Who are the main characters that St. Luke points out?

2) What things have you possibly forgotten about that first Christmas?

3) Thinking of where the Holy Family stayed, what might their surroundings have been like?

REFLECTION
Las Posadas is a very old custom that began in 1587 in Mexico and it continues today in many Spanish-speaking countries. When I was a kid, I had many Hispanic friends and they allowed me to be a part of the traditions of Las Posadas. 'Posada' translated to English means 'inn', or 'a place of lodging'. All my friends and their parents would walk through their neighborhood, going from door to door. And the person answering their door would be dressed up in ancient garb and pretend to be the 'innkeeper.' We would ask the 'innkeeper' if they had any rooms available, and the innkeeper would say, "No! Go away – there's no room for you here!" and he'd shoo us away. And so, chased away from that house, we'd pray together and then journey to the next house, finally making our way to a home that would welcome us, and then enjoying treats together to end the night.

That was *our* part to play as wayward pilgrims looking for shelter. But the *innkeeper's* part really began *after* he shooed us away. After closing the door, the one dressed in the ancient garb of the innkeeper would then gather his family together, and they would read together this passage from St. John's Gospel, "[Jesus] was in the world, and though the world was made through him, the world did not recognize him. He came to that which was his own, but his *own did not receive him*. Yet to all who received him, to those who believed in his name, he gave the right to become children of God." (John 1:10-12) And then the family would kneel and pray for God's love and mercy to enter their hearts.

4) **Read Luke 2:7** How *simple* was that first Christmas?

Mary and Joseph can't find a place to stay, so more than likely they were in a cave – basically the 'starter home' of first century Judeans. Back in those days, when you were first starting out, you couldn't afford to build, and since there's very little wood in Israel, the only things you had to build with were simple stones. But before you could build, you had to save up. In the meantime, your home was very likely what already existed – a cave. So, you'd mark out one place for the family to sleep, another to eat, and another to be a makeshift pen for the animals. Then, when you could afford to build, you built on top of that cave with stones, leaving the animals more space down below. So, its highly likely that the person who let Mary and Joseph stay with them, moved them to their 'starter home' below their house. The place where the animals slept.

And remember, since there's very little wood in Israel, a manger in their day would have either been a cut out notch in a cave wall, or a depression in the floor. The manger was the place where the animals' food was placed. Which is where our Savior, Jesus, would have been laid. You can't get more simple and humble than that. Or lower. Showing all people for all time that there was *no* place too low, that our Savior wouldn't go.

5) **Read Romans 5:8** How have we 'shooed God away in our hearts'?

6) Think about the Christmases you've celebrated as an adult. What traditions have kept Jesus close to you? What traditions might be pulling your focus off of Him?

REFLECTION

In case you missed it, the innkeeper is really *you and me*. St. Luke tells us that there was no room for Jesus and Mary in the 'posada' – in the 'inn'. (Luke 2:7) But that's only *part* of what St. Luke is telling us. He's not just pointing out that the inn suffered from a lack of square feet. He's pointing out that the innkeeper suffered from a lack of room in the *heart*. On our own, we are a lot like the people who play the role of 'innkeeper' during the festival of 'Las Posadas' – sinful hearts that will not receive the Christ-child on our own, even if He were being born in our world today. More than likely, we wouldn't have the *time* or the *need* for Him beyond December 25th. The reality is, if we wait on our sinful hearts to willingly receive Jesus, then Jesus would have never been born in the first place.

So, Jesus takes it upon Himself to save our sinful hearts – and *be born*. St. Paul says, "But when the fullness of time had come, God sent forth His Son, born of woman, born under the law, to redeem those who were under the law, so that we might receive adoption as sons." (Gal 4:4-5). But our adoption would come at a terrible price. Jesus was still in Mary's womb when He heard the words from the innkeeper – "We don't have room for you here." The 'posada' of Jesus' birth shows us just how unwelcome He was to the world from the very start. If any of you have ever worked on a farm, you know what a feeding trough looks like <u>all</u> the time: it's where the farm animals <u>drool</u> while they eat! It's dusty; it's crusty and full of all kinds of filth. No parent in their right mind would *ever* place their 'bundle of joy' in something like that, unless there was no other choice. Unless they weren't welcome *anywhere else*.

The manger was a bad enough place but think about the stable where Joseph and Mary stayed. Most mothers spend *months* preparing a nursery for their baby. People hold baby showers and throw parties for their new arrival. If a binkie gets dropped on the floor, mom runs to the stove to boil it in water and sanitize it. In Mary's day, the birth of a son was cause for great celebration, too. But all she had for party favors were unclean strips of cloth to wrap her son in, as she cleared some of the manure away to make a place for him. Mary and Joseph were alone, far from home, with complete strangers for visitors. Because they weren't welcome *anywhere else.*

7) Think about your Christmas calendar. How might our Christmas plans *complicate* our lives, instead of simplifying them?

8) Think about the Christmas parties and plans you make – how might those things be simplified?

9) Have a family meeting when the season of Christmas rolls around. Come up with a plan to keep Christmas simpler. Start a morning or evening devotional for the season of Advent. Be intentional in keeping Christ at the center.

BRINGING IT HOME

When Jesus grew up, He would live to hear the threats of the Pharisees, the accusations that He wasn't God in the flesh, but had a demon in Him. His ministry was rejected from the start, even in His own village – a place He should have been welcomed. And He Himself would say, "Only in his hometown, among his relatives and in his own house is a prophet without honor." (Mark 6:4) He would feel the spit on His face, the whips on His back, the nails in His hands and feet. All these things would shout at Jesus from the top of their lungs, "*We don't have room for You here!*"

And that is the point of St. John's words to us today, "He was in the world, and though the world was made through him, the world did not recognize him. He came to that which was his own, but his own did not receive him. Yet to all who received him, to those who believed in his name, he gave the right to become children of God." Jesus doesn't wait until *you and I* are ready for him. He doesn't wait until our hearts are full of love for Him. Jesus didn't wait for something that could *never* happen – for the 'posada' of our hearts to be ready to make room for Him.

This is the real miracle of Christmas – not that the world was ready to receive Jesus, but that Jesus saw a world that was *not* ready to receive Him – *and He came anyway*. To endure everything that came with our rejection of Him.

And by His coming to a world that would not receive Him, by His suffering, death and resurrection, He gives us 'innkeepers' a new name: 'children of God'. This is the incredible gift of Christmas. And that's why, as Christians, we aren't just "Christmas People" or "Epiphany People" – we are "Easter People" – sharing our lives with others, restoring brokenness, being 'living previews' of the Resurrection – celebrating the Gospel truth that our salvation has come – Christ has come to the 'posada' of our hearts and forgiven us our sins.

And best of all – through the forgiveness that He dared to bring to a world that didn't want Him, you and I will one Day enter in to the 'posada' that Jesus is preparing for us in Glory—a new heavens and new earth (Revelation 21 and 22). And there, with Jesus as our 'eternal innkeeper' - *we* will, never, *ever* be turned away. A promise that was made—and was kept—in a cave, with animals and shepherds nearby, at ground zero of your salvation – where a dirty manger hosted the Son of God – to welcome *you*.

10) Think of your church home. What is it about your church that welcomed you?

11) Think of a time when you visited an *un*welcoming church. What made it feel that way?

12) How might God's people *unintentionally* be unwelcoming? How can we create an 'awareness of welcome' when we gather together?

13) In what ways might God's people welcome others as Christ has welcomed us in our daily lives?

> O come, O come, Immanuel,
> And ransom captive Israel
> That mourns in lonely exile here
> Tntil the Son of God appear.
>
> Rejoice! Rejoice! Immanuel
> shall come to you, O Israel.
>
> O come, Thou Key of David, come
> And open wide our heavenly home.
> Make safe the way that leads on high,
> And close the path to misery.
>
> Rejoice! Rejoice! Immanuel
> shall come to you, O Israel.
> O come, O King of nations, bind
> In one the hearts of all mankind.
> Bid all our sad divisions cease
> And be Thyself our King of Peace.

Rejoice! Rejoice! Immanuel
shall come to you, O Israel.

—Lutheran Service Book,
357, public domain

Closing Prayer: *Lord God, Your Son, Jesus, came to this world, knowing it would not receive Him – because He loved us that much. Help us as Your forgiven people, to welcome You into the manger of our hearts all year long – living Your Christmas welcome and Your forgiveness to those we encounter in our world. In Jesus' Name. Amen.*

CHAPTER 3
'You prepare a table before me...' – The God of Relational Hospitality – Part 1

Matthew 25:40
"And the King will answer them,
'Truly, I say to you, as you did it to one of the least
of these my brothers, you did it to me.'"

Psalm 23:5
"You prepare a table before me in the presence
of my enemies; you anoint my head with oil;
my cup overflows."

SETTING THE TABLE

"*God desires all to be saved and come to the knowledge of the truth.*" (1 Tim. 2:4) This is the heart of the God's Mission on earth. The Church doesn't have a Mission — but God has a *Church* for *His* Mission![6] If mission is the heart of God, then it would follow that His Church – you and me – are called to engage that Mission. Yes, God is already active in the world, but people have tons of different ideas about what God is, Who He is, and what He's come to do among us. That's where His Church—His community of people—come in.

God's mission is making Jesus Christ known through His Church. Sometimes it's through His people sharing His Word, sometimes it is through the Sacraments (how God gives His Grace to people) in our Baptism and at the Lord's Supper. That's why the most visible plan on earth where God's heart is revealed to everyone is when God's people gather as a community around Word and Sacrament. So, what God's people say and do – both verbally and non-verbally—in their church, at home and in their community—tell the story of God's welcome and hospitality to the world.

So, just what was God's original plan and purpose for hospitality among His people? As we will see, God's mission for us has been about *restoration* and *relationship.* God longed to restore us from the beginning – and you can see it all throughout the Bible. God wanted deeply in His heart to welcome us as His children – and He was willing to pay the ultimate price to make that possible.

Prayer: *Lord, from the beginning, You have been a hospitable Host. You welcomed us to this world and continue to welcome us through Your Son. Open our minds and hearts to be welcoming of one another as brothers and sisters in Christ. Help us, in turn, to be welcoming to those You place in our paths. Amen*

TABLE TALK

Take a moment to discuss the following together:

1) How has God been a 'hospitable Host' to you?

2) **Read Psalm 15:1-5 and Matt 5:23-24.** What does our relationship with one another as God's people have to do with our relationship to God?

3) Thinking about those Scriptures above, what 'heart condition' is

God asking us to be in towards our brothers and sisters? How soon should we reconcile with them?

REFLECTION

The act of living as God's community in the world is an extension of God's redemptive work through Christ, His restoration of relationships and welcoming others into the community via hospitality. The biblical story makes it clear that the *whole world* matters to God, especially fallen humanity. The Lord gathers His saved people in worship to receive His gifts of forgiveness in Word and Sacrament but He also uses His gathered people to live as a community of faith in the world — to serve as a means by which the whole world can hear of His mighty works and be gathered into Christ's saving work. This focus is echoed throughout the Psalms, which tell of God's people praising the Lord while telling others of what He has done—not just for His people, Israel, but for the whole world. Ps. 145:4 is a good example: "One generation shall commend your works to another and shall declare your mighty acts."

Martin Luther saw early on the need for connection among people and for a distinctively Christian sharing of hospitality. In fact, Luther saw this unique connection among the baptized saints of God as an extension of God's grace and mercy in the world:

> God is superabundantly generous in His grace: First, through the spoken Word… Second, through Baptism. Third, through the Sacrament of the Altar. Fourth, through the Power of the Keys. *Also, through the mutual conversation and consolation of the brethren*, 'Where two or three are gathered' (Matt. 18:20) and other such verses [esp. Rom. 1:12].[7]

Luther saw relationships as almost *sacramental* in nature – that our living and loving as a community of faith conveyed the grace of God to each other. That's a pretty amazing thing to say – and an amazing thing to contemplate. That means God's intentions for His people are to live as His redeemed community.

TABLE TALK

1) How does confessing specific sins to those you've hurt, heal people? How does confession reflect humility in our relationship with God and each other?

REFLECTION

God is all about relationships from the very beginning – literally.

From the beginning, God calls His Creation "very good."[8] This means that from the beginning, God's Creation was inherently uncorrupted, without sin, held great value to the Lord, and had a special purpose. In His creative work, God shows that He is actively engaged in His creation. By the end of the creation narrative of Genesis 1–3, and ultimately at the end of the biblical narrative, He will redeem creation and restore it through a Savior. God first prophecies of His redemptive work in Gen 3:15: "I will put enmity between you and the woman, and between your offspring and her offspring; he shall bruise your head, and you shall bruise his heel." We read of creation restored through the Savior in Rev. 21:1: "Then I saw a new heaven and a new earth, for the first heaven and the first earth had passed away, and the sea was no more."

As each day of the first five days of the creation narrative come to pass, God's Word shows us that He has been building up to something special. That special something is shared on the sixth day of creation when the focal point of His creation is revealed: man and woman made in His image: Gen. 1:26 "Then God said, "Let us make man in our image, after our likeness. And let them have dominion over the fish of the sea and over the birds of the heavens and over the livestock and over all the earth and over every creeping thing that creeps on the earth." God builds a world — a home — for His children. Through the creation act, we see that God Himself is the author and perfecter of hospitality.

God is also the author of community. Before time began, He is a living expression of community: "In the beginning, God created the heavens and the earth. The earth was without form and void, and darkness was over the face of the deep. And the Spirit of God was hovering over the face of the waters. And God said, 'Let there be light,' and there was light." (Gen. 1:1–3) God the Father is present in the creative act as well as the pre-incarnate Christ, the Word, being spoken to create,[9] and finally the Holy Spirit hovering over the waters, participating in this divine trinitarian act of creation. The Holy Trinity's interaction is quite literally a 'common unity' from the very beginning, first and foremost through the interaction of the persons of the Holy Trinity as expressed in His creative acts.

God's creation was designed for the enjoyment of Adam and Eve in the Garden of Eden, which becomes the home where God interacts with them, serving as the basis for community between God and His crowning creative achievement, man and woman. The mission of God is then given to Adam to take care of the land and guard His creation. Adam (and later, Eve) are the visual extension and representation of God's work in the world – truly the image of God.[10] The *Missio Dei* of community is also given to Adam (image of God) when Eve is created.[11] Adam's rejoicing at Eve's arrival echoes the joy of communion with God and His people when he cries out: "This at last is bone of my bones and flesh of my flesh; she shall be called Woman, because she was taken out of Man." (Gen. 2:23)

This special community of Adam and Eve in communion with God will become the gold standard for how God views the special covenant community of marriage and later referenced by Jesus as God's standard for marriage in the face of divorce, where Matthew clearly states: "[Jesus] answered, 'Have you not read that he who created them from the beginning made them male and female, and said, 'Therefore a man shall leave his father and his mother and hold fast to his wife, and the two shall become one flesh?'" (Matt. 19:4–5)

Adam and Eve and the Lord—a tri-unity—communing together in a home built by God's own hand, living in harmony, enjoying the Creator's hospitality — truly *relational hospitality* — a deep expression of the community that existed between man and God and is echoed within the Holy Trinity itself.[12]

TABLE TALK

2) If God's people are made in the image of God and called to be His image to the world, what happens if we cut off a brother or sister, instead of working through difficulties we've had with them?

3) **Read James 5:16** – what two things can bring healing when our relationships are difficult?

REFLECTION

When the guarding and stewardship of creation fails through Adam's disobedience and a part of the image of God is lost by the Fall into sin,[13] we immediately witness a broken community and hear one of the most tragic lines of the entire Bible. God is in the Garden of Eden and asks of Adam, "Where are you?"[14] This question clearly shows that community has been broken. The tri-unity of Adam, Eve, and God has collapsed. Their fellowship is lost. Not only communion with God but also the deep relationship between Adam and Eve, as evidenced by their dialogue of placing blame upon one other for their disobedience towards God, tainting all future relationships between men and women.[15] Man has become thoroughly corrupted, right down to how he interacts in relationship to community. He has no power to restore what once was.

Therefore, God takes action—in a heavenly mission to search for His people, to restore His people and to regain community with them through the sacrifice of His Son, Jesus.[16] This question by God in the Garden of Eden— "Where are you?" — is the one question that drives everything else in the Bible and even gives us the forthcoming answer within that question — that God will go to the ends of the earth, making a people for Himself by His mercy[17] and mobilizing His people to seek out and welcome all people into His community — ultimately realized through the incarnation of Jesus Christ as foretold by His prophets.[18] A Christocentric community lives out relational hospitality unlike any other community on earth.

A vivid expression of this relational hospitality is in the Book of Acts:

> And they devoted themselves to the apostles' teaching and the fellowship, to the breaking of bread and the prayers. And awe came upon every soul, and many wonders and signs were being done through the apostles. And all who believed were together and had all things in common. And they were selling their possessions and belongings and distributing the proceeds to all, as any had need. And day by day, attending the temple together and breaking bread in their homes, they received their food with glad and generous hearts, praising God and having favor with all the people. And the Lord added to their number day by day those who were being saved.[19]

TABLE TALK

4) **Re-read Acts 2:42-47.** What special characteristics are present in God's community of people?

5) **Read Ephesians 4:25-32.** What kind of problems can happen in relationships, now that we live in a fallen world? What does St. Paul say we are called to do to avoid relationship problems?

REFLECTION

God redeeming mankind begins with Adam and Eve and continues when He calls a man named Abram.[20] God calls Abram to make a great nation from him — with the sole purpose of restoring the whole world to Himself. Abram's call by God is not solely for Abram's benefit nor is it solely for the purpose of what would later become the nation of Israel. The primary goal is that by choosing Abram, he would ultimately be a blessing to the whole earth, which is fully revealed, later in Genesis. Gen. 15:5–6. "And [God] brought [Abram] outside and said, 'Look toward heaven, and number the stars, if you are able to number them.' Then he said to him, 'So shall your offspring be.' And he believed the LORD, and he counted it to him as righteousness."

Reading Gen. 12:1–3 shows who the primary actor is in redeeming the world. It is not Abram. It is God. The primary pronoun in Gen. 12:1–3 is the word, 'I.' Five times in three verses, God shows that He is the actor. Abram is passive. God is ushering in the action and making things happen. The mission of God has been and continues to be the Lord God—as the primary actor, reclaiming the whole world for Himself through a restored relationship with Him by His Son.

Genesis 12:2 and especially Abram's renaming to 'Abraham' by God in Gen. 17:5 to be the 'father of many nations,' alludes to the final restoration of the world into one community under God: "After this I looked, and behold, a great multitude that no one could number, from every nation, from all tribes and peoples and languages, standing before the throne and before the Lamb, clothed in white robes, with palm branches in their hands, and crying out with a loud voice, 'Salvation belongs to our God who sits on the throne, and to the Lamb!'" (Rev. 7:9-10)

As the Bible continues to tell the story of God's mission, the question God asked in the Garden of Eden, "Where are you?" begins to have answers. God is choosing to act and to seek out His people. From the very beginning with Abram, then Isaac and Jacob, God is the One drawing people to Himself. The Book of Genesis closes with Joseph and the enslavement of Egypt, leading to God's calling of Moses for His mission.

In the remaining books of the Pentateuch, we see key verses alluding to God's plan to create global community through the community of faith He has created. This includes reaching out with relational hospitality. We read in several places, both during and after the Exodus, of God's intentions for the world: "You yourselves have seen what I did to the Egyptians, and how I bore you on eagles' wings and brought you to myself. Now therefore, if you will indeed obey my voice and keep my covenant, you shall be my *treasured possession* among all peoples, *for all the earth is mine*; and you shall be to me a kingdom of *priests* and a *holy nation*. These are the words that you shall speak to the people of Israel."[21] "The *alien* who resides with you shall be to you as the *citizen* among you; you shall love the alien as *yourself*, for you were aliens in the land of Egypt: I am the Lord your God."[22] "You shall also love the *stranger*, for you were strangers in the land of Egypt."[23]

Several key words stand out here. God has made Israel His 'treasured possession.' Israel's salvation is completely God's action and special work with a special purpose. God then reveals what that purpose is by saying, "…for all the earth is mine." This phrase tells us that God's sole purpose for saving Israel is not *only* for Israel. God is saving Israel out of Egypt *because the whole world is at stake*!

All the world, and therefore all people, are called into relationship by God through His saving work. Israel's communal purpose is to gather the world to its doorstep, to learn of the saving work of God—living in relationship to God and one another. As a 'kingdom of priests,' they are to be a reflection of God's reconciliation to the world.

The Levites (the tribe God sets apart to be His first priests) instructed the people in the Word of God and led the people in prayer. This makes Israel a living witness to what the new life in God looks like—not only to His gathered people but also towards all people.

Deut. 4:5–7 reads, "See, I have taught you statutes and rules, as the LORD my God commanded me, that you should do them in the land that you are entering to take possession of it. Keep them and do them, for that will be your wisdom and your understanding in the sight of the peoples, who, when they hear all these statutes, will say, 'Surely this great nation is a wise and understanding people.' For what great nation is there that has a god so near to it as the LORD our God is to us, whenever we call upon him?" In Isa. 49:6 "he [God] says: 'It is too small a thing for you to be my servant to restore the tribes of Jacob and bring back those of Israel I have kept. I will also make you *a light for the Gentiles*, that my salvation may reach to the ends of the earth.'"

St. Peter will later make this connection to the New Testament people of God in his description of the 'new Israel' (i.e., those saved in Christ): "But you are a chosen race, a royal priesthood, a holy nation, a people for his own possession, that you may proclaim the excellencies of him who called you out of darkness into his marvelous light." (1 Pet. 2:9) A passage in Exodus 12 foreshadows St. Peter's words: "And the people of Israel journeyed from Rameses to Succoth, about six hundred thousand men on foot, besides women and children. *A mixed multitude* also went up with them, and very much livestock, both flocks and herds." (Exod. 12:37–38)

These 'mixed multitudes' represent the foreigners who were likely citizens of Egypt, present during the ten plagues visited upon Pharaoh. They were also centripetally gathered by God and at the Exodus have now joined Israel to become part of His "holy nation, a people for his own possession, that you may proclaim the excellencies of him who called you out of darkness into his marvelous light." These foreigners are not just fleeing the plagues — they are included in the Exodus community as a pan-national gathering of God's people.

TABLE TALK

6) I've heard it said that Israel is a special nation. Based on what

we just read, what made Israel special? What was their primary purpose?

7) **Re-read Genesis 12:1-3** and **Deut. 4:5-7**. How does God view Israel's primary purpose?

8) **Re-read 1 Pet. 2:9**. As the 'new Israel' today – what is our primary purpose?

REFLECTION

Solomon's prayer at the dedication of the Temple gives us more insight into Israel's purpose. No other location on earth best signified the 'ground zero' location of God relating to His people than the Temple. God's words to Moses in Exodus 25 regarding construction of this holy place illustrates the significance of God dwelling with His people. Exod. 25:8–9 "And let them make me a sanctuary, that I may dwell in their midst. Exactly as I show you concerning the pattern of the tabernacle, and of all its furniture, so you shall make it."

If God's plan for Israel was to gather them alone and *no one else*, there would be no need to talk about anyone other than Israel—particularly at the dedication of the Temple, where God's people would worship. Solomon's words tell us exactly where God's heart is and His mission of relational hospitality. God's mission has two parts: towards the gathered people of Israel and towards the *not-yet-gathered Gentiles* who need the Presence of the Living God. This is why Solomon's prayer at the dedication of the Temple in 1 Kings is so powerful:

> Likewise, when a foreigner, who is not of your people Israel, comes from a far country for your name's sake (for they shall hear of your great name and your mighty hand, and of your outstretched arm), when he comes and prays toward this house, hear in heaven your dwelling place and do according to all for

which the foreigner calls to you, in order that all the peoples of the earth may know your name and fear you, as do your people Israel, and that they may know that this house that I have built is called by your name.[24]

So, according to Solomon's prayer, the foreigner is allowed to pray towards the Temple because he has first heard the Word of God from His people or possibly, even by reputation from other nations sharing stories of God's work in the world. Think about this for a moment: Solomon's prayer is saying that not only is the foreigner allowed to pray, but he can also rest assured that God will hear his prayer! God hears the foreigner's prayer—and He will hear him *the same way* as God's people when they pray! A relationship with the Lord to the foreigner, made by God's hospitality and reflected in God's community of people.

This relationship of the foreigner with the Lord is an incredible disclosure, especially since the king of Israel could have quite easily declared God's work with people finished. After all, His people had been safely gathered at the building of His Temple. This kingly prayer at the Temple clearly indicates that God's work in the world is, in fact, *not finished*. What has been implicit from Genesis is now explicit in this prayer: from the beginning and most especially at the establishment of the Temple, God's purpose, and plan of salvation all along has been to gather to Himself *everyone* on earth! The Temple design itself bears this out in first-century Judaism, with the Herodian inclusion of the building of the Court of the Gentiles[25] with the sole purpose of allowing the stranger, as well as God's People, to hear the Word of God.

We continue to see this promise of God proclaimed through the prophets, where they chastise the people of God for rejecting the commission to act like His community of people who welcome others to relational hospitality. The prophets warn that if they refuse to act like God's people, then God will make for Himself a new people. This warning would also be a promise where God would ultimately use

Israel as a way for Him to make for Himself a new people – calling all nations to Himself through Israel. We see this played out in matters of Israel and their gathering together for worship. The worship of God is truly not complete until *everyone* is doing it. It involves God's call to the world — then, the peoples' response over all the earth.

In the writings of the prophets we read that God's ultimate purpose — and His true purpose all along — is to have His eye on all the nations of the earth and to show us what He has in mind for the whole world. Isa. 49:5–6 is a good example: "And now the Lord says, he who formed me from the womb to be his servant, to bring Jacob back to him; and that Israel might be gathered to him — for I am honored in the eyes of the Lord, and my God has become my strength — he says: 'It is too light a thing that you should be my servant to raise up the tribes of Jacob and to bring back the preserved of Israel; I will make you as a light for the nations, that my salvation may reach to the end of the earth.'"

This theme continues with Isa. 56:3–8 directly instructing the foreigner/outsider to come to God and be welcomed by Him into the community of faith. It is relational hospitality in action:

> Let not the *foreigner* who has joined himself to the LORD say, 'The LORD will surely separate me from his people'; and let not the *eunuch* say, 'Behold, I am a dry tree.' For thus says the LORD: 'To the *eunuchs* who keep my Sabbaths, who choose the things that please me and hold fast my covenant, I will give in my house and within my walls a monument and a name *better* than sons and daughters; I will give them an *everlasting* name that shall not be cut off. And the *foreigners* who join themselves to the LORD, to minister to him, to love the name of the LORD, and to be his servants, *everyone* who keeps the Sabbath and does not profane it, and holds fast my covenant — these I will bring to my holy mountain, and make them joyful in my house of prayer; their burnt offerings and their sacrifices

will be accepted on my altar; for my house shall be called a house of prayer *for all peoples.*' The Lord GOD, who gathers the *outcasts* of Israel, declares, 'I will gather *yet others* to him besides those *already* gathered.'[26]

In Isaiah 19, God promises that even when He strikes down Egypt, He will still send to them a Savior and make Himself known to them. Then God promises something truly remarkable — He plans to bring in the barbarian people of Assyria, along with Israel and Egypt: "In that day, there will be a highway from Egypt to Assyria, and Assyria will come into Egypt, and Egypt into Assyria, and the Egyptians will worship with the Assyrians. In that day Israel will be the third with Egypt and Assyria, a blessing in the midst of the earth, whom the LORD of hosts has blessed, saying, "Blessed be Egypt my people, and Assyria the work of my hands, and Israel my inheritance."[27]

The incredible promise here, not to be overlooked, is that by the grace of Almighty God, the phrase "my people" now applies even to Egypt, the one-time enslavers of Israel — and moreover, Assyria is now counted among God's handiwork — incredible Gospel that includes even the *enemies* of Israel! This is hospitality that goes beyond anything humanly possible.

TABLE TALK

9) **Read Matt. 5:43-48**. Think about what we just learned about God's purpose for Israel and His welcoming of all people. How does this impact Jesus' words in these verses?

10) What about **Matt 5:48**. What do you think Jesus means by His words? How does this tie into God's relationship to His people?

BRINGING IT HOME

Towards the end of Zechariah 8, we see a direct connection between

God's call to welcome the foreigners and gathering them in: "Thus says the LORD of hosts: 'Peoples shall yet come, even the inhabitants of many cities. The inhabitants of one city shall go to another, saying, 'Let us go at once to entreat the favor of the LORD and to seek the LORD of hosts; I myself am going.' Many peoples and strong nations shall come to seek the LORD of hosts in Jerusalem and to entreat the favor of the LORD.' Thus says the LORD of hosts: In those days ten men from the nations of every tongue shall take hold of the robe of a Jew, saying, '*Let us go with you*, for we have heard that God is with you.'"[28]

These verses from Zechariah even allude to the shepherds' later response in the Gospels when they saw the heavenly hosts: "And the angel said to them, 'Fear not, for behold, I bring you good news of great joy that will be for all the people. For unto you is born this day in the city of David a Savior, who is Christ the Lord.' When the angels went away from them into heaven, the shepherds said to one another, '*Let us go over to Bethlehem* and see this thing that has happened, which the Lord has made known to us.'"[29]

God has always had a heart for mission to the entire world — for gathering in, not just the nation of Israel, but all peoples of the earth. As we have seen in the Old Testament, God also intended His community of faith to one day include all the nations of the earth, where extending hospitality, that is — welcoming in the stranger, the foreigner, the outcast and *even the enemy* — have always been His missiological and Christological plan.

ENEMIES AND PSALM 23

One text that has significant meaning to just about every person, no matter their faith – is Psalm 23. There's a line in that Psalm that goes, "You prepare a table before me in the presence of my enemies." (Psa. 23:5) We tend to skip over this verse and go to the lines about 'green pastures' and 'the Lord is my Shepherd.' But this line is significant. When enemies attacked someone in the Old Testament, it was common practice to attack from an elevated position. It's common military strategy, today.

So, if the Lord is setting a table before His favored 'in the presence of our enemies', the implication is, He's doing so at an elevated position—with our enemies being down in the valley. Instead of attacking our enemies from an elevated position, like they would do, we dine in God's Presence on a high place—free from attack by our enemies.

Our good, powerful and ever-present God gives comfort to His people – food, safety, rest, and peace to His people—even as we are in the midst our enemies. Our Almighty God is with us in all moments—moments of trial, temptation, sleeping, eating and in fellowship. Even our enemies cannot reach us, when God has placed us on high, by lifting His Son high on the cross! So, what is there to fear in this life? Why not welcome the stranger—even *our* enemies—in our midst, at our table? As one author put it:

"God has a habit of waging war with strange weapons. He fought Egypt with frogs, gnats, and boils. He defeated the Midianite army with Gideon's clay pots and torches. Strangest of all, He defeated sin and death using a tree. So, it should be no surprise to us that Jesus calls us to take up forks and spoons to fight back Satan and his legions."[30]

Let's set a table—and see how God blesses it—for *all people*!

TABLE TALK

11) **Read John 3:14-17**. In light of what we've just discussed, how does Jesus' words tie all of this chapter together?

> The King of love my shepherd is,
> Whose goodness faileth never;
> I nothing lack if I am his
> And he is mine forever.

Where streams of living water flow,
My ransomed soul he leadeth
And, where the verdant pastures grow,
With food celestial feedeth.

Perverse and foolish oft I strayed,
But yet in love he sought me
And on his shoulder gently laid
And home rejoicing brought me.

In death's dark vale I fear no ill
With thee, dear Lord, beside me,
Thy rod and staff my comfort still,
Thy cross before to guide me.

Thou spredst a table in my sight;
Thine unction grace bestoweth;
And, oh, what transport of delight
From thy pure chalice floweth!

And so through all the length of days
Thy goodness faileth never.
Good Shepherd, may I sing thy praise
Within thy house forever.

—**Lutheran Service Book**
709, public domain

Closing Prayer: *Lord, I sometimes struggle with welcoming people I have problems with. I struggle with welcoming people I claim to 'get along' with. I struggle with past hurts, past hates, past sins – both against me and the ones I've committed against others. I've been betrayed and I've made enemies. Send Your Spirit, Lord, to call me to You and Your ways of welcome, forgiveness and reconciliation. Amen*

CHAPTER 4
A Woman, A Well and A Holy Welcome

John 4:13-14
"Jesus said to [the woman at the well],
'Everyone who drinks of this water
will be thirsty again, but whoever drinks of the water
that I will give him will never be thirsty forever.
The water that I will give him will become in him
a spring of water welling up to eternal life.'"

SETTING THE TABLE

You gotta love the writing style of St. John the apostle. In his Gospel, he records Jesus' ministry in such a way that you can't help but be drawn in by it. And his account of the woman at the well is no exception. But the only real way to take in all the things that are going on in this text - with a woman, a well and living water, is to look at the *context*.

During our time together, we will take a look at the story *behind* the story, to see not only what it means for this Samaritan woman drawing water, but what it also means for you and me and our welcome of others, today.

Prayer: *Heavenly Father, this story has a lot of beautiful parts to it.*

That is, until I recall all the ugly ways I've treated people or ignored them just because I felt they were 'below me' in some way. Open my mind and heart to the truth You want to show me in Your Word, as I look to You as the Living Water to quench my soul's thirst. Amen.

TABLE TALK
Take a moment to discuss the following together:

1) How does our society 'make distinctions' between one group of people and another?

2) Have you ever experienced a time when someone 'looked down' on you, or know someone that this happened to? What surprised you about your experience or what that person shared about their experience?

3) How do we evaluate someone's 'worth' in our society? How do *you* evaluate someone's 'worth'?

4) How have you wrestled with welcoming someone who you know isn't living how God wants them to live?

AT THE TABLE
5) **Read aloud John 4:3-42. Take turns reading, if you like.** What parts of this story stick out for you? Does anything 'unexpected' occur?

6) How does Jesus act in a way you *would* expect? In a way you *wouldn't* expect?

7) What about the woman – what questions does she ask Jesus that you didn't expect?

REFLECTION

The best place to start with this story, is to take a look at how much the Jews and Samaritans *hated* each other. 'Hate' might be a strong word for you and me, but it's not strong *enough* for Jews and Samaritans in Jesus' day. Their hatred for one another made the relationship between the Hatfield's and McCoy's look like a *simple misunderstanding*! It was a blood-feud going back 500 years before 'the woman at the well'.

Way back in 721 B.C., the Northern Kingdom of Israel fell to Assyria and most of them were exiled. Refugees soon took their place and began to inter-marry with the people who were left behind. This region became known as Samaria. 200 years passed, and the Southern Kingdom of Judah was also conquered, but these Jews came back home just a few years later, so they hadn't had time to inter-marry and were therefore considered 'pure'. The Judahites' first project when they arrived at Judah was to rebuild the Temple in Jerusalem. The Samaritans offered to help rebuild the Temple, but the Kingdom of Judah wanted nothing to do with them. Because they now considered the Samaritans to be '2nd Class' citizens – unclean rebels, who for 200 years had been marrying Gentiles - and in their eyes, they were worthless.

And that's when the trouble *really* started. In response, the Samaritans built their *own* temple on Mount Gerizim. They created their own priesthood, and rejected all the books of the Old Testament, except the Torah (the first five books of the Bible). To add insult to injury, they claimed they had the *oldest* copy of the Torah, so that made them *better* than the so-called 'pure' Jews from Judah. Not to be outdone, the king of Judah invaded Samaria and destroyed their temple. In response, the Samaritans snuck into Jerusalem at night and left a dead pig on the altar at *their* Temple, defiling it, since the Law stated that pigs were unclean animals.

In response, the Judahites made a decree that a Samaritan was *lower* than a Gentile, and that they would *never* be allowed to convert to Judaism. Things got so bad, that by the time of Jesus, when a Jew traveled from Judea to Galilee, they made a point to take a long detour *around* Samaria, just so their *feet* wouldn't have to touch Samaritan soil.

8) **Read John 4:4 again.** What is interesting about this verse and the description of Jesus' behavior?

9) Fun Fact: Sychar exists in what is now modern-day Palestine. Jacob's well is located in an Eastern Orthodox church. It is widely considered one of the most accurate archeological locations of the Holy Land, because you can't move a well. To this day, you may draw water from this well and have a drink.

10) **Compare John 4:4 with Luke 9:51-53.** The expression 'set his face' is the same one used in John 4:4. What does this tell you about Jesus' actions to head to Sychar?

REFLECTION

It was the sixth hour, according to the Jewish clock, which is another way to say, 'six hours after sunup' or 'high noon', if you're from Texas. To everyone else, that's 12p.m. If you've been in the Middle East in the Spring or Summer, the heat of the day is oppressive, to say the least. Who in their right mind would draw water at that time? The women in Jesus' day certainly knew better. They typically went to the well in the cool of the morning or after dark. And if they didn't, they could expect immoral men hanging around the well at midday, looking for something else, *besides* water, from a woman.

So, the time of day tells us a lot about this woman. She's not just an outcast Samaritan by *Jewish* standards, she's an outcast woman by *Samaritan* standards! Not even Samaritan women would have anything to do with her or allow her to draw water when they ordinarily did. So, from a cultural standpoint, you can't get any lower than this woman.

So, it likely didn't surprise her that Jesus asked her for water, because other men had probably tried that line on her before. What surprised her was Jesus' *accent*. He sounded like a Jew, and a Jew should know *better* than to speak to the likes of *her*, especially with her social standing. So, she calls Him on it, thinking that would end the issue (4:9). But Jesus calls her to the mat on the *real* issue – the issue of her heart: "If you *knew* the gift of God, and who it is that is saying to you, 'Give me a drink,' you would have asked him, and he would have given you *living* water." (v.10)

The *real* issue with the woman at the well is that she knows *nothing* of the true God or His ways. From a spiritual standpoint, you can't get any lower than this. Truly, this woman can't get any *lower* – period.

11) Do you know anyone in your life that is living like this Samaritan woman? How might this woman's behavior give you insight into the behavior of a person who lives like her?

This woman doesn't like Jesus' words and so, she isn't going to take it *lying down*. She shoots right back at Jesus, with the words, "Are you *greater* than our father *Jacob*? *He* gave us the well and drank from it *himself*, as did his sons and his livestock." (v.12) Why bring *that* up? Well, she knew that Jews hated to admit that Jacob was the father of the Jews <u>and</u> the Samaritans. And the Samaritans had their common ancestor's well!

In other words, she's saying to Jesus, "Not only is Jacob *our* father, too, but we drink from *his* well every day, and *you* can only get some of it by asking for *a Samaritan's* help." Do you see what she's trying to do? She's trying to make Jesus mad. She doesn't want anything from

Him: doesn't want water, doesn't want *living* water, either. She just wants Him to go away! But the 'Word made flesh' will not be denied. If she doesn't want any *living water*, then His Words will make her *thirsty for it*. His words will force her to realize she is caught up in sin. That she needs a Savior. That she needs *Him*.

Jesus says to her, 'Go, call your husband, and come here." (v.16) She pauses, then blurts out, "I have no husband.' "You are right in saying, 'I have no husband'; for you have had five husbands, and the one you now have is not your husband. What you have said is true." (v.18) Jesus could see *right through her*.

12) God's Word carries power – and we've all felt its effects. Discuss a time when you did something you knew was wrong and tried to convince yourself it was justified under the circumstances. But then there was this nagging voice within you that wouldn't keep quiet. And despite your best efforts to silence it, you kept hearing the word, 'guilty', so you fell at Jesus' feet.

13) Discuss a time you knew God was asking you to do something you didn't want to do, and you tried to ignore His voice. How soon was it before you got so bothered over it that you eventually did it?

A Samaritan woman, who likely started her conversation with Jesus suspecting that he was trying to seduce her, like so many others – hearing power in His words, her heart knew, he *had* to be a man of God to know so much. "Sir, I can see that you are a prophet." (v.19) Maybe this was her chance to get the answers to the questions welling up insider her. Maybe this man would know how a worthless, Samaritan woman could receive forgiveness for five husbands, five divorces - and a broken life.

'Our fathers worshiped on this mountain, but you say that *in Jerusalem* is the place where people ought to worship.' (v.20) She wanted forgiveness but wondered whether it could only be found in the Temple in Jerusalem, like she'd been told. And if that was true, it wouldn't do *her* any good - because Samaritans were forbidden from that place.

Side Note: This text should not be used as an argument for *not* going to church, 'since I can worship God in my own way wherever I am.' This Samaritan woman *was* worshipping – just in the wrong place, at Mt. Gerizim. She had been denied access to the One True God, Who had located Himself at the Temple for all the nations. Jesus was about to change the terms of the Gospel by bringing the Temple to *her*.

14) **Read John 1:14.** In the Greek, this could translate as, "The Word became flesh and *tabernacled / pitched His tent* among us". In light of the conversation between Jesus and the Samaritan woman, how is this relevant to her statement in John 4:20?

15) Reflect on this statement: You might be able to find God in a boat on the lake, in a beautiful sunset or anywhere among His beautiful creation. But you *won't* find forgiveness there.

'Woman, believe me, the hour is coming when neither on this mountain nor in Jerusalem will you worship the Father. You worship what you do not know; we worship what we know, for salvation is from the Jews. But the hour is coming, and is now here, when the true worshipers will worship the Father in spirit and truth, for the Father is *seeking* such people to worship him.' (4:21-23). Suddenly, it sounded like she didn't have to go to Mount Gerizim OR to Jerusalem to seek forgiveness. It sounded like God was seeking people – seeking *her*. God was *bringing* His forgiveness *to her*, *right here*. And if that was true - the world would change. *Her* world would change.

> 16) Reflect on this statement: If Jesus is the Divine Pursuer, the 'hound of heaven', then the reality is not that *we* can't find God - the reality is, we can't get *rid* of Him!

This woman of Samaria was beginning to realize - maybe this prophet in her midst was saying that the day of the Lord had come. God was sending the Savior. Right now. 'I know that Messiah is coming. When he comes, he will tell us all things.' 'I who speak to you am He.' His words penetrated her soul like cool, refreshing water. Right there, by a well in the midday sun. Culturally outcast, ritually impure, spiritually dry and blatantly unholy, she stood *exposed* before the Messiah. He knew *everything* – about *her* – and even when she confessed her sins, He *didn't* reject her. The Temple of God had been made into flesh – had come to her and met her right where *she* was at - and He didn't leave her there.

> 17) How does God deal with sinners – does He wait for them to 'get their act together' before He will love them? How has He dealt with you?

> 18) Just as important: Does God love people right where they are at – and then go on His way? How does He 'not leave' someone where they are?

> 19) Reflect on your life: How might you have demanded someone change their ways before you will welcome them into your life? In what order does Jesus act towards those living sinful lives? How might His order reprioritize *your* order?

WHEN WELCOMING IS HARMFUL

Question 19, above, is *not* asking you to 'be a doormat for Jesus'. That is not the Christian calling.

To 'be a doormat for Jesus' is to treat the Christian life like mistletoe.

Have you ever stolen a kiss under the mistletoe at Christmas? Mistletoe might be pretty to look at, but did you know that mistletoe is actually a parasite? Typically, when birds eat the white mistletoe berries, they'll fly over to a high tree and sit there. When the bird leaves his droppings on that tree, the sticky mistletoe seeds stay on the branch. Before long, the seeds start growing into the wood. The mistletoe starts to take water and nutrients from the tree, eventually killing the tree. If you try to get rid of mistletoe by pulling it off, the root stays inside the tree and grows back. You have to cut it out by removing the branch or twig so the tree can survive.

Therefore, I want you to carefully—*carefully* contemplate this question—are there any friends or family that you might need to cut out of your life?

These are the people, who, despite countless years and your best efforts to have a healthy relationship, continue to take and never give – continue to hurt you, say unkind things and really aren't sorry? Do they manipulate you, lie to you or take advantage of your kindness? Do you have to emotionally prepare yourself before you see them, just because you know its going to sap your energy? Do you need a couple weeks to recover after you see them, just because they took from you in countless ways? Do they do things that truly hurt your family and friends? And worst of all—do they physically, verbally or emotionally abuse you?

Those kinds of people are 'mistletoe' growing in your 'people tree'.

(Where marriage is concerned—*please* see a counselor or a pastor before jumping ship. God calls us to take our wedding vows seriously.)

Yes, God's Word tells us to do all we can to reconcile with others, to forgive others and seek peace with others. To love one another and serve one another. But never—*never* at the expense of your safety and your soul. You cannot be responsible for other peoples' bad choices and harmful behaviors in their lives. But you absolutely can set healthy boundaries in yours.

There are other verses that deal with the unrepentant person who continues to hurt you or refuses to change their sinful ways after hearing what God's Will for them is (see Matthew 18:15-20, Romans 12:18 and Titus 3:10-11, among others). If, after loving them and sharing Jesus' love with them, they *still* are stirring up division and hurting you, for your own sake (and sometimes safety) you must withdraw from this person – but never stop praying for them that one day they might see God's love for them and the forgiveness that is waiting for them.

There is a difference between forgiveness and reconciliation. God commands us to 'forgive one another as God in Christ has forgiven you' (Ephesians 4:32). However, forgiveness does not *always* mean reconciliation. Not all relationships can or should be reconciled. Parasitic relationships that suck the life out of us are, by nature, 'one way'. And not healthy.

Check the pulse of your relationships and see if there's mistletoe that needs to be cut out.

You are God's child – and you are worth more to Him than to be a doormat.

20) Discuss the phrase, 'blood is thicker than water'. How might this phrase excuse the harmful ways family is allowed to treat others? How have you allowed this phrase to give people license to hurt you and those you love?

21) Check the pulse of *your* life—and be brutally honest with yourself—are *you* being 'mistletoe' in someone's 'people tree'?

Are *you* draining to others? Do *you* suck the life out of other people with negative talk and behaviors?

22) Ask a trusted friend or family member if they see 'mistletoe' in you. If so, how might you repent and quit draining the life out of people? How might you *speak* life and *give* life to others, instead?

BRINGING IT HOME

"…the woman left her water jar and went away into the town." (v.28) Her reason for going to the well was gone, and her water jar stayed empty – because now she was *full of living water*. Applied to her *very soul*. Soaking her in forgiveness and eternal life. She wasn't spiritually dry anymore – because she *drank deep* from the *source* – the spring of eternal life. And she had *enough water to spare* for others: "Come, see a man who told me all that I ever did. Can this be the Christ?" (v.29) Not just a Savior of the Jews. He was the 'living water', the Savior of the *world* – and *her* Savior.

And He is *your* Savior, too. When we couldn't climb the mountain of salvation, Jesus brought the 'mountain' to us – becoming flesh and dwelling among us. He already knows everything you've ever done or ever *will* do, and standing there, exposed before Him – He doesn't reject you. He dies for you instead. Pouring His forgiveness over you, to cleanse you of sin, to mend all your hurts and remove all your fears. Filling you with the living water of eternal life - filled to overflowing! By His grace, you will always be able to draw from His well of forgiveness, because, like the woman at the well - Jesus' love for *you* – will *never* run dry.

23) Take a moment to reflect on the 'Samaritans' in your life. Who might God be calling you to welcome? Encourage? Reach out? Write a letter? Reconcile?

24) Who might God be calling you to 'let go of', for your sake or for your safety? How often have you set aside your own worth as a beloved child of God for all the wrong reasons?

25) What toxic relationship has damaged your soul, that needs to be bathed in prayer, confessed to others, so the healing and peace only Jesus can grant might take root in your life?

> Come to Calvary's holy mountain,
> Sinners ruin'd by the fall;
> Here a pure and healing fountain
> Flows to you, to me, to all,
> In a full, perpetual tide,
> Open'd when our Saviour died.
>
> Come in poverty and meanness,
> Come defiled, without, within;
> From infection and uncleanness,
> From the leprosy of sin,
> Wash your robes and make them white:
> Ye shall walk with God in light.
>
> Come, in sorrow and contrition,
> Wounded, impotent, and blind;
> Here the guilty free remission,
> Here the troubled peace may find;
> Health this fountain will restore,
> He that drinks shall thirst no more.

He that drinks shall live for ever;
'Tis a soul-renewing flood:
God is faithful;—God will never
Break his covenant in blood,
Sign'd when our Redeemer died,
Seal'd when he was glorified.

—Lutheran Service Book
435, public domain

Closing Prayer: *Lord, through Your Son, Jesus, You pursued me while I was still a sinner and Your enemy. Help me, by Your Holy Spirit, to know when to love people, when to welcome people and know when to let them go in peace. Grant that I might always be a reflection of Your mercy, which loves people right where they are at – and yet, doesn't leave them there. Amen.*

CHAPTER 5
'Bearing With One Another' - The God of Relational Hospitality - Part 2

Colossians 3:12-13
"Put on then, as God's chosen ones, holy and beloved,
compassionate hearts, kindness, humility, meekness,
and patience, bearing with one another and,
if one has a complaint against another,
forgiving each other; as the Lord has forgiven you,
so you also must forgive."

1 Corinthians 12:25-27
"But God has so composed the body...that the members
may have the same care for one another.
If one member suffers, all suffer together;
if one member is honored, all rejoice together.
Now you are the body of Christ
and individually members of it."

SETTING THE TABLE

Back in 2018, Michigan State Troopers received a call from dispatch that there was a man standing at the guard rail of an overpass on I-696, ready to jump.

What the troopers didn't expect was local truckers in the area hearing the call go out over their radio – and what they would do next:

Thirteen semi-truck drivers pulled on to I-696, coordinating their efforts by radio to line up, side-by-side, underneath the overpass, reducing the man's possible fall from a fatal twenty-eight feet – to just six feet.

Effectively making it impossible for the man to end his life.

For four hours, the semi-truck drivers stayed parked under the overpass, while troopers talked to the man. At one point, a trucker hollered from his window below to the distraught man hanging above him, "Buddy, if you fall – you won't fall far!" At the end of four hours – the man walked off the overpass to waiting officers and to seek medical help.

"Buddy, if you fall – you won't fall far!"

What a rallying cry for the *Christian life*.

That picture perfectly shows how not only Christianity, but how the very first Christians viewed their faith – as an act of restoration and bearing with one another, and everyone they met - no matter the cost.

To a dying, hopeless world, they took up the cry, "If you fall – you won't fall far!"

And it literally changed the world.

Prayer: *Jesus, so many times I'm willing to engage my brother and sister in Christ, but I don't know how to start. I want to welcome those around me but sometimes I'm afraid. Help me to risk sharing radical, relational hospitality, where the world hears our cry in Christ, "If you fall – you won't fall far, with Jesus!"* Amen

RELATIONAL HOSPITALITY IN THE NEW TESTAMENT

As modern-day Westerners, we tend to have a 'closed' view of hospitality, limited to public functions or house parties — where hospitality boils down to no more than entertaining. Rarely does a function or party center around relationships outside of family gatherings. On the contrary, in the culture of Jesus' day, hospitality went far beyond the public setting and was vital to the daily life of the people.

Hospitality was not an exclusive practice to Judaism but was also woven into the fabric of the Greco-Roman world. Greek custom mandated that a person was not to ask the name of a guest until the guest's feet had been washed and food had been offered, as a way to honor the gods. Roman politicians recognized hospitality as a means of diplomacy and of greasing the wheels towards forming treaties with surrounding nations. To Roman citizens, hospitality was instrumental in helping them not only to welcome the stranger but also to overcome the fears that often go with interacting among citizens who came from a variety of nations yet were collectively under Roman rule. Most, if not all, of these interactions were centered around the dining room table while a meal was being hosted.[31]

Hospitality was also necessary for survival in the ancient world. When people traveled, they often took their lives into their own hands, because of the dangers of the terrain and the perils they faced from robbers on the road. This present danger is reflected in Jesus' parable of the Good Samaritan.[32] In nomadic tribes, a mandate was that people host the traveler in their midst, as part of a sacred duty. When travelers stayed in the homes of their host, they came under the protection of the host as if they were family.[33] We see an Old Testament example of this when Lot refuses to hand over his two guests to the mob outside his door, even offering his own daughters in their place.[34]

At the wedding at Cana that Jesus attends,[35] most weddings in that day lasted for seven days,[36] with the host inviting the entire village to celebrate with him and his family. The comments made by the master of the wedding feast in this Gospel point to the opulence of the wedding, since good wine of large amounts was used at the very beginning, with the cheap wine being held until the end of the day. Hospitality was embedded in the culture of the people of Israel.

Jesus Himself uses hospitality as a means to begin His mission on earth. When Jesus sends out His disciples, He instructs them to stay in homes where a person of peace welcomes them.[37] For those who reject hospitality towards them, Jesus tells them to move on to another home to be welcomed by another.

The hospitality of banquets and meals were bookends for Jesus' teachings, for Gospel moments and to highlight special events. Examples include the great wedding banquets[38] and the great celebration that occurs when the prodigal son comes home.[39] These meals of relational hospitality and celebrations of guests are imagery for what the kingdom of heaven looks like. When Jesus instructs His disciples about who is the greatest in the kingdom, it is around a meal, where the image of the greatest is tied to who also show the greatest hospitality.[40] Even at the end of time, we see the image of a marriage feast where the Lamb welcomes His Bride, the Church.[41]

When Jesus teaches around a meal, He occasionally uses hospitality as an image of how correctly or incorrectly to receive Him in faith. Luke chapter seven begins and ends with the issue of receiving Jesus in faith.[42] Furthermore, Jesus points out the sinful woman who welcomes Jesus in repentance, juxtaposing her to Simon, who did not welcome Jesus in hospitality, i.e., by faith, using the various signs of welcoming the visitor by pointing them out to Simon as an illustration of faith:

> Then turning toward the woman he said to Simon, 'Do you see this woman? I entered your house; you gave me no water for my feet, but she has wet my feet with her tears and wiped them with her hair. You gave me no kiss, but from the time I came in she has not ceased to kiss my feet. You did not anoint my head with oil, but she has anointed my feet with ointment. Therefore I tell you, her sins, which are many, are forgiven — for she loved much. But he who is forgiven little, loves little.'[43]

Jesus also uses hospitality as an illustration of how not to receive Him in faith, during a time when He stayed with Mary and Martha in their home:

> Now as they went on their way, Jesus entered a village. And a woman named Martha welcomed him into her house. And she had a sister called Mary, who sat at the Lord's feet and listened to his teaching. But Martha was distracted with much serving. And she went up to him and said, 'Lord, do you not care that my sister has left me to serve alone? Tell her then to help me.' But the Lord answered her, 'Martha, Martha, you are anxious and troubled about many things, but one thing is necessary. Mary has chosen the good portion, which will not be taken away from her.'[44]

The issue is not that Martha was doing anything wrong, *per se* — after all, she was welcoming the guest and practicing hospitality under her roof according to the cultural norms of the day, including pointing out to Jesus that Mary was not doing her cultural duty of showing hospitality. While Martha was busying herself with hospitality (i.e., entertaining guests), she was neglecting the *relational hospitality of God* — to simply be still and attend to the Word Made Flesh right in her midst and to hear what He had to say.

This theme continues in the missionary journeys of St. Paul and others, who rely on the offerings and community of the faithful in order to preach the Gospel. For example, in Acts 16, we read of Lydia, who welcomes St. Paul into her home, where it would later become a place where deeper connections of hearing the Gospel would occur.[45]

In the Book of Hebrews, the author encourages the gift of hospitality, going so far as to claim the practitioner of hospitality may be "entertaining angels, unaware,"[46] pointing the reader back to the Old Testament where Lot welcomed the two strangers who were themselves, angels.[47] As Revelation closes out the canon of Scripture, hospitality (or the lack thereof) is pointed out to the church at Laodicea, to receive Jesus as a guest Who stands at the door and knocks, waiting to be let in to dine with them in the intimacy of a meal, suggesting the receiving of Jesus in faith and fellowship.[48]

REFLECTION

I saw a picture online, once, that I think perfectly illustrates why God's people bear one another's burdens:

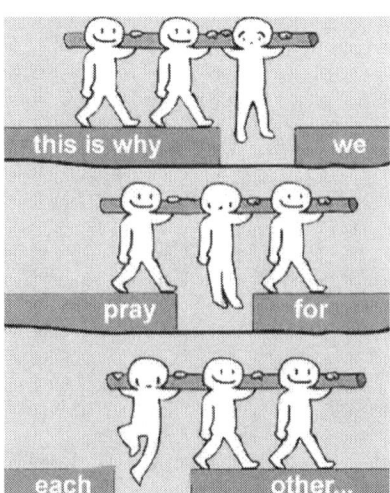

Simply put, the church does not exist for itself. The church exists to ask the question, 'for whose spiritual well-being are we responsible?' The answer lies in looking at a map.

I remember one of my vicarage pastors pointing to a map of the surrounding community near our vicarage church and telling me, "We claim this for Christ!" In short, he was telling me that my calling was not only to the baptized in our flock but to the immediate surrounding community God had placed me in. This not only included welcoming guests when they came through our doors but also engaging others in our *community*, where the stranger was most comfortable, as well as inviting others into our *lives*.

TABLE TALK

1) What would it mean to take out a map of your neighborhood or your city and pray, "Jesus, we claim this for You!"

2) **Read 2 Cor. 10:3-5**. How does this passage inform the cry, "Jesus, we claim this for You"?

3) Reflect on this thought: My experience has been that people are most resistant to engaging the stranger, inside or outside of church, largely because *they* would be the ones who were uncomfortable doing so.

4) Reflect on this thought: Throughout the ages, the home has been the battlefield Christians have used to catechize, evangelize and disciple those in the faith – primarily through the framework of relationships and hospitality.

5) Have you seen families leave the catechizing of their children to their pastor and youth director? What are the consequences of this?

REFLECTION

To be a church that is rooted in the restoration of relationships calls us to be a church that is building relationships with other people through relational hospitality. This means 'doing life together' as a church — not just where we gather to receive Word and Sacrament but where we gather to experience day-to-day life together. This kind of 'life on life' happens out in the world and in the home, as a community centered on relationships and welcoming others to join us on this journey.

Salvation by grace through faith compels our hearts not only to live a life of repentance but it also then directs us to the world to welcome and love others. The love of our neighbor, empowered by the Holy Spirit, is the response to Jesus' command to love our neighbor as ourselves.[49]

This heart knowledge prompted by the Holy Spirit calls on God's people to joyfully and humbly serve in Christian love to our neighbor and to one another. Through the gift of Jesus on the cross, we have received a forgiveness we didn't earn or deserve—and that calls us to live out our love for our neighbor in the world.

The strange things about this is, if you were to line up the Christian sharing his love for his neighbor with the mercy a non-believer shows others, it would be almost indistinguishable. So, if mercy looks the same between a Christian and a non-Christian, what is the difference?

The difference is the motivation of the heart.

God's people serve in love because God in Christ has loved us[50] — with no ulterior motives.

Sadly, we Christians haven't done a very good job portraying this love to the world. Accusations are often leveled against believers for serving their neighbor in the secret hopes of 'getting a notch in their belt for Jesus.' If that is the primary goal, then our accusers would be correct, for this confuses the reasons why we welcome others.

While we should welcome opportunities to share the Gospel with our non-Christian neighbors out of love for them, this is not the *initial reason* for loving them.

Let me say it another way – if we make everything we do around non-believers as another way to win converts, we have missed the point of Ephesians 2:10 "For we are God's workmanship, created in Christ Jesus to do good works, which God has prepared in advance, so that we might walk in them."

We serve our neighbor in love, simply because God calls His forgiven people to do so.

No strings.

TABLE TALK

6) How can God's people keep 'the main thing the main thing' when loving our neighbors?

7) How have you been told to engage non-believers? As a 'project', a 'potential Christian' or a 'notch in the Jesus belt'?

8) What difference would it make to engage people as just 'people'? How freeing would that be?

9) Think of times when Jesus engaged 'sinners.' How did He interact with them? Where did He interact with them? In public? In private? In their homes?

DOING LIFE TOGETHER[51]

From 1935 to 1937 Dietrich Bonhoeffer served as pastor, administrator, and teacher at an underground seminary at Finkenwalde, Germany (now modern-day Poland). Bonhoeffer insisted that if seminarians were to learn about and lead within the Christian community they must also enter into and learn the practical disciplines of the Christian faith in community. This commitment led to the formation of a 'community house' where those involved in seminary education would share 'life together.' At Finkenwalde, Bonhoeffer invited students and all involved in their education into a 'life together' marked by being intentional in living a life that cultivated a shared life of discipleship. The book, *Life Together*, records Bonhoeffer's experiences from his time at this seminary.[52]

"Christianity means community through Jesus Christ and in Jesus Christ. No Christian community is more or less than this. Whether it be a brief, single encounter or daily fellowship of years, Christian community is only this. We belong to one another only through and in Jesus Christ."[53] Bonhoeffer's assertions point to the deep relationship opportunities that are unique to a Christian community. To paraphrase Bonhoeffer, in Christ, Christians belong to one another and this belonging cultivates opportunities for relational hospitality. Even the unique Christian language used to refer to one another is based on close family relationships.

For example, sixteen times, St. Paul addresses the Christians in 1 Thessalonians as "brothers and sisters." This intentional use of the language of belonging reminds these new Christian converts of their changed identity and of the new set of relationships this change brings. Both their new identity and their relationships are bestowed by baptism into Christ and extend beyond their family of origin. Christian community is therefore not an ideal that we must work to realize; it is rather a reality created by God in Christ through His mission of salvation – a mission in which we may *participate*.

We are bound to one another because of what God has done for us in Jesus Christ, not even through shared interests or like-mindedness or common experiences. This unique community transcends the usual relationships seen in the world, where people gather together primarily through commonalities. This new spiritual reality in Christ creates a space for deep relationships centered in a fellowship that reflects the real cares, needs, joys, thanksgivings, petitions, and hopes of the community. In this faith community, peoples' prayers become our own, through these relationships. And all relationships are bound together by the one commonality that holds the community together: our baptism into Christ.

TABLE TALK

10) Reflect on this statement: "Christians are not bound by common interests or political loyalties. We are bound by our baptism into Christ."

Bonhoeffer further speaks of ministry itself as living out *redemptive relationships* in community.[54] Christians learn what it means to be the body of Christ in the world as they minister to and with one other in relationships that welcome one another. This relational hospitality is reflected in the New Testament, characterized by the practice of a "radical togetherness."

FILL IN THE BLANKS ON THE FOLLOWING LIST:

The Christian community is a community of persons who:
1) live in _____ with one another (Rom. 12:16),
2) _____ one another (Rom. 15:7 and 1 Pet. 4:9ff),
3) through love, _____ one another (Gal. 5:13),
4) _____ one another, (1 Thess. 5:11), _____ up one another (1 Thess. 5:11),
5) _____ to one another (1 Thess. 5:15),
6) _____ to one another (Eph. 5:21),
7) _____ to one another (James 5:16)
8) _____ all trespasses (Col. 2:13),
9) _____ one another earnestly from a pure heart (1 Pet. 1:22),
10) clothe one another with _____ (1 Pet. 5:5),
11) _____ for one another (James 5:16),
12) have _____ with one another (1 John 1:7).

- Have you experienced any of these things in your church family?

- Which ones in the list are harder to live out? Which are easier?

- What parts of this list would you like to experience more of?

The relational hospitality that Christ calls us to share, also extends to our fellowship around a meal. A meal together takes us back in time to similar practices of the ancient Church. God's people prepare for Jesus when they gather for fellowship at meals, at table fellowship of the Lord's Supper, and at the final table fellowship in the kingdom of God at the life of the world to come.

BRINGING IT HOME

As we have seen, God's people have received a tremendous gift of relational hospitality from our Lord and as a result, we now live out our faith in this unique community centered in Christ. The mission of God calls His people to be intentionally aware of others and to welcome the engagement of others in our everyday lives — first with the gathered saints and then by loving our neighbor through our vocations.

If all people matter to God, then as His people, they matter to *us as well*! This calls the Christian community to cultivate a culture of hospitality and a heart for welcoming others, trusting the Lord to determine the harvest and who among His people He will raise up to reap it[55]. Equipped with Word and Sacrament, we seek to welcome the stranger as we ourselves have been welcomed in Christ. We practice the relational hospitality of welcoming the stranger through first welcoming one another in the Body of Christ, living out our connectedness through the blood of Jesus.

We save no one through hospitality and no one is 'discipled into conversion' — only Jesus can do that through the power of the Holy

Spirit coming down to save sinful people. He continues to do this today, through the power of the Word, whether read, preached or present in the Sacraments.

But, like semi-truckers parked under an overpass, crying out to the world, "If you fall – you won't fall far!" - the highway the Holy Spirit can travel on just might be through God's people joyfully sharing hospitality in a post-Christian age.

> My hope is built on nothing less
> Than Jesus' blood and righteousness;
> I dare not trust the sweetest frame,
> But wholly lean on Jesus' name.
> On Christ, the solid Rock, I stand;
> All other ground is sinking sand.
>
> When darkness veils His lovely face,
> I rest on His unchanging grace;
> In every high and stormy gale
> My anchor holds within the veil.
> On Christ, the solid Rock, I stand;
> All other ground is sinking sand.
>
> His oath, His covenant, and blood
> Support me in the whelming flood;
> When every earthly prop gives way,
> He then is all my Hope and Stay.
> On Christ, the solid Rock, I stand;
> All other ground is sinking sand.

When He shall come with trumpet sound,
Oh, may I then in Him be found,
Clothed in His righteousness alone,
Faultless to stand before the throne!
On Christ, the solid Rock, I stand;
All other ground is sinking sand.

—**Lutheran Service Book**
575, public domain

Closing Prayer: *Lord, we live in a world that seems pretty apathetic towards You, at times. And that can frustrate me, when I know how wonderful Your love is. Don't let it get to my heart, so that I will be open to welcoming the hurting, the broken and the poor in spirit, just as You welcomed me. Help me by Your Holy Spirit, to come alongside those Who need to know You love them and take up the cry, "If you fall – you won't fall far!"* Amen

CHAPTER 6
A Good Neighbor and a Godly Welcome

Luke 10:29, 36-37
"[A lawyer], desiring to justify himself, said to Jesus, "… who is my neighbor?" [Jesus told him a parable and asked], "Which of these three, [the Priest, the Levite or the Samaritan] do you think, proved to be a neighbor to the man who fell among the robbers?" [The lawyer] said, "The one who showed him mercy." And Jesus said to him, "You go, and do likewise."

SETTING THE TABLE

Other than the parable of the Prodigal Son, there's probably no other parable that is more familiar to people than the parable of the Good Samaritan. It's a powerful image of one person helping another person. In fact, it's such a powerful image, our society has "Good Samaritan Laws", named in its honor - laws that let citizens help other people in need, without fear of prosecution. Ultimately, what our world thinks this story is about, is that everyone is called to be a good neighbor, and if you see someone in trouble, you're supposed to be a good neighbor and help them out.

And that's very appealing, because it *would* be nice if everyone would treat people with decency and help them out if they found someone in need. But is there more to this parable? That's what we'll be exploring during our time together and how, learning who the Good Samaritan is, calls us to view Jesus' words in an entirely new light.

Prayer: *Merciful Lord, this parable is rich with mercy, grace and welcome. Open my mind and heart to the true Gospel You wish to show me in Your Word, so that I might be the kind of neighbor that lives by – and rests in - Your mercy. In Jesus' Name. Amen.*

SETTING THE TABLE

Take a moment to discuss the following together:

1) How have you heard friends and neighbors describe the parable of the Good Samaritan?

2) Why do you believe our culture is so fascinated with this parable?

3) Do you know someone who seems to personify the parable of the Good Samaritan? What is it about this person that brings them to your mind?

4) Have you ever experienced a time in your life when someone showed undeserved mercy to you? What about that moment stands out for you?

TABLE TALK

This parable has not only fascinated our culture, but it has also held the attention of the Christian Church for generations with the dynamic nature of the story. Lots of books – secular and religious - have attempted to pull apart this parable to mine its treasures. In fact, many

Christian books and many Christian churches have boiled down this parable in to a 'morality tale' that commands: "Be a good neighbor." I bet you thought this book was trying to do the same thing (*gotcha!*)

Of course, the theme of caring for others is present in this parable, but is that *all* that Jesus is saying here? Is His command to 'love your neighbor as yourself' the *only* thing Jesus is telling us? Because if that's *all* Jesus is saying, there's not much *Gospel* in telling His followers to be a good neighbor. It's just a story telling us to do something. In Lutheran circles, we call that the Law - where we're told to do something or be something for God. No matter how *nice* it would be if everyone would love their neighbor as themselves – to see this parable only as a command to do something is still a 'Law statement' – it is *not* the Gospel. And doing *more* Law won't save us.

Now, I'm not saying that we just throw up our hands, draw the blinds on the windows, lock the doors and 'ride it out till Jesus comes back'. Of course, we are called to love our neighbor as followers of Jesus. However, thinking this is the only point to the parable of the Good Samaritan actually takes us out of the original conversation Jesus had with His audience, and it removes the reasons *why* He told this story in the *first* place.

A friend once told me, "All Scripture is written *for* us but not necessarily *to* us." In other words, God's Word is meant for all to convey the Gospel of Jesus and is meant for our instruction. But there is also the original audience that the words of the Bible were written to, and to know the audience helps us to better understand the meaning of the words. So, in order to fully understand the meaning of this parable, we first need to understand the *audience* Jesus is speaking to.

5) Go over the text of **Luke 10:10-37**. What was happening in verses 10-24 to lead up to this parable?

6) Side Note: the word, 'parable' comes from the Greek word

παραβολή (parabolay). It's a verb that literally translates as, "To throw around". It was a verb used when someone in Jesus' day got dressed for the day. Taking a robe, they would 'throw around' the robe across their body, wrapping it around themselves. They would wear the robe throughout the day, and as they did so, it became a part of them. You've probably experienced the same thing with the clothing you wear! So, a 'parable' differs from a 'story' in the sense that it is a tale that you are meant to 'wrap around your heart', take it with you and let it become a part of you in your daily life.

REFLECTION

In this passage, we find Jesus being approached by a lawyer. A lawyer in Jesus' day was an expert in the Old Testament Law, and this lawyer is *really* worried. He's heard that seventy-two of Jesus' disciples have been going around proclaiming the Gospel. (Luke 10:1-24) He's *really* worried, because Jesus seems to be giving away the Kingdom of God - *for free*! And this lawyer's been spending his whole life trying to *earn* that kingdom! So, he asks Jesus a question to *test* Him (v.25): "What <u>must I do</u> to inherit eternal life?" When someone tests Jesus, it usually isn't a question asked in faith. It's asked to see if they can either trip up Jesus or get some information from him. So, likely the underlying question the lawyer is asking Jesus is, "What *else* is required for my salvation? I've done a lot, already. There must be *some* 'extra Law' I need to follow here! Some extra-credit I can do to really nail it!" Do you see how off base this guy is, already?

As only Jesus can do, He patiently asks the lawyer, "What is written in the Law? How do you read it?" And he replies, "You shall love the Lord your God with all your heart and with all your soul and with all your strength and with all your mind and love your neighbor as yourself." The Lawyer first asked Jesus a 'Law' question, so Jesus now gives him a 'Law' answer, "You have answered correctly; *do this*, and you will live." (Luke 10:26-28) 'Love God completely, totally, constantly - love your neighbor *perfectly*, too - and you will live!' That's IT!

Now, at this point, there should be a 'flag on the play' in your mind. On the surface, Jesus' words many not *seem* to be that difficult. But once we pull apart Jesus' words and plop them down into our daily lives, following the Law gets *hard*:

"You know there's a lot of neighbors out there that *aren't* like me. A lot of neighbors don't *look* like me or *act* like me. They practice the religion of Islam or they practice no religion at all. They make less money than me. Some are homeless. Some are cranky. Some are alcoholics or drug addicts!" Add in the rest of the words Jesus said: "*All* your heart." "*All* your soul." "*All* your strength." "*All* your mind." "Your neighbor as *yourself*." Now, we're looking at doing something that's a monumental task!

To be the Good Samaritan in this story means that's *all* you can *ever* be! You can't go to the movies, anymore – because if you did, then you're not loving your neighbor. You must be the Good Samaritan, *all* the time - *perfectly*. In *all* that you say and think and do - to *everyone*. Give *no* thought to yourself. *Always* live for your neighbor. Be nothing but the Good Samaritan – 24/7. "This 'loving your neighbor' stuff gets *hard*, if not impossible!"

But that doesn't mean we won't try…

7) Looking at this parable from our new perspective, how does that impact what you 'thought' you knew about the parable?

8) Do you know of any churches/denominations that focus on doing things to show their worth to God? What do they do? How about churches that think if they 'save the whales', 'the environment', etc that this is the gospel? (Hint: it's good to be a good steward of the environment. It's even biblical (see God's

commands to Adam in Genesis 2) – but it's not the Gospel)

Since our hearts believe 'there's no free lunch', we are naturally disposed to wanting to 'do' something. So, when we bump up against something that we believe to be impossible, we try to change the rules:

"What if we could narrow down the *definition* of the word, 'neighbor'? Then maybe I could love just *those* neighbors, instead of ALL neighbors!"

And that is *exactly* what the lawyer tries to do – he tries to find a 'loophole' in the Law.

9) Have you ever tried to find a 'loophole' to excuse a behavior that you know God doesn't approve of?

10) Recall a time when you tried to 'bargain' with God. What was the circumstance and how did it shake out?

When the lawyer realizes that 'loving your neighbor' is going to be *really hard*, he tries to narrow down the *definition* of the word, 'neighbor' with Jesus. And that made total sense to him.

You see, in his day, it was normal practice for the teachers of the Law to reject *certain people* as their 'neighbor': people like the Gentiles and *especially* the 'blood sucking Samaritans'. We covered them in a previous chapter. The Samaritans were outcasts from Israel - excommunicated former brothers. Just to avoid walking on the land that the Samaritans *lived on*, the Jews would walk over *twenty miles* out of their way! So, just to be *absolutely sure* which 'neighbor' Jesus is referring to - and to try and weasel out of doing an impossible task, the lawyer asks the question:

"And <u>who is</u> my neighbor?" (v. 29)

Jesus answers him with the parable of 'The Good Samaritan'.

11) Who are the main characters in the parable? What background information do we know about each character that can give us some insight into this story?

I said earlier that knowing the context of a story helps us better understand it. Here is a picture of the setting of Jesus' parable:

This is the desert region between Jerusalem and Jericho. As you can see, it's very sparse. Down in the canyon, stands a Christian monastery built into the side - still in use, to this day. Along the top of the ridge, you can just make out the original trail that would've been used in Jesus' day to get from Jerusalem to Jericho. As you can see, there's nowhere to hide and nowhere to run if you get jumped by bandits. This area was notorious for people getting robbed, beaten and then thrown over the side of the cliff. It was very common for thieves to travel in caravans, appearing to be 'good neighbors' who would offer protection for wayward travelers. Then, as they gained the person's trust, they'd jump the guy, rob him and leave him for dead. So, Jesus is telling a story that everyone who traveled from Jerusalem to Jericho would've been familiar with.

People ensuring safe passage for one another and helping injured travelers was part of the culture of the day as a matter of survival.

What's so shocking to the lawyer's ears *is who stops to help* in the parable.

The Samaritan – an outcast of Jewish society - is being 'good' and taking care of his neighbor.

Let's recap: our lawyer friend has been shown through Jesus' words that he *can't* be a good neighbor, because he doesn't love his neighbor as himself *all the time.*

So, back to you and me.

If the lawyer can't be the Good Samaritan in this parable, then guess what? Odds are high that we can't be the Good Samaritan, either.

12) Part of the purpose of a parable is to 'put yourself in the story'. Since we can't be the Good Samaritan, who else from our cast of characters must we consider?

13) The Priest and the Levite walking along the road represent the Law – the rituals, sacrifices and orders of the Temple. Based on what we've talked about, what function does the Law serve?

14) If the Priest and Levite represent the Law, what does the Law do, for a beaten up, half-dead man lying on the side of the road?

> That's right - the Law - passes *right on by*. When it comes to the Law, the message is still the same: the Law can't save anyone. Jesus is telling the lawyer and you and me, that we will never find salvation by doing *more* Law.

> 15) If we *can't* be the Good Samaritan in this parable, and the Priest and Levite represent the Law - then what role is left that you and I can play?

The only role left is the beaten up, half-dead man. A man who considers a Samaritan his 'blood-sucking enemy'. Totally helpless, unable to defend himself or heal himself. In fact, so helpless, all he can do is lie there and bleed. Someone *must* take action *FOR* him – even someone he considers his enemy!

Not a very appealing role, is it? After all, we're red-blooded Americans. We *like* to 'pull ourselves up by our bootstraps', to 'do something' for our salvation:

"We can do it, Jesus! All we need is a little direction - something to *do*, something to *try*, forty days of purpose, a WWJD bracelet. *Something*!"

How many times have our requests to God shown our hand to Him? How many times have we behaved exactly like the lawyer?

Then, to drive home the point, Jesus asks the lawyer, "Which of these three, do you think, proved to be *a neighbor* to the man who fell among the robbers?" The lawyer grits his teeth and says, "The one who showed him mercy." And Jesus says, "*You* go - and do likewise." (Luke 10:36-37)

The only conclusion left for the lawyer to draw was: "Go and do likewise?!? I *CAN'T* go and do likewise."

And guess what?

You.

Can't.

Either.
Because *you* aren't the Good Samaritan in this parable.
That role has already been taken...
...*by Jesus*.

The Samaritan is moved with <u>compassion</u> when he sees the half-dead man.

And that single word gives away the secret of the story.

Throughout the New Testament, the word for 'compassion' is *only* used to refer to *God* having compassion upon *sinners*. The Samaritan in this parable is God *Himself*. God, Who 'became flesh and dwelled among us' (John 1:14), Who moved in to our neighborhood and 'became a Good Neighbor for *us*'.

Jesus is the "Samaritan": the outcast, the despised One – the One that the Priests and the Levites had rejected. As the Samaritan, we were *His* enemies, "but God shows his love for us in this: while we were *still* sinners, Christ died for us." (Romans 5:8) The Good Samaritan, Who perfectly loves God with all *His* heart, *His* soul, *His* strength and *His* mind – and Who loves us as *Himself*. He has come to our aid. He binds up our wounds. He places our burdens upon Himself. He carries us and brings us to the "inn."

And that "inn" – is in God's House.

Gathered together with God's church family. It is *here*, with Him, that *we* are cared for. Nursed along. Washed with water and the Word. Wounds mended and tended. Fed with bread and wine and true body and true blood. And everything we receive has already been *paid for* by Jesus.

And as if that's not enough - to the 'Innkeeper' – to God the *Father* Himself – Jesus says on our behalf, "Take care of him, and whatever more you spend, I will repay you, when I come back." (Luke 10:35) Just think - as if His suffering, death and resurrection were not payment *enough* for your sins, your Good Samaritan is *so* 'good' that Jesus would do even *more* than what is required for you – to win you back for the Heavenly Father!

16) What difference does it make in this parable to see it through the lens of the Gospel, rather than the lens of the Law?

Now, that we've seen this parable through the lens of the Gospel and the original context, we see the true meaning much more clearly.

Because of Jesus and the forgiveness of your sins, you don't *have* to love your neighbor – you <u>GET</u> to love your neighbor! We Lutherans call that the 'third use of the Law'.

"But I thought you said the Law was bad!"

No, I said the Law can't save you. The Law isn't bad – but it's not going to cover the distance from yourself to God. Doing *more,* being *more* will not get you closer to the Kingdom of God. So, why do good works at all?

Let's take a look at the beautiful Gospel words of Ephesians 2:8-9:

"For by grace you have been saved through faith. And this is not your own doing; it is the gift of God, not a result of works, so that no one may boast."

Incredible Gospel words. But I wish people would go one verse further to verse ten:

"For we are his workmanship, created in Christ Jesus for good works, which God prepared beforehand, that we should walk in them." Verse ten gives us the full picture of our place in the world as God's forgiven people.

Our works *are* important. But the *why* is very different from what we believe.

Being a good neighbor *does* matter – but *not* to get you to heaven.

Jesus has done the work *for* you – and so now, you are *free.*

You are free in Christ to do good works, not to earn your way to heaven, but because your neighbor *needs* you!

17) Reflect on the words of this statement: You don't *have* to do good works – you *get* to do good works!

BRINGING IT HOME

And just who is *your* neighbor, you ask? Turn to your left – turn to your right. Take a look at who sits at your dinner table. Walk outside your door. Take a good look around. Wander the cubicles at your job. Lo and behold – you've found them. Not just any neighbor - *your* neighbors!

Forgiven by Jesus, you simply live as God has called you to live, in the everyday, ordinary life that you lead – in His forgiveness. Not 'one more thing' for you to do – but 'living life that is truly life' (1 Timothy 6:19) Embrace the fact that you *can't* be a good neighbor, no matter how hard you try – but at the same time, embrace the eternal truth that there was One Who, for *you*, as the Ultimate Good Neighbor - took your punishment on the cross and set you free.

Instead of pretending you've 'got it all together', be honest with people about how tough life can be. How you're just as messed up as they are. You make mistakes. You hurt. You struggle. But Thank God, Jesus took care of all that, and more for us! Because of that sweet Gospel, you are free to do your job with pride and in humble service, taking care of your neighbor, whatever their needs.

18) I've heard it said, 'Love the sinner, hate the sin.' God's Gospel is more radical than that. "Love the sinner, hate your *own sin*, and say, 'Let's get through this together, with Jesus.'" What difference would it make in your life to engage people with those words written on your heart?

As you live free in Christ to love your neighbor – with His Peace in your heart, there will come a time when people will ask you, 'Why did you do this for me? Why would you care, when no one else does?'

You can say, 'Come and see. Come with me to the Inn – to God's House. Come and meet Someone, Who truly is a *Good Neighbor*. He would *really* like to meet you.'

A *truly* Good Samaritan. A *truly* Good Neighbor—Jesus Christ—Who forgives us of our sins, freeing us for service in this world. A truly Good *Savior*, Who promises one Great Day, to return to the "Inn" - for *you* – and take you home.

> My song is love unknown,
> my Savior's love to me,
> love to the loveless shown,
> that they might lovely be.
> O who am I, that for my sake
> my Lord should take frail flesh and die?
>
> He came from his blest throne,
> salvation to bestow;
> but men cared not, and none
> the longed-for Christ would know.
> But oh, my Friend, my Friend indeed,
> who at my need his life did spend!
>
> Sometimes they strew his way,
> and his sweet praises sing;
> resounding all the day
> hosannas to their King.
> Then "Crucify!" is all their breath,
> and for his death they thirst and cry.

Why, what hath my Lord done?
What makes this rage and spite?
He made the lame to run,
he gave the blind their sight.
Sweet injuries! Yet all his deeds
their hatred feeds; they 'gainst him rise.

They rise, and needs will have
my dear Lord sent away;
a murderer they save,
the Prince of Life they slay.
Yet willing he to suff'ring goes,
that he his foes from thence might free.

In life, no house, no home
my Lord on earth might have;
in death, no friendly tomb
but what a stranger gave.
What may I say? Heav'n was his home,
but mine the tomb wherein he lay.

Here might I stay and sing,
no story so divine;
never was love, dear King,
never was grief like thine.
This is my Friend, in whose sweet praise
I all my days could gladly spend.

—Lutheran Service Book
430, public domain

Closing Prayer: *Jesus, I can't thank you enough for being a Good Neighbor, a Good Samaritan and a Good Savior to me. Help me to focus, not on being 'perfect' but on being grateful – for your gift of salvation and the chance to share that mercy and grace with the neighbors You have placed in my path along this journey of life. Amen.*

CHAPTER 7
Entertaining Angels - Welcome as Worship

Hebrews 13:2
"Do not neglect to show hospitality to strangers, for thereby some have entertained angels unawares."

SETTING THE TABLE

Sometimes *you just know an angel when you see one.* For example, if you see a statue with wings, a halo, and a white robe – odds are high you're looking at - an angel. During the Christmas program it's easy to tell who the angels are because they're the little kids with paper mâché wings strapped to their backs and a coat wire hanger in the shape of a halo above their heads. The Bible works much the same way. When people saw these 'holy messengers' of God - they knew *instantly* who they were. When Isaiah the prophet saw the seraphim, the six-winged angels who dwell in the presence of God, he didn't ask for their ID. He took one look at them and immediately cried out, "Woe is me!" St. Mary, the Mother of our Lord, stood face to face with the angel Gabriel, trusting his message that she would carry the Son of God. The Shepherds in the field on that first Christmas night, saw the sky filled with angels as the heavenly host sang at the birth of Christ - and they were terrified. They all knew what they saw – they saw angels.

But it's not always like that. In Proverbs we read: "It is the glory of God to conceal a matter." (Proverbs 25:2) When you're dealing with angels, sometimes, in His infinite wisdom, God *conceals* the identity of angels among us. So, just because we don't always recognize them, doesn't mean there are *no* angels among us. In fact, they sometimes look like *strangers* – strangers that God calls on you and me to entertain, or welcome, with our hospitality. The writer of Hebrews tells us, "Do not forget to entertain strangers, for by doing so some people have entertained angels without knowing it." (Hebrews 13:2)

In this chapter, we will look at how the Early Church embraced God's plan for *relational hospitality*, even in the face of persecution, and how the saints of old can teach us what it means to 'welcome the stranger' today.

Prayer: *Heavenly Father, as we look back on the saints of old and how Your Spirit moved among them, open our hearts to see Your way of welcome as an offering of praise to welcome others in Your Name. Amen*

TABLE TALK

Take a moment to discuss the following together:

1) When you think about the way God reveals Himself throughout Scripture, what are your favorite pictures of Him?

2) Who has been most influential in your walk of faith? Why?

3) Who are the people you credit with teaching you the practices of hospitality? Why?

4) What role do you think hospitality should play in our mission to make disciples?

5) How does our view of God affect our relationships with others - particularly with those who are strangers?

REFLECTION

In the Greco-Roman world, hospitality was a way of life. In a world where hotels and hostels were nonexistent, the hospitality of others was vital to survival. The culture of that day did not only supply the basics of food and shelter to others; it also lavished hospitality upon the guest, seeing them as an extension of worshipping the gods.[56] This 'worship' was manifest in the great lengths the host went to in welcoming their guests. In typical practices, the host usually took the guest by the hand into their home, which was an ancient sign of officially beginning the host-guest relationship.[57] Offering either a bath or foot washing upon entry into the house, the guest provided elaborate meals, often with the guest staying overnight in a special guest room with the understanding they were welcome for lengthier stays. Any animals that traveled with the guest were welcomed and pampered. In more elaborate hospitable settings, new clothes, provisions for their continuing journey, even unique entertainment and a parting gift were offered.[58] As a final gesture, the host would often escort his guest out of town to protect them from thieves, his enemies or attacks from animals.[59]

However, these fantastic shows of hospitality had one ultimate goal – *reciprocity*. Guests were rarely random people off the street but were either the upper crust of society or those high in political stature. In a hostile world, you never knew what day would be your last, with political and social enemies everywhere, no guarantees of safety while traveling and never knowing if one indeed pleased the gods. Therefore, the Greco-Roman world lived in constant fear of reprisal from the gods that dwelt in the heavens or the underworld and lived with the threat of harm from among their own people.[60]

In return for this lavish caring of the guest, the host expected that his hospitality would be returned to him in some way, whether it was the basic needs of lodging and food or even extenuating circumstances, such as obtaining legal counsel in court or gaining advantages through receiving insider information on the latest political intrigues.[61] Grand gestures of hospitality assured that the guest would remember their hosts in the immediate future, either for hosting them or for advancing their status within society.

If the saying, 'the more things change, the more they stay the same' remains true, then Greco-Roman practice of hospitality looked very much like the ulterior motives behind the modern business practices of hospitality and generating business. As we discussed in our last session, the world sees hospitality as 'entertaining,' where doing just the right things in just the right ways creates a place of welcome but not necessarily a place where relationships are formed.

TABLE TALK

6) What other similarities do you see in our modern-day culture, when compared to hospitality in the ancient world? Any differences?

7) How has our advances in technology helped with hospitality? Hindered it?

8) How has technology in your home helped with hospitality? Hindered it?

REFLECTION

Jesus gives us some insight into who these angels might actually be, that we are called to welcome: "When you give a luncheon or dinner, do not invite your friends, your brothers or relatives, or your rich neighbors. If you do, they may invite you back and so you will be repaid. But when you give a banquet - invite the poor, the crippled, the lame, the blind, and you will be blessed. Although they cannot repay you, you will be repaid at the resurrection of the righteous." (Luke 14:12-14) We have no trouble believing that there are angels surrounding those *we love*. But it's harder to imagine angels among the *outcast* in our world, among the *lowest* of the low; among those people we usually don't have *any* dealings with. But the Lord calls us to *entertain* – or *welcome* - these strangers - for by doing so, we just might be entertaining a holy messenger of God.

Now, there's a possibility that you don't know *anyone* who is poor, crippled, lame or blind. But even if that's the case, you're *not* off the hook.

TABLE TALK

9) Recall a time when you were welcomed by someone when you were in great need. How did their 'taking you in' when you had nothing to offer in return impact you?

10) Reflect on this statement: "Take a look in the mirror – there stands someone poor, crippled, lame and blind."

CHRISTIAN PRACTICES IN THE GRECO-ROMAN WORLD

The ancient church had a different motivation from the Greco-Roman world in welcoming guests. While safety and protection certainly benefited Christians, welcoming others went deeper than that. Christianity distinguished itself even from the Jewish world, who under Old Testament prescriptions understood hospitality as relating only to one's extended Jewish family or towards someone of Jewish descent[62], keeping their guests in the Greco-Roman world limited to those they knew or most frequently for someone with a Jewish background.[63]

While Greco-Roman society offered hospitality to appease the gods as an act of 'worship' or for reciprocity among the upper echelon of society, while their Jewish predecessors welcomed only those of similar ancestry, early Christians saw guests, not as a person to be worshipped or to help themselves in future travels or political aspirations. Instead, they viewed the welcoming of others as a means of showing reverence and honor towards God – an act of worship, associating the guest with 'entertaining angels.'[64] As Christianity began to take hold in the ancient world, so did their unique approach towards hospitality and the welcoming of others.

Modern Christians, when thinking of the first Christians, often perceive them as hiding in upper rooms or caves, living on the fringes of society, in constant fear of persecution or death. While this is undoubtedly part of Early Church history, what we find overall is the exact opposite – followers of Christ who engaged the stranger, and their world, with a bold conviction and boundless love.[65]

Early Christians saw themselves as the very incarnation of God's hospitality, not only in sharing His salvation with others but as the embodiment of Christ's presence among His people and in the world – a living preview of Christ's coming hospitality in the new heavens and new earth.[66] This was reflected in their love for one another as well as love for their neighbors.[67] This Gospel called them out of the caves and hiding places and into the communities where they lived, caring for their Christian brothers and sisters – including welcoming the stranger in their midst, regardless of social standing or need, doing so often at the risk of death.

When a devastating plague afflicted the Roman empire in the mid-third century (AD 250–270), averaging five thousand deaths a day in Rome, Cyprian, the North African Bishop of Carthage, called believers out into society to tend to the sick and the dying, while the pagans around them were fleeing the city for fear of dying from the disease themselves.[68] Cyprian charged the Christians of all social levels, from the wealthy to the poor among them, to enter the villages and walk the streets, entering the homes of the sick and dying to offer aid.[69]

Fifty years before Cyprian, the Church father Tertullian (AD 160–220) stood in the gap against accusations that Christianity was a secretive cult that would not bend the knee to Roman gods and defied the state.[70] This led to Tertullian writing his *Apologia*, or 'defense,' in AD 197, which not only attempted to clear up society's misconceptions of these followers of 'The Way,' but also spoke about the support network established by Christians to help those in need, as an extension of God's mercy and hospitality towards all people. Here he writes one of his most compelling defenses of the distinction to be made between pagans and Christians in their motivations behind loving their neighbor:

"We don't take the gifts [from the church treasure chest to aid those in need] and spend them on feasts, drinking-bouts, or fancy restaurants. Instead, we use them to support and bury poor people, to supply the needs of boys and girls who have no means and no parents. We support the elderly confined now to their homes. We also help those who have suffered shipwreck. And if there happen to be any in the mines, or banished to the islands, or shut up in the prisons – for nothing but their fidelity to the cause of God's Church – they then become the nurslings of the confession they hold [as we take them in to help them]. Primarily it is the acts of love that are so noble that lead many to put a brand upon us. 'See,' they say, 'how much they love one another.'"[71]

Christian mercy and hospitality turned Greco-Roman ideologies on its ear, subverting the core of Hellenistic societal practices in the home with the incarnational, tangible love and grace of Jesus that was self-sacrificial - with no underlying motivation of reciprocity, no expectations of being repaid or benefiting from their hospitable practices.

AT THE TABLE

11) **Read Ephesians 4:13, Romans 12:12-13; Romans 15:32; 1 Thessalonians 5:11; 1 Timothy 5:10; Hebrews 10:25** – according to

these verses, what is hospitality?

12) **Read Psalm 145:4, Proverbs 13:20, Acts 8:27-31, 35, Colossians 1:27-28, Titus 2:3-5** – according to these verses, what is hospitality?

13) **Read Psalm 105:1, Matthew 28:18-20, Romans 1:15-16** – according to these verses, what is hospitality?

TABLE TALK
Hospitality, according to God's Word, has three key purposes:

- The first purpose of hospitality is to encourage and build up the saints, providing hospitality to fellow believers.
- The second purpose of hospitality is discipleship and mentorship.
- The third purpose is to share the Gospel with people.

Would you agree with these purposes? Any other purposes you'd like to add?

REFLECTION
In the book, *Unchristian*[72] researchers Kinnaman and Lyons found 'Only one-third of young outsiders believe that Christians genuinely care about them (34 percent). And most Christians are oblivious to these perceptions—64 percent of Christians said they believe that outsiders would perceive their efforts as genuine.'

This is especially significant because Christians were very accurate in anticipating many of the negative perceptions of outsiders but being perceived as insincere surprised believers.'[73] Furthermore, Kinnaman states these young 'outsiders' often believed that Christians engaged them with the sole purpose of 'saving them' – where they weren't treated as persons but as trophies: "Even if our intentions seem pure to us, outsiders often feel targeted, that we merely want another church member or a new notch in the 'get-saved' belt."[74]

TABLE TALK

14) What things stand out for you in Kinnaman and Lyons' research?

15) What practices in the Early Church could be used by God's People to engage our world, today?

REFLECTION

There are strangers deserving of your hospitality. Just look around you. How many people in your church family do you know only by name and nothing else? Sure, you may say hello after church on your way to the car or nod your head as you make eye contact on the way into church, but God intends something *more* for His people. The author of Hebrews calls on God's people to get to know one another. To *really* welcome others - not only into our church, but into our *homes* and into our *lives*. To share our meals with them, to be generous with them, and to expect nothing in return. By doing so, we just might be entertaining an angel sent from heaven.

Read Acts 2:37-47

16) Describe the shape of the life of the new community in Acts. With what activities does the new community of faith involve itself?

17) What elements of the life of your congregation relate to the description given in Acts 2?

18) **Read 1 Thessalonians 4:9-10 and 2 Thessalonians 1:3** What two elements of growth had taken place in the Thessalonian

believers?

19) **Read 1 Thessalonians 3:12-13** What relationship causes us to be able to increase in love for one another?

20) According to the Scripture above, what reason is given for love to grow?

21) **Read 1 Peter 1:22-23; 1 John 3:23; 1 John 4:7 and 1 John 4:11** According to these Scriptures, what action is needed to love some people?

22) Circle the characteristics of love in the following passage:

1 Corinthians 13:4 Love is patient, love is kind. It does not envy, it does not boast, it is not proud. 5 It is not rude, it is not self-seeking, it is not easily angered, it keeps no record of wrongs. 6 Love does not delight in evil but rejoices with the truth. 7 It always protects, always trusts, always hopes, always perseveres. 8 Love never fails. But where there are prophecies, they will cease; where there are tongues, they will be stilled; where there is knowledge, it will pass away. 9 For we know in part and we prophesy in part, 10 but when perfection comes, the imperfect disappears. 11 When I was a child, I talked like a child, I thought like a child, I reasoned like a child. When I became a man, I put childish ways behind me. 12 Now we see but a poor reflection as in a mirror; then we shall see face to face. Now I know in part; then I shall know fully, even as I am fully known. 13 And now these three remain: faith, hope and love. But the greatest of these is love.

23) What impressions do you get from what you have circled?

24) What are some examples of childish thinking that keeps us

from maturing?

25) Now, **Read 1 Corinthians 12:13-31**. Knowing that these verses precede the passage above, how do these verses help you understand the context of 1 Corinthians 13:4-13? How does this impact your understanding of what St. Paul means by 'love'?

REFLECTION

It is fascinating that the Early Christians' outreach in the world was not really all that special or novel when compared to the approach of the Ancient World.

Most of the Greco-Roman world already offered hospitality to people of influence and had state programs to care for the poor, the widowed and orphaned.

What made the difference - in addition to the Holy Spirit leading the way - was the Early Christians took hospitality, caring for the poor, widowed and orphaned and coupled it with their rock-solid passion and conviction in Christ, engaging everyone with it, not just people of influence.

And the Lord blessed that passion and conviction so that Christianity *outlived Rome*.

How might God's Church look differently if His people engaged their community with Christ's passion, love and conviction?

How might God's Church act differently, if they remembered that His Church had its greatest explosion of growth under a pagan government that was hostile to their beliefs and way of life?

TABLE TALK

26) If it seems too much to open your arms and your heart to a *complete* stranger; if it's too great a struggle to make new friends among your fellow believers; then the best place to start is to entertain

the strangers that you know *the best*.

- Think of people you *used* to know very well but have lost touch with them.

- People you spent most of your free time with but for some reason, you've drifted apart.

- That friend who stabbed you in the back, and so you've never spoken to her again.

- That confidant who suddenly turned on you for no reason at all.

- That best friend who you now shun because you're holding a grudge over something they did.

- Maybe the stranger for you is your wife – your husband – your children.

Take some time to ponder how you might be able to reconnect with these people and welcome them into your heart, again.

BRINGING IT HOME

When we're content with the fact that our brothers and sisters in the faith remain strangers to us, we break the bond of fellowship that makes us one in the faith. When we refuse to build bridges with our brothers and sisters who have sinned against us - we break the bond of fellowship with Jesus - Who calls us to welcome the stranger in our midst. When we ignore our spouse and refuse to listen to their needs, we sin against our God, Who created marriage to bless His people. When we ignore the hurting, the broken and the needy, we sin against Christ and His command to welcome those we normally wouldn't think of spending time with. And that sin grows and takes root deep within our souls when we let old grudges live, nurse our hurts and wounds and refuse to entertain the stranger who used to be our friend. Without even knowing it, we sin against the angels of God sent for our protection and companionship, and in so doing we make ourselves strangers to God Himself.

That's why, Jesus became a stranger for us. On the cross, He became a stranger to His own Heavenly Father. As He hung there, He cried out, "My God, my God, why have You forsaken Me?" Covered in all *our* sins of ignoring those who we think are unworthy of our love; clothed with our wickedness of refusing to share our lives with those we don't know or don't like. Christ died on the cross as a stranger - to His Heavenly Father; a stranger to the world and as an *angel* – as 'God's Messenger' - that almost no one recognized. He did this, so you would *always* be recognized by God and welcomed by Him!

In dying a stranger's death, Christ has destroyed everything that makes the stranger among us, strange. He paid the price for our poor treatment of strangers. By taking the lowest place and putting Himself where no man would want to be, Christ earned His own exaltation. After His death, He didn't remain a stranger to His Father. In His love and mercy, God the Father raised Him up from the dead and restored their relationship to its rightful honor - seating Him at His right hand, at the head of the 'table of heaven'. And as we welcome the stranger in our midst, we take comfort that through Jesus, God is now pleased with us – granting us, who once were strangers, ourselves – a seat at His own table through gifts of bread and wine - His true body and true blood; a foretaste of the eternal banquet to come in His heavenly kingdom.

God's grace empowers us to do His good work of reaching out to the stranger and reconciling with those who we've made into strangers. So, go ahead - call up that friend that you've ignored for too long. Take the hand of the person you vowed to love until the day death parts you and say, "I'm sorry". Open your door once again to the stranger in your life. Welcome that new neighbor across the street you don't know. Be willing to entertain even the strangest of strangers, for by so doing, some have entertained angels unawares. Because we are forgiven and declared righteous by our Righteous Stranger, Jesus - our welcoming of strangers is now pleasing to God.

27) Think of the 5 closest homes, apartments or workspaces where you live, work and play. Write down the names of the people you know who live, work and play there and what you know about them.

1. _____
2. _____
3. _____
4. _____
5. _____

28) This week spend time in prayer for these people. Ask the Lord to open an opportunity for you to have a conversation, a kindness, or interaction with one of them.

29) Think of a person who came alongside you, mentored you or was there for you when you needed them. Attempt to track that person down. Send them a note, give them a call – thank them for investing in you.

> Crown Him with many crowns
> The Lamb upon His throne;
> Hark how the heavenly anthem drowns
> All music but its own.
> Awake, my soul, and sing
> Of Him who died for thee

And hail Him as thy matchless King
Through all eternity.

Crown Him the Virgin's Son,
The God incarnate born,
Whose arm those crimson trophies won
Which now His brow adorn;
Fruit of the mystic rose,
As of that rose the stem;
The root whence mercy ever flows,
The Babe of Bethlehem.

Crown Him the Lord of Love.
Behold His hands and side,
Rich wounds, yet visible above,
In beauty glorified.
No angel in the sky
Can fully bear that sight,
But downward bends his wondering eye
At mysteries so bright!

Crown Him the Lord of Life
Who triumphed o'er the grave
And rose victorious in the strife
For those He came to save.
His glories now we sing
Who died and rose on high,
Who died eternal life to bring

And lives that death may die.

Crown Him the Lord of Heaven,
Enthroned in worlds above,
Crown Him the King to whom is given
The wondrous name of Love.
Crown Him with many crowns
As thrones before Him fall;
Crown Him, ye kings, with many crowns
For He is King of all.

—Lutheran Service Book
525, public domain

Closing Prayer: *Lord, the Christian community is called to live out Your hospitality in the world. We welcome the stranger best when we first welcome one another in the Body of Christ. May our joyful sharing of hospitality be the highway on which the Holy Spirit can travel on to other people. Amen.*

CHAPTER 8
"And You Welcomed Me...", Whatever My Need

2 Timothy 2:1, 3
"You then, my child, be strengthened by the grace that is in Christ Jesus. Share in suffering as a good soldier of Christ Jesus.

Matthew 25:35
"I was a stranger and you welcomed me..."

SETTING THE TABLE

Whenever I think about the sound of gentle humming by a windowsill and old Dr. Pepper bottles made out of glass - I think about J.J.

J.J. was my uncle and he was born just a few years after my father. At first, he seemed just like any other healthy baby boy, but as time passed, the doctors noticed that something was wrong with J.J. He acted different, he didn't speak, didn't comprehend things well and would hurt himself when he got frustrated or angry. The doctors eventually came up with a diagnosis and informed my grandma that J.J. was 'retarded' – a cruel description by our standards today, but in grandma's day, that's the only term they had. And the doctors also had a suggestion for how to handle him: put J.J. in an institution so he wouldn't be a burden on the family.

Now, grandma was a God-fearing Christian lady, and she lived out the phrase "WWJD", long before it became a cultural buzzword. And Grandma knew all about those kinds of places – they weren't nice facilities at all, but places where people dumped the leftovers of society, the ones nobody wanted – the ones that people were ashamed of, where they were abused and neglected in nothing more than a modified prison cell; abandoned and left to slowly fade away in to nothing.

Because of that, grandma knew what had to be done. She got in that doctor's face, swung her purse at him and told him flat out that J.J. was a child of God – not trash, that He had a purpose for J.J. and the only way he was gonna go to a place like that was over her cold, dead body. And with that, she took J.J. home and did the one thing she knew to do – she picked up the phone and called her pastor.

Prayer: *God in heaven, even as Christians, we struggle with seeing people the way You see them. Our own discomfort, at times, keeps us from making connections with others who need Your love and grace. Open my mind and heart to the truth You want to reveal to me in Your Word this day, as we 'share in the suffering' of others to honor Your Name. Amen.*

SETTING THE TABLE

Take a moment to discuss the following together:

1) How does our society positively see people with 'special needs'? Negatively?

2) Have you ever experienced a time when a friend or relative with special needs was neglected or ignored? How did your friend or relative react?

3) How might your experiences of being neglected or ignored mirror the experiences of people with special needs? How might your experience differ from their experience?

REFLECTION

That story with J.J. happened many decades ago – and what a blessing that things didn't stay that way. There are so many great organizations out there that help people with special needs, and our communities are working to advocate for them. But there is still much work left to be done. You only need to look at how our world still treats the weakest among us. When the world gets a little sloppy with its moral behavior, it then decides it's okay that an unborn baby should die so that other people can live how they wish.

Tests in the womb try to determine if a baby has Down Syndrome, and if that test (which is highly inaccurate anyway) comes back positive, the world demands that the baby's life end so it won't be a burden. Sadly, that's the world's attitude toward most things that it sees as an inconvenience – *including* people: "Let's get rid of those *inconvenient people*. And if we can't cure them, then let's call up Dr. Kevorkian and get rid of those *inconvenient people* so they won't have to suffer and be a *burden* anymore."

Burdens are a matter of perspective. St. Paul once wrote, "We rejoice in our sufferings, knowing that suffering produces endurance, and endurance produces character, and character produces hope…" (Romans 5:3-4)

TABLE TALK

4) What might happen if society saw everyone not as 'people with problems' but as 'people with potential'?

5) How might God's people be more outspoken about defending the weak and helpless (the elderly, the infirm, the unborn)?

6) How might God's people better demonstrate forgiveness and mercy to the women and men hurting from the pain of an abortion? How might our words speak life into their heart?

What about the suffering our world *can't* see? People with epilepsy, mental illness, depression, attention-deficit disorder, autism, even severe food allergies? Often, the world is even *tougher* on those kinds of ailments. Because the world often blames the *person* who has it or tells the person who is suffering to 'work through it', that 'it's not so bad' or the worst one of all - 'you look fine to *me.*' May God have mercy on us for knowingly and unknowingly *crushing the spirit* of the weakest among us.

7) How might your home be a haven for those with special needs? How might your heart?

8) If you have a friend or family member with special needs, how might you honor them when you're at a restaurant? In your home? In your daily life?

9) Side Note: Many Christians are embarrassed or uncomfortable approaching their friends or family with special needs about their challenges. But it is an incredible gesture of love to ask your friend or family member how you can meet their needs in advance. You show them, in word and deed, that you value their *participation* – not just their *observation* - in your life.

My Grandma called her pastor – because she knew St. Paul's words to Timothy, "You then, my child, be strengthened by the grace that is in Christ Jesus. Share in suffering as a good soldier of Christ Jesus." (2 Tim. 2:1) She knew that Jesus had impacted this world forever with His innocent suffering and death, saving her, and J.J., from sin. And that also meant He had impacted other Christians who were called to act different than the rest of the world. That the Church was called to 'bear one another's burdens' and that they *would* 'share in her suffering' as 'good soldiers for Christ'. And they did. They prayed for her and J.J. They included him in the life of the congregation. They connected her with another organization that saw J.J. like grandma did – as a forgiven child of God, who deserved dignity and respect. That organization built J.J. up, they taught him to speak and all the while, J.J. grew in his faith. And he became the man and the child of God the he was called to be.

My first memory of J.J. was when I was around seven years old. I went in to my sister's room and I saw him leaning on a windowsill, looking up at the sky, holding an old glass Dr. Pepper bottle. He was humming the tune, 'Amazing Grace' and spinning that Dr. Pepper bottle in his hands. So, I asked, "Uncle J.J., what'r you doin'?" And he smiled and said, "God's gonna make it rain for me!" and he kept spinning that bottle. Now, it was a clear blue sky that day, but sure enough, about 15 minutes later, a short cloudburst sprang up and dumped rain on our block for about a minute. And you could hear J.J. laughing through the whole house. My uncle was the first person to show me what beautiful, childlike faith looked like. And I would have missed out on that… if the world had had its way with J. J.

10) Why do we have handicapped pews, ramps and wheelchair access for people at our church? Is it because the 'Americans with Disabilities Act' requires it? Or is there something more?

11) St. Paul says in Christ, we are called to 'share in the sufferings of others as a good soldier of Christ'. So why does God's people make the effort to wait for those with canes and walkers and wheelchairs as they make their way to the communion rail? Why do we offer gluten free wafers? Why do we raise the communion cup to the mouths of those who need it lifted to

their lips, or to take Christ's very body and blood to the pew where someone is sitting?

12) Reflect on this statement: As Christians we see every person as someone for whom Christ died, whatever their needs, and they have *value* – not because of what they can *do*, but because of whose they *are*!

BRINGING IT HOME

Whether someone has OCD, ADD, or ALS, they have *value* in Christ's Church and in our lives. What people suffer will *never* make them a 'second-class citizen' among Christ's people - because the Great Suffering Servant became a '*nameless* citizen' for us - hung on a Roman cross to save us from sin. Living in that forgiveness, God's people offer a place you can call home –in His House – and in ours. That's why in Christ, we not only get to 'share in the *sufferings*' of others, we get to take part in something the world can't comprehend - 'sharing in heavenly *blessings*' here on earth.

The highlight of my Christmas one year was hearing a little girl with Down Syndrome tell everyone loud and clear, "Merry Christmas!" at the Children's Christmas Program - when the world thought she would never be able to speak. I once served where a man with special needs named Andrew, enthusiastically greeted everyone he met, and would proudly tell me almost every time I saw him that he'd invited someone to church. And he often brought them with him – living out his name, as Andrew, the disciple who brought people to Jesus.

I'd have very likely never known how the Minnesota Twins were doing, if it wasn't for an elderly man with mental challenges, who made a point to consistently feed me the scores on Sunday. I can't tell you the personal blessings it's brought to my own family to have so many Christians surround *us* with care and concern throughout one of our child's challenges with special needs over the years: through her epilepsy, her special diet, her countless hospital stays and ER visits.

God's people, through their prayers, cards, visits, meals – through 'sharing in _our_ sufferings' created Christian blessings because of it. But the greatest joy of all is seeing so many of God's people watching out for one another, bearing one another's burdens, and sharing in the sufferings of others. By faith, may the Lord's Church continue to openly share His love with the weakest of His children, to make this House of God a true 'Bethesda' – a 'house of mercy', where every single person, whether they're someone like my Uncle J.J. or someone who carries a hurt we *can't* see, or someone like *you* - that you know you are *valued* to God and to His People - not because of what you can *do*, but because of what has been done *for* you in Jesus. That means you are a beautiful and forgiven child of God – not trash – who will always have a purpose and a place in His Son's Kingdom, whatever your needs might be.

13) Pretend for a moment, that there were no ministry staff at your church (because it is our nature to think that ministry is *only* done be them). How might your *church family* be more attentive to the members who need it?

14) Do an 'access assessment' of your church. Are there people at the entrances who can hold open the door for those who need it? Are there wheelchairs within reach, should someone need one? Can everyone who wants to come up for communion physically have the means to do so? Can they reach the things they need to reach?

15) Do a 'spiritual inventory' of your congregation. Are the families of children with special needs welcomed in your congregation? Is it acceptable in your church culture to

allow random outbursts, hollering or crying? Do you talk *to* the children who can't respond to you, instead of talking *at* them? Do you hold in your church culture that the highest priority be all God's people gather together – warts and all, inconveniences, interruptions and all?

16) Do a 'spiritual inventory' of your home. Is it a place where people with special needs will know their requests will be heard? Will they be respected and loved there? Will they be welcomed just like any other person? Will they not be known as 'your special needs friend', but 'your friend'?

17) Side Note: Special needs ministry is varied and multi-faceted. But some general rules of thumb that may help you engage:

1 - Do not touch someone with special needs (i.e. hold their hand, touch their shoulder, give a hug) unless given permission to do so. Physical contact not only makes some special needs individuals uncomfortable; it can even physically hurt.

3 – If a person with special needs is okay with being touched, shaking their hand and saying hello is quite appropriate. By touch, you show them you welcome and accept them just as you would any other individual.

4 – ALWAYS talk *to* the person with special needs – do not talk *at* them or speak to others as if they aren't there. Acknowledge their presence. *Especially* if they can't respond verbally. They will respond in other ways.

5 – As a wise person once told me, "I own my struggles – my struggles do not own me!" The same applies for people with special needs. They are amazing, insightful individuals who often carry the deepest connection to God's mercy and grace.

6 – LEARN, don't teach. The best way to get to know a person with special needs is to be a good student. Don't assume you know their one-of-a-kind situation or what they need. Ask. Listen. Respect. Love.
7 – Here's a thought – ask them to pray for *you*. We are *all* handicapped with sin and we all struggle. These special people, as the saints of God, are mighty prayer warriors, when you entrust them to strap on their armor and go to battle for you.

> I am Jesus' little lamb,
> Ever glad at heart I am;
> For my Shepherd gently guides me,
> Knows my need, and well provides me,
> Loves me every day the same,
> Even calls me by my name.
>
> Day by day, at home, away,
> Jesus is my Staff and Stay.
> When I hunger, Jesus feeds me,
> Into pleasant pastures leads me;
> When I thirst, He bids me go
> Where the quiet waters flow.
>
> Who so happy as I am,
> Even now the Shepherd's lamb?
> And when my short life is ended,
> By His angel host attended,

> He shall fold me to His breast,
> There within His arms to rest.
>
> **—Lutheran Service Book**
> *740, public domain*

Closing Prayer: *Dear God, You have blessed me with so many people in my life that can teach me so much. Keep my heart open to welcome those with special needs. Widen the boundaries of my soul, to know that I carry my handicaps, as well and would be lost, were it not for Your love and mercy through Your Son, Who handicapped Himself on the cross to make me free. Use me as Your instrument, so that I may learn of the mercy and grace shown through all of Your people. Amen.*

CHAPTER 9
"When Peace Like a River…"
Welcoming Adversity When Life Hurts

Job 1:21b
"The LORD gave, and the LORD has taken away;
blessed be the name of the LORD."

2 Corinthians 12:9
"But he said to me, 'My grace is sufficient for you,
for my power is made perfect in weakness.' Therefore
I will boast all the more gladly about my weaknesses,
so that Christ's power may rest on me."

Romans 15:4
"For everything that was written in the past was
written to teach us, so that through endurance and the
encouragement of the Scriptures we might have hope."

SETTING THE TABLE

The sounds had become almost deafening: the beeps coming from the machines around me and the soft hissing of oxygen that was swirling inside my newborn daughter's incubator. Our daughter was four hours old – four pounds, four ounces. Nine weeks premature. The size of my hand. My wife said she hadn't felt our daughter kicking in the womb, and our hospital visit to determine the cause ended up in an emergency c-section to try and save our daughter's life.

As they prepared my wife for surgery, I was sitting in a chair in the hallway, when our doctor came out of the operating room. Having an intense look on her face, she approached me and said, "I just want you to know – this is *serious*." Dumbfounded, trying to process everything, I simply asked, "How serious?" Without hesitating, she said, "*Very* serious. I need you to do two things for me: keep your wife calm – and pray like you've never prayed before." Without waiting for a response, she wheeled around and entered the pre-op room.

And I was left in the hallway, alone.

I was a fourth-year seminary student, just two quarters away from graduating and being ordained as a pastor. I'd been taught countless collect prayers that I would later use to lead the church in prayer. I'd learned the systematic forms to plan for public prayer and for writing devotions. A real treasure trove of ways to pray.

But sitting there, in that cold and grey hallway - I had… nothing.

Stripped to my most basic of human needs, I went to the one place I *knew* I could go.

I went to the prayer I'd learned since I was a boy.

In a choked voice, I prayed as the words echoed around me in the hallway…

"Our Father, Who art in heaven, hallowed be Thy Name…"

When I finished, I uttered a whispered cry to my Lord, over and over—not knowing what else to say…

"*Jesus, I trust You…Jesus, I trust You…*"

"Sir, we're ready for you."

I hadn't even noticed the anesthesiologist standing next to me.

Standing up, I followed him into pre-op where my wife was prepped and waiting, a blue medical drape covering her.

"Everything okay?" she asked. There's a reason I don't play poker. I wear my emotions all over my face. It was obvious to her that I knew more than I was telling. Not wanting to lie but also wanting to keep my promise to the doctor to keep my wife calm, I simply nodded a 'yes', tears welling up in my eyes. That was all my wife needed to know – things were *not* okay.

But I silently prayed with all my heart that it would be. After suffering the heartache of infertility for years, only to suffer the heartbreak of a miscarriage, God blessed us with our first daughter, Addisyn - a living, breathing miracle that we adored. We had our own medical scares with her, too; at one point, we were told they couldn't locate her in the womb, and we would need to terminate the pregnancy. My wife adamantly refused and asked our friends and family to pray.

Two weeks later – there she was, our tiny baby girl with a strong and regular heartbeat.

After birth, Addisyn developed such severe jaundice that she was brought to the ER where discussions at one point involved replacing all of her blood to get the bilirubin count down. Miraculously, she pulled through. I can't imagine our household without this beautiful, intelligent, musically talented, follower of Jesus who brightens our world with love, music and laughter.

Our house would feel so empty without her in it.

Leslie and I felt God's Presence throughout the medical scares with Addisyn. Now, as we held each other's hands in the operating room with our second daughter on the way – not knowing what the future held – we held on to the One Who held the future…

"*Jesus, I trust You…Jesus, I trust You…*"

As terrible as things were in that moment—as challenging as things would be, years later—we were *never* far from God. Our relationship with Him, built over time and prayer and through God's Son, Who took our place on a cross – we knew He would see us through – no matter what the future held.

Maybe you've heard stories like the one I've shared, before. Maybe you've *lived* one just like it. Regardless of your life situation, if you live on this big blue ball, we call Earth, long enough - you *will* be touched by pain and heartbreak. Be it large or small – adversity eventually comes to us all. And no matter how strong your faith in Jesus is, it can sometimes leave you with deep and haunting questions during those quiet nights of the soul.

"Does God care?" "What is His plan?" "Why would He allow something like this to happen to me?"

Let's seek the answers, together. And I pray it will more clearly reveal the loving heart of our Heavenly Father, Who has a far greater plan, in the midst of our pain, than we can possibly comprehend.

Prayer: *Lord, so many times in my life, I don't have a clue as to what Your plan is for me. I think partly, it's because I'm so focused on my own timeline, I forget to focus on eternity. Help me, as Your child to remember eternal things - the adversity endured for me at Your Son's cross – so that an empty grave would be awaiting me, too, one Great and Glorious Day. Amen.*

TABLE TALK

Take a moment to discuss the following together:

1) What coping mechanism do you have to handle situations in life that are a trial? What coping mechanisms are positive? Negative?

2) How do you deal with adversity when it comes to you? Is there a 'go-to' prayer you use? Scripture passages?

REFLECTION

Not many people know the story behind the well-known Christian hymn, "When Peace, like a River" (Lutheran Service Book 763). This hymn was written by a man named Horatio Spafford. Spafford was a very successful Chicago businessman, until the great Chicago fire of 1871 wiped out all his real-estate holdings. About that time, his only son, just 4 years old, passed away from scarlet fever. Horatio drowned his grief in work, pouring himself in to rebuilding the city of Chicago and helping the over 100,000 people left homeless from the great fire.

Two years later, Spafford and his family were planning to vacation in Europe and to help with evangelism of the Gospel there. When last-minute business threatened to delay their trip, Spafford decided to send his wife, Anna and their 4 daughters, Maggie, Tanetta, Annie and Bessie on ahead of him. In the middle of the Atlantic, their ship, the *Ville du Havre*, was struck by another ship, the *Lochearn*. The *Ville du Havre* sank.

All four of Spafford's young daughters drowned.

Mrs. Spafford was found nearly unconscious, clinging to a piece of the wreckage. When the 47 survivors landed in Wales, Mrs. Spafford cabled her husband with two haunting words:

"Saved."

"Alone."

Immediately, Spafford sailed to Europe to join her. One day during his grief-filled voyage, the ship's captain called for Spafford to come up to the bridge. The captain told Spafford that he estimated they were at the location of that tragic shipwreck. It's hard to imagine the emotional hell that Spafford must have been going through at that moment. After taking it all in, Spafford said to himself, "It Is Well. The Will of God be done."

He went back to his cabin and he wrote down these words: "When peace, like a river, attendeth my way; When sorrows, like sea billows, roll; Whatever my lot, Thou hast taught me to say, It is well, it is well with my soul." And he put these words to the tune, *Ville du Havre*, the name of the ship that took his 4 remaining children…

How on earth could Spafford, on that high, blustery ocean, buffeted within by unbelievable grief, be able to take it all in and finally say, "It is well, it is well with my soul"? To know that answer would be of great help to you and me, don't you think? Because we, too, are tossed about on the seas of life. Finances. Health. Relationships. Loss of people and things dear to us. What howls on the *outside* can churn our emotions on the *inside*: Fear. Worry. Anger. Grief.

There's not one of us who doesn't know these emotions and knows them well. Philosophers have observed that it's not the storms outside that bother us so much, as the way we respond to them inside. We are often blindsided, buffeted by unseen storms, broken and driven to our knees in despair. But one thing we are *not*, is *alone*. God comes to us when we need Him most. In those moments, we cling to His promises, by faith…

***

The emergency c-section was over. But our struggles had just begun. Our daughter's umbilical cord was wrapped three times around her body, once around her right arm and twice around her neck. Miraculously, she was alive. In fact, our doctor pulled me aside and said, "I want you to know—in all my years of doing this, I have *never* had a situation turn out like yours just did." I was overwhelmed with gratitude to the Lord, for sparing our daughter's life! But there was more news to come.

I'll never forget the drawing that our NICU doctor put before us, as he sketched out on a napkin, the map of Chloe's brain, showing the damage she had suffered. The immense strain in the womb, essentially being straightjacketed by her own umbilical cord, had caused her to suffer a stroke, resulting in a grade-four intraventricular brain hemorrhage in the left hemisphere, which we would later find out would mean that the left side of her brain would never form. And now, my wife was in post-op and I was standing over our daughter – alone – watching her tiny body cling to life.

Three hours before this, Doug Chinberg, my vicarage pastor and dear brother in Christ, came to the NICU to officiate while I performed my very first Baptism on my little girl. I will never forget Doug's kindness, as he came in the middle of the night, to ensure my daughter was claimed by Christ.

As I adjusted to standing over Chloe's incubator, I heard a man's voice behind me, so I turned to see where it came from: a man about my age, standing over another incubator. He had watched me give my daughter the sacrament of Baptism, using purified water from a vial and speaking God's Word of forgiveness. That man's son was six hours old – a little over *one pound* – tubes and IV's all over his little frame – and fighting for his life, too.

We both exchanged a knowing glance and a thought that we didn't need to put into words – what a journey this day had been! Just a few hours ago, we were joyful, expectant fathers. Now, we were in a place we had never been before, talking to people we had never met before. All the while, living in a haze of heart monitors and oxygen tubes, praying that our children would see another day. Then my mind finally heard the words that the man had spoken to pull my attention away from my child.

A simple question. A haunting question.

"*Do you feel like God's abandoned you?*"

What comfort could I give to someone who was in the same situation I was in? What do you say to someone who is wondering 'why' as much as you are? What hope could I give to him in such a seemingly hopeless place?

TABLE TALK

3) **Read 2 Corinthians 12:2-10**. In verse 2, St. Paul is talking about himself in a tremendous vision he had from God. Since Paul was a Hebrew, he describes his vision in Hebrew terms:

   a. **The first heaven** - where the birds and the clouds were.

b. **The second heaven** - where the sun, the moon and the stars are.
   c. **The third heaven** – where God lives. We see a vision of *exultation* in heaven before a discussion on *struggle* in this life.

4) **Look at 2 Cor. 12:7 again**. The Greek word St. Paul uses for 'thorn', is literally, 'tent peg'. All we have to do is look at Paul's missionary life to know that he had quite a few 'tent pegs' in his career:

   a. He was beaten on three occasions with a 'cat of nine tails', which involved 39 lashes each time. "40 lashes, minus one" punishment was reserved for Roman citizens, like Paul.
   b. He sustained five beatings with Roman rods, a torture designed to break the back and crush the vertebrae.
   c. He was stoned several times within an inch of his life. He probably walked bent over, with a hunched back, and more than likely was horribly deformed.

5) Besides physical pain and suffering, what else might the 'tent peg' be that St. Paul discusses?

6) Discuss this thought: "If you ask most folks today how they're feeling, you'd better grab a chair, because it could take a while to get the whole answer. I think that if one of us had written this epistle instead of Paul, more than likely we would have told everybody, "Here's my problem. Here's what I'm suffering. Here's my sickness." We love to talk about our sicknesses and problems and troubles, but not Paul. Not a word. We don't know what this thorn in the flesh actually was. That would have taken the focus off Jesus."

7) How easy is it to complain about circumstances in this life? Do you catch yourself living in a 'glass half empty' state? What helps get you out of this cycle?

REFLECTION

My wife and I saw many people without hope over the two months that Chloe was in the NICU. Parents with questions, with fear and despair in their eyes as they longed to hold their children, but couldn't reach through the incubator to touch them, for fear of infection. Parents like me who watched in horror while tubes were inserted through their little ones' nose to reach their tiny stomachs and force feed them just three milliliters of breast milk – and praying they could keep it down. The endless IV changes and blood draws done through the only available veins large enough to do so – in their heads.

Not even being able to see their child's face, because of the large eye patches to protect their eyes under the purple lights that helped to keep their weak liver from elevating their bilirubin count and killing them. The anguish of leaving their child alone to come home to a sleepless night of lying in their beds and thinking about their child and hoping they wouldn't receive a late-night call that their baby had a setback, or a seizure, or wasn't eating right – or was dead.

My wife and I were one of the few couples that could *smile* in that place. And when new parents just coming in with their child, or doctors or nurses would wonder why it was that we could do such a thing in such a seemingly hopeless place, we could tell them about the hope that we both had in Christ. It was the same thing that I told that desperate man beside his one-pound son's incubator during the first four hours of Chloe's life. I told him, "What you saw me doing tonight was Christ coming to my little girl in her Baptism. And whatever she faces now, one day at the resurrection, none of this will matter."

A hospital chaplain baptized his little boy the next morning.

Eighteen days later, his son was with Jesus.

***

No doubt you can recall some point in *your* life where you were handed a situation, you prayed to escape it, but couldn't get away from it. And like St. Paul with his 'thorn in the flesh', one way or another you had to settle down and live with the pain. But what Paul is telling us today is that no weakness we have, no pain we endure, can compare to the strength that we receive in our Savior. Paul says, "Three times I pleaded with the Lord to take it away from me. But he said to me, 'My grace is sufficient for you, for my power is made perfect in weakness.' Therefore, I will boast all the more gladly about my weaknesses, so that Christ's power may rest on me. That is why, for Christ's sake, I delight in weaknesses, in insults, in hardships, in persecutions, in difficulties. For when I am weak, then I am strong." (2 Corinthians 12:8-10)

There was another man, Who became well-acquainted with thorns, Who didn't look all that strong to the world. When Jesus willingly wore His crown of thorns, He assured us that we would *never* have to. He endured the greatest of suffering for our sake. He had the *ultimate* cross to bear – one that held the sins of the world – including yours and mine. And it is because of *His* strength, *His* sacrifice, *His* love, that we can boast about Jesus and His power to save us, in spite of our weaknesses. It is why St. Paul could say with confidence, "For the foolishness of God is wiser than man's wisdom, and the weakness of God is stronger than man's strength." (1 Cor. 1:25)

I'm convinced that Paul would never have been Paul *without* that terrible 'tent peg' in his flesh.

Take some shining specimen of manhood who has never had a handicap, who's had fortunate circumstances and never known a sick day in his life, and however energetic he may be in his service to others, there are things he could *never* do that Helen Keller *could*. Whatever your ailment may be on this earth, know that you are a unique, one-of-a-kind instrument that the Lord is using to shape and mold the lives of those around you. Because of Christ, we have the assurance that God's grace *is* totally sufficient for all of our thorns, our tent pegs, our handicaps, our problems and our troubles. And when you're weak, when you need God most, through Jesus, the strength of His grace will be there to see you through.

And that is something that *all* of us, by faith, can boast about.

TABLE TALK

1) **Read Isaiah 53:3-5**. How does the prophet describe Jesus?

2) What 'tent pegs' have you prayed for God to remove, but He didn't? Looking at 2 Cor. 12:9, what possible reasons might God have for His choice?

3) Reflect on this statement: "God answers prayer in three ways: 'Yes.' 'No.' 'Grow.'"

4) I had a friend who was a pediatric cardiologist. He and his wife had a child who was deathly allergic to certain foods. One wrong food item could have killed their child. One day, when his wife was particularly down over their child's condition, he gave her a tour of the pediatric care wing of his hospital. Why do you think he did this?

REFLECTION

As the weeks of Chloe's hospitalization wore on, we were starting to feel the emotional and physical strain. Our family lived five states away, and I was trying to get school done during the day, while Leslie worked. Dear friends from seminary took Addisyn while Leslie and I would meet up after she got off work to go to the hospital to stay by Chloe's incubator. We'd return to get Addisyn in the evening, then head to bed, trying to sleep. Then we'd repeat the process the next day.

In short - we were exhausted.

A couple of friends from our vicarage congregation came by our house to visit one day. One of them, a faithful elder, asked me if there was anything that we needed. I instinctively responded, "No, I think we're doing okay."

That's when the elder's expression changed to one of complete seriousness. He put a hand on my shoulder and said, "Rance, don't rob your fellow Christians from being *Christian*. What do you need?" It was then that the walls came down and I told him everything: Our struggles of late. Being so tired. Scared for Chloe, even in the midst of entrusting her to God's care. Once we shared our pain, our vicarage church responded. They brought meals over. They sent cards. Some helped us with bills. We were overwhelmed with God's care of us, through His people.

In the midst of NICU visits, I had forgotten a very important piece of Christianity—that being Christian isn't only in the *giving*—it is also in the *receiving*. Not just in *giving* help but in *accepting* it.

I have never learned so much about faith and trust in God as when I've allowed others to help me!

TABLE TALK

5) How difficult is it for you to accept help from others? From your church family? What makes it difficult?

6) Reflect on this statement: "Don't rob your fellow Christians from being *Christian*."

7) Reflect on this statement: "I have never learned so much about faith and trust in God as when I've allowed others to help me!"

***

So, back to Horatio Spafford - and back to you and me. How

can we be buffeted by all sorts of trials and emotions and still say, "It is well, it is well with my soul"? We can only do this when we live by faith – faith that stands on the solid Word of God. St. Paul says, "Whatever was written in former days was written for our instruction, that through endurance and through the encouragement of the Scriptures we might have hope" (Romans 15:4). To hope in Jesus Christ, we have to be anchored to what's written in Scripture. That faith – that Word of God, gives you and me the strength to go on, even when our emotions are buffeted by the storms of life.

One man who recently had to weather a terrible storm was the Christian singer, Steven Curtis Chapman. On May 17, 2008, his five-year-old adopted daughter, Maria, was struck and killed by her seventeen-year-old brother, who was backing his SUV out of the family's driveway. Knowing in their hearts that their daughter might be dead, Chapman and his wife gathered Maria up to take her to the hospital. As Chapman and his wife backed out of the driveway with their broken daughter, he said, "I suddenly had this overwhelming need to let my son know that this accident wasn't his fault – to let him know that Jesus, and his parents, had already forgiven him. And while we might have lost a daughter, he was still my son. So, I rolled down my window and shouted to him, as he was sobbing in the driveway, 'Will Franklin – your father loves you!'"

In the midst of an emotional hell, a broken father shared the love of the Heavenly Father to heal his son.

Four days later, on May 21st, Maria Sue went to the arms of Jesus. Chapman wasn't sure he'd ever sing again, but on the day his daughter died, he sang "Blessed Be Your Name". Inspired by the story of Job, at one point the lyrics repeat, "He gives and takes away." Chapman said, "As I sang this song … it wasn't a song, it was a cry, a scream, a prayer, and I found an amazing comfort and peace that surpasses all understanding." Several months following Maria Sue's death, Chapman would perform in concert again. And he would add a verse to this hymn, and it goes like this, "I've walked the valley of death's shadow - so deep and dark that I could barely breath - I've had to let go of more than I could bear and I've questioned everything that I believe - Still even here in this great darkness - a comfort and a hope comes breaking through - as I can say in life or death - God we belong to you."[75]

With everything buffeting and swirling - within and without in your life, where can we go for real hope – to renew our faith? Doesn't it make sense to locate yourself in God's Word, in God's house, among His people—*your people*—through worship and Bible study and prayer together, celebrating the truths of faith – which are an anchor that holds you fast, in rough seas?

Without God's Word—without His Son, Jesus—without His People—how else can you imagine that it will be 'well with your soul'?

TABLE TALK

8) At a recent Celebrate Recovery meeting, one man shared that his favorite Bible verse was from Joel 2:25 "I will restore to you the years that the swarming locust has eaten." What do you think he meant by choosing that verse?

9) Discuss this quote by C.S. Lewis: "We can ignore even pleasure. But pain insists upon being attended to. God whispers to us in our pleasures, speaks in our conscience, but shouts in our pains: it is His megaphone to rouse a deaf world....No doubt pain as God's megaphone is a terrible instrument; it may lead to final and unrepented rebellion. But it gives the only opportunity the bad man can have for amendment. it removes the veil; it plants the flag of truth within the fortress of the rebel soul."[76]

10) Discuss the following story: After the tragic events of 9/11, I watched a memorial service on T.V. At one point in the chaplain's sermon, a man stood up in the crowd and cried out, "Where was God the day He took my son from me?!" The chaplain called the grieving man forward, put his arm around him and said, "The same place that He was the night soldiers came and took His Son from Him."

11) Discuss the following story: During a hospital visit to a church family member, right before surgery I asked the man if he was scared, since the surgery was very serious and could end his life. He said, "The way I see it, if the surgery works – I win. If it doesn't work – I *still win*. I'm ready, either way."

12) Discuss the following statement: Some scholars believe that the book of Job, a book that talks about the problem of pain and suffering in the world, may be the first book of the Bible that was actually written down. Why do you think this book would be the first one written down by God's people?

13) **Read Job 2:11-13**. How do Job's friends initially react to his pain and suffering? It is interesting to note that God never rebukes Job's three friends for being present with him – He only rebukes them later—for opening their mouths.

14) **Skim Chapter 11 in the Book of Hebrews**. What promises and hopes did God's people have? What difference did it make for them to live 'by faith'? What difference does that make for you?

BRINGING IT HOME

Chloe continues to be a blessing in our family's life. Yes, there have been many trying days of epilepsy, ER visits, therapy, years of being on the ketogenic diet, learning challenges and more. But I wouldn't trade any of those struggles, for they taught me, and our family, to rely on my Jesus, even more. Struggles have taught me more about God's care than at any other time in my life. He taught me patience, a deeper empathy for others, and gratitude for each day we receive in this life.

Chloe has taught me a great deal, herself. She has risen above every challenge put in her path. She has blessed our family through her unique perspective on the world, her sense of humor and her deep faith in Jesus. Not only that, God saw fit to add Brett and Tressa to our family, a few years after Chloe. Brett is a wonder with his deep thinking, his ability to build almost anything out of Legos, his engineering mind, his huge heart and deep compassion. Tressa is a joy with her spunky ways and fun-loving nature, who speaks her mind and has an audacious outlook on life. We continue to be blessed by all four of our children.

Addisyn learned from an early age what it meant to be the 'big sister', and the responsibility that went with it. I am continually in awe of the quiet grace she exuded throughout our struggles, not once complaining about our unique family situation. One week before Chloe was to have a seizure, Addisyn had seen a safety video in her 2nd grade class about flashing the front porch light to give firefighters a better chance of seeing your home in case of emergency. On the day Chloe had her seizure, I turned to see Addisyn, on tip toe, turning our front porch light on and off until the firefighters arrived. When Chloe had another seizure while we were on a road trip, it was Addisyn who gently patted her sister's cheek as she was seizing, saying, "It's okay. It'll be okay", as we waited for the ambulance.

I learn so much from all four of our children – no matter the joys or sorrows, highs or lows. Our family has been blessed beyond measure by our loving God. I've learned much during life's challenges.

When Leslie and I were in the NICU, a nurse handed us a poem called, "Welcome to Holland", by Emily Perl Kingsley, that compares a family with special needs to planning a trip to Italy and landing in Holland, instead. The poem states that at first, you're shocked and overwhelmed, because you'd been planning this awesome trip to Italy, only to find yourself totally unprepared for Holland. But as you get used to your surroundings, you start to appreciate the beautiful windmills and tulips and the different pace of life. And while you'll hear your friends talking about their amazing trips to Italy, and at times you do wish you could see Italy yourself, if you spend all your time wishing you'd been able to go to Italy, you'd never appreciate the unique beauty of Holland.

Truth is – in this life, you can't have a rainbow, without the rain.

And I've learned, by faith, to trust God's promises, in Christ, when the rain comes.

Praise God that by faith, we are anchored to the Lord - Who parted the sea with a blast of His nostrils, and Who calmed the sea with a Word of command. It is that Word that St. Paul and Horatio Spafford and countless saints who have gone on before us—hand to *you now*, to keep you on solid ground when you are buffeted by life. "Whatever was written in former days was written for our instruction, that through endurance and through the encouragement of the Scriptures we might have hope." Real hope that can only come through Christ.

Welcoming adversity in this life doesn't mean we say, "Bring it on, God."

Welcoming adversity means we say that, by faith, when life hurts—we will lean into *Christ*—and *each other*, saying together…

"Thy Will be done, Lord" …

Knowing that one Great Day – it *will* be well with our souls – *forever*.

SOME THOUGHTS ON ENGAGING PEOPLE IN THEIR PAIN

1) Go visit people in the hospital. Embrace *your* discomfort and

go do it - your discomfort is *far* less than their pain. Your *presence* means far more than having the right words.

2) Honor people's pain. For instance, don't tell someone who's had a miscarriage, "you can always have another." They'll never have *that* baby, again, this side of Glory. They'll never stop being a mother or father to *that* baby. Remember, even if their children are now with the Lord, they *remain* parents, forever.

3) There's a mile-wide difference between telling someone, "I'll pray for you", and telling someone, "How about we pray right now?"

4) There's a mile-wide difference between telling someone, "If you need anything, just ask" and telling them, "I'm going to bring by dinner sometime this week. What day works best for you?"

5) Write someone who is hurting a letter or send a card. In a digital world, a handwritten note carries with it more hope, encouragement, and meaning than ever before.

6) It's okay to say, "I don't know what to say." Your hurting friend probably doesn't know what to say, either. Be like Job's friends at the beginning of his book—and just *be present*.

7) In a crisis visit, follow these simple steps:

   a. Start by telling the person, "It's good to see you."

   b. Ask them, "Can you tell me what happened?" So many times, people go into a crisis thinking they know the full story. Not only can the story be incorrect, but the story has never been told to you by the person who is *living it*. They need to tell you *their* story.

c. Tell them, "I'm so sorry." How many words are wasted by well-meaning people trying to 'explain away' pain! Call a thing what it is – say how sorry you are that this happened to them.

d. Ask if you could pray together. Your prayer doesn't need to be as eloquent as Shakespeare – it just needs to be *honest*. (See Luke 12:12 for trusting the Holy Spirit to lead the way with prayer). The simpler the prayer, the better. Name the pain. Name the Savior. Close in Amen. For example, "Lord, we are so sad that this terrible thing has happened to my friend. Help us to trust You, Jesus, and the promises You give us at the cross. In Your Name, we pray. Amen." "Lord, help! Amen!" also works.

When peace like a river attendeth my way,
when sorrows like sea billows roll;
whatever my lot, thou hast taught me to say,
"It is well, it is well with my soul."

It is well with my soul;
it is well, it is well with my soul.

Though Satan should buffet, though trials should come,
let this blest assurance control:
that Christ has regarded my helpless estate,
and has shed his own blood for my soul.

It is well with my soul;
it is well, it is well with my soul.

My sin oh, the bliss of this glorious thought!
my sin, not in part, but the whole,
is nailed to the cross, and I bear it no more;
praise the Lord, praise the Lord, O my soul!

It is well with my soul;
it is well, it is well with my soul.

O Lord, haste the day when my faith shall be sight,
the clouds be rolled back as a scroll;
the trump shall resound and the Lord shall descend;
even so, it is well with my soul.

It is well with my soul;
it is well, it is well with my soul.

—Lutheran Service Book
763, public domain

Closing Prayer:
Our Father, Who art in heaven
Hallowed be Thy Name
Thy Kingdom come
Thy Will be done
 On earth, as it is in heaven.
Give us this day our daily bread
And forgive us our trespasses
As we forgive those who trespass against us.
And lead us not into temptation
But deliver us from evil.
For Thine is the Kingdom, and the power and the Glory, forever and ever. Amen

CHAPTER 10
Putting Out the Welcome Mat — Hospitality and Households of Faith

Romans 15:7
"Therefore welcome one another as Christ has welcomed you, for the glory of God."

SETTING THE TABLE

want to start our time together today with a quiz. Don't worry – you'll pass.

Take a minute to look at the following pictures:[7]

What do you see? For me, other than the time period that the two pictures were taken in, there's really not a whole lot of difference.

Putting these pictures beside one another clearly illustrates one important thing about human nature: the more things change, the more they stay the same.

Regardless of what the 'technology naysayers' claim, being distracted by our glowing smartphone screens and tablets is as old as time, itself. All humanity has done over the years is trade one mode of distraction for another, whether it be drawings on cave walls from ten thousand B.C., kaleidoscopes from the fifth century A.D., newspapers, radio, 'moving pictures' (what would later be called 'movies'), 'talkies' (when movies added sound), television, the Internet and more – we are a people that crave entertainment and are easily distracted. And that desire, while spurring mankind to incredible feats of creativity and innovation – is also our Achilles heel. These distractions can keep us from 'tuning in' to each other – even while we're right next to one another – whether it's waiting for a carriage in the 18th century or a tram in the 21st century.

One great distinction in the 21st century is, while in other centuries peace and quiet was readily accessible, in our world today there never seems to be one single moment where we can *unplug*. We have a myriad of distractions at our fingertips: Our Fitbit wakes us up, Alexa gives us the headlines while we brush our teeth, smartphones give us our itinerary and maps to get around traffic on our way to work. Emails, phone calls, texting throughout the day, not to mention surfing the Internet for work or pleasure. The day ends, we go home streaming our Spotify playlist or favorite podcast (after all, who wants to listen to *someone else's* music selections on the radio?), we stream a show or two on Netflix during our Peloton workout and wrap up the day with a shower as our custom playlist is on in the background. We set our Fitbit alarm for a wakeup call the next day – and the routine repeats itself.

Distractions of life are constant. Plugged in. Never ending white noise—in ways previous generations couldn't have imagined. And the damage is starting to show, especially in our homes and in the spaces where we have the greatest opportunity for meaningful and lasting connection – the dinner table:

'We eat one in every five meals in our car. One in four of us eat at least one fast-food meal every single day. US households spend roughly the same amount per week on fast food as on groceries. Sixty years ago, the average dinnertime was ninety minutes; today it is less than twelve minutes. The majority of US families report eating a single meal together less than five days a week. And even then, our 'dinners together' are mostly in front of the TV. No wonder the average parent spends only 38.5 minutes per week in meaningful conversation with their children. We are losing the table.'[78]

These sobering words from author Leonard Sweet show just how much has changed in our world these past few decades, especially in our households investing time with each other. In this chapter, we will look at the culture shifts that have impacted our homes and ways we can reclaim our homes as places of welcome in Christ.

Prayer: *Heavenly Father, You call us to be in the world, but not of it. Open our eyes to see ways that we can reengage our families to be different from the world and love our neighbors in the world, for the sake of the Kingdom. Amen.*

TABLE TALK

Take a moment to discuss the following together:

1) Was your childhood home a place of welcome and nurturing conversation? If so, what made it that way? If not, what kept it from being that way?

2) In a typical week, how often do you gather around the table with family or friends?

3) Who are the people you credit with teaching you the practices

of hospitality? Why?

4) If you could change several things in your life that would open the door to practicing relational hospitality, what would those things be?

REFLECTION

Worldly distractions and the feeling that we have no time to spare has wreaked havoc on our families. In the past 20 years, the frequency of family dinners has declined 33 percent. In addition, a recent poll by YouGov found that 62% of parents with children under 18 wish they had family dinners "much more often" or "somewhat more often." Here are some additional sobering statistics that show just how much our family time around the dinner table has changed:

- According to a recent study, Americans now spend a higher percentage of their food budget on restaurants (50.3%) than they do on groceries (49.7%).

- 97 percent of the children's restaurant meals studied by the Center for Science in the Public Interest did not meet the expert nutrition standards for children's meals.

- Less than one-fourth of family dinners include a full serving of vegetables, according to a recent survey by Birds Eye.

- In 1970, Americans spent 26 percent of their food budget on eating out; by 2010, that number had risen to 41 percent. During that time, rates of obesity in the United States more than doubled.

A poll by NPR, the Robert Wood Johnson Foundation, and the

Harvard School of Public Health found that:

- Busy family schedules are cutting into family dinners together—46 percent of those surveyed said eating together is difficult to do on a regular basis.

- Fewer than half the parents surveyed admitted that they had eaten together six or seven nights out of the previous week.

Here's the results of what happens when families make dinner table time a priority:

- Family dinners are more important than play, story time and other family events in the development of vocabulary of younger children. (Harvard Research, 1996)

- Frequent family meals are associated with a lower risk of smoking, drinking and using drugs; with a lower incidence of depressive symptoms and suicidal thoughts; and with better grades in 11 to 18-year olds (Archives of Pediatrics and Adolescent Medicine, 2004)

- Adolescent girls who have frequent family meals, and a positive atmosphere during those meals, are less likely to have eating disorders. (University of Minnesota, 2004)

- Kids who eat most often with their parents are 40% more likely to say they get mainly A's and B's in school than kids who have two or fewer family dinners a week. (National Center on Addiction and Substance Abuse at Columbia University)

- "More frequent family dinners are related to fewer emotional and behavioral problems, greater emotional wellbeing, more trusting and helpful behaviors towards others and higher life satisfaction." (Journal of Adolescent Health, April 2012)

And families would agree with the positive outcomes of time together around the dinner table. Despite the feelings of being overwhelmed and the claims of lack of time, 89.9% of families surveyed claim that it is very important for families to eat dinner together regularly!

So, where's the disconnect? How did families arrive at a place where they felt they could no longer have the time to be at the dinner table together?

The answers are many. But we'll focus on just a few to see how we got here.

SUNDAYS, MOVIE HOUSES AND JOHN WAYNE

A study done by Hauerwas and Willimon[79] of the decades between the 1960s-1980s attempted to find the answer as to how and when the American culture shifted the most radically in our morality and connection with one another.

They discovered that, in the 1960s, blue laws emphasizing Sabbath rest and creating space for people to gather for worship became overturned. Businesses prided themselves on '24-hour service' and movie houses were open on the weekends, giving people plenty of reasons not to attend church and 'join John Wayne at the Fox.'[80]

While the removal of blue laws certainly shifted Sunday priorities in the public square in recent decades, one fundamental change that began centuries before had already begun to diminish hospitality in the home. I am referring to the advent of the modern-day restaurant.

HOSPITALITY AND *MATHURIN ROZE DE CHANTOISEAU*

What we now know as the modern-day restaurant could very well trace its origins to the 1700s. Before this era, the choices for eating publicly were limited in scope and style. The taverns, inns and other similar establishments had no menu, for only one item was served, along with irregular and limited hours of operation. No separate tables were available, for everyone ate at a communal table and paid one set price for whatever was served at the moment.[81] But in 1766, a man named Mathurin Roze de Chantoiseau (mAE-thuu-rahn rOHz day shan-twah-ZO) opened what could rightly be described as the first modern-day restaurant – and it forever changed what it meant to 'eat out' and the dining experience. And, one could argue, it shifted the culture's perception of what hospitality was and how it was to be expressed in the home.

As the Enlightenment gained influence in exploring matters of anatomy, philosophy, exploration, and expansion of the sciences, Chantoiseau capitalized on this by generating interest in a public dining experience that further promoted the belief that 'a food or remedy…has the property of restoring lost strength to a sickly or tired individual.'[82] His restaurant was open for long hours, prided itself on catering to the needs of Enlightenment proponents, serving food that was 'restorative' on the finest china. This practice resulted in 'the creation of a new market sphere of hospitality and taste.'[83] And therefore, what used to be considered 'getting something to eat' became all about the *location* and *atmosphere* where one consumed it. Hospitality began to lose out to the art of *hosting*. And public places to dine would never be the same.

As the 18th century dawned, Paris became a front runner on the 'restaurant as experience' mentality, with restaurants popping up everywhere, specializing in just about whatever the heart desired.[84] America was not far behind. As the specialty restaurants came into vogue, inside of one hundred years, eight percent of all Americans were dining out 'on a regular basis.'[85] While this percentage may not seem like much to our modern-day ears, understand that at the time, around fifty percent of all Americans did not live in cities but in rural areas.[86]

However, restaurants creating custom menus, flexible hours and dining experiences surely are not enough to explain how hospitality moved from the home to the public square motif of 'hosting.' Why would people, living in the era of the Enlightenment, feel the need to dine in public when they could have done so at home? The innovation of the restaurant is not enough to explain this. Changing architecture provides further answers.

HOSPITALITY AND ARCHITECTURE

A structure came into fashion in the home of the eighteenth century that had not existed before: the 'dining room.' Most of Europe and America embraced this structure as homes expanded in their use of square footage – a design utterly alien to the early Christians living under Roman rule. Large dining room tables, capable of accommodating dozens of guests, because a chic extension of houses that mastered the art of hosting. The intimacy of shared spaces and group culture revolving around closeness and need for one another was becoming a foreign concept. As disposable income, square footage expansion of the home and the desire to entertain in the home caught on so did the declination of genuine relational hospitality.[87]

Social constructs of hospitality and caring for one another in a 'guest-host' relationship began to decline, in favor of mimicking the Enlightenment push for trade and expansion of borders.[88] Development of this sort became the breeding ground for creating distance between individuals, even so far as creating distance among family members. And Christianity, known for centuries as being countercultural, chose to embrace this new trend, rather than speak out against it. Christians who once took care of friends, neighbors and the stranger in their midst – offering food, housing, clothing, even protection while they traveled – become more and more like the world around them. With no one left to champion the cause of relational hospitality – *hosting* took hold. Therefore, the advent of the restaurant as 'experience' ultimately seems to be the result - not the cause - of hospitality becoming lost in the home. As Christianity fell victim to the Enlightenment, it behaved more and more to the stranger like the culture they had once vowed to live counter towards.

Our modern world now embraces dining as an '*experience*,' the welcoming of people as human beings is traded for welcoming people as *patrons*, food as life for the wayward traveler is exchanged for fare to be *reveled* or *critiqued*, the relationship of *life-on-life* replaced with a *menu, ambiance* and a *check*. Is it any wonder why the Christian witness in the world struggles so much in our modern society when absent are the practices that the early church embraced in the home? It leaves little to the imagination as to why the lost among us see Christian attempts to engage them as 'forced,' ingenuine and manipulative.

TABLE TALK

5) Thinking of today's modern Christian church, how do you think God's people *lost* their place in society, while the Early Church *solidified* their place in it?

6) Thinking about the Early Church, what do you see as different when comparing their practices to modern Christian churches today? What practices are similar? What practices could we re-embrace from the Early Church?

BARNA AND HOSPITALITY

In 2019, Barna research[89] released a years-long study on hospitality, the home and its impact on Christian families. Regardless of household types - nuclear family, roommate, couple, single-parent and multi-generational – the common threads that *vibrant* households shared (i.e. that talk about God or faith together weekly, pray together every day or two, read the Bible together weekly and welcome non-family visitors several times a month) were:

- Faith Formation is Connected to and Increases with Hospitality – households that regularly host non-family guests are more likely to talk about faith, pray or read the Bible together.

- Generally, Active Households are Spiritually Active Households, and Vice Versa – Shared meals, work and play are common in households that also carve out time for faith interactions.

- Spiritually Vibrant Households are Characterized by Fun and Quality Time – Games, singing, reading and sports are common group activities among households that are vibrant.

One in four U.S. practicing Christians live in households that qualify as vibrant. While Barna's research is encouraging to show these vibrant households, at the same time it shows the majority of American Christian families have been negatively influenced by the culture's perception – and their own perceptions – about the true nature of hospitality as God designed it. In particular with the interaction they have – or don't have – with the people who matter most to them. Their families.

In short, Christian households that 'do life together' embrace relational hospitality together. Those that don't – *won't*.

Putting out the welcome mat – begins with your family first putting out the welcome mat for *each other*.

TABLE TALK

7) Look up the following passages and note what food or table is

discussed. Then note what the purpose of each is:

- **Exodus 25:23-30**

- **Psalm 23:5**

- **John 21:12-19**

- **Revelation 3:20**

8) Read the following passages and complete the sentence:

    - **Mark 10:45** "The Son of Man came…_____"

    - **Luke 19:10** "The Son of Man came…_____"

    - **Luke 7:34** "The Son of Man came…_____"

9) Looking at the above answers, why did Jesus come? Which purpose starkly stands out against the rest?

10) Might we have missed one key method that Jesus uses to connect with others? With our families?

11) Discuss the following statement: Jesus 'doing life' around a table was one way to enact change. Change that can take place in our families, with Christ at the center.

12) How has God called us to 'take back the table' in our households? Brainstorm ways your table could be a 'better battlefield' for the Gospel.

13) **Read 2 Timothy 2:1-2** – In this passage, St. Paul poured into St. Timothy, as a young pastor for the early Christian church. As God's People, the Lord calls on you and me to pour into others.

14) Who is God specifically calling you to pour in to? To influence? To pray for? **Read 1 Corinthians 3:5-7** – In this passage, St. Paul states that the Gospel of Jesus did not begin with him and will not end with him, either. Furthermore, while he planted the seed of the Gospel in some, others might come along and water that seed. But it is God alone Who receives the glory for the Gospel.

15) Think back to those who taught you about Jesus. Who were those strong links in your Gospel story? How might it help you to know you are 'one strong link' in someone else's Gospel story?

REFLECTION

I have a few special memories of baseball games I played when I was a kid. I remember some of the trips we took as a family and the extracurricular activities I did. Those are all special memories for me. But the thing I remember most – the memory I hold most dear – is just about every evening my family would get together to tell jokes and stories, just before our night prayers.

I also remember meals together in the evening, no matter what. I remember Mom reading to me. I remember working with Dad and our conversations on how to be a man. The thing about taking a 'once-in-a-lifetime vacation' with your family is – they happen only once in a lifetime. But 'life-on-life' – spending time together now, is welcoming one another with the relational hospitality of Christ.

I have never met a CEO of his company who climbed the ladder of success and lost his family along the way, say at the end, "It was worth it."

Your children will not look back on this formative time in their lives and say, "I wish I'd done more activities." But in their hearts, they'll look back and say, "I wish I'd spent more time with my family."

BRINGING IT HOME

16) Think of the 3 daily routines your family shares. How could you be more intentional about making these routines a time to better enjoy one another? What distractions need to be removed to allow for that enjoyment?

17) Make a 'cellphone bucket' for your family, where everyone puts their phones in the bucket on the counter, to focus on one another during the meal. You'll be amazed at how much you *don't* miss by not having your phone handy in the amount of time it takes to make and enjoy a meal together.

18) Has social media on your smartphone 'chipped away' at family time? What boundaries do *you* have in place to model your social media behavior to your family? Do you have a timer on your app, to ensure you don't allow this to distract you from the people who matter most?

19) Do a 'once over' on your house. How has the architecture/layout hindered your ability to connect as a family? How has the architecture/layout helped it? How could you be more intentional to make your home more welcoming of one another?

20) Think of your personal routine in the morning. What changes could you make that would invite your family into your life?

What about your evening routine? What things are helping or hurting the opportunity for your family to connect?

21) Host a 'family meeting'. Ask for their input on what they see is keeping them from connecting as a family. Ask them what they believe *you* are doing that keeps them from connecting with you. If they pointed out those things, would you take them to heart?

22) What is the one thing you could do differently this week that would create opportunities for relational hospitality within your family?

23) How could meal planning the week help alleviate the stress of preparing the dinner table after work? How would being intentional address the dreaded question, "What's for dinner?"

24) Use family-friendly apps like OurGroceries, where not only can everyone who uses the app input items they need to get at the store but meal planning items are automatically added by their ingredients in to your shopping list and synced across one account.

25) Ask your children (if they're old enough) to take one night of the week to prepare the family meal. If your children are not old enough, have them walk through the making of dinner together. You'll be amazed at the conversations that will take place as you prepare the meal.

26) If your children have grown and left home, plan a night or two each week to prepare a meal with your spouse and savor dinner together.

27) If you are single, invite some friends or family over one night this week to prepare and enjoy a meal. See how God uses this moment to pour into one another.

> **On my heart imprint Your image,**
> **Blessed Jesus, King of grace,**
> **That life's riches, cares, and pleasures**
> **Never may Your work erase;**
> **Let the clear inscription be:**
> **Jesus, crucified for me,**
> **Is my Life, my hope's foundation,**
> **And my glory and salvation!**
>
> **—Lutheran Service Book**
> *422, public domain*

Closing Prayer: *Heavenly Father, we invite You into our lives. We make ourselves available to Your holy will. Help us become living examples of Your love in the world. Open our hearts to the areas of our lives that need to change—so that we carry out the mission of Your church—Connecting People to Jesus. Inspire us to live the Christian life in ways that are dynamic and engaging. Bring renewal to our church. And make us hunger and thirst for more of Jesus. Give us courage when we are afraid. Hope when we are discouraged. And clarity in times of decision. Clear the distractions and clutter from our lives, so that we can see more clearly the loving family and friends you've placed there. Open our hearts to see that the first mission field you have given us is to the people who share life with us inside our homes. Amen.*

CHAPTER 11
Welcoming Those Who Are Late to the Party

Jonah 3:10-4:1,11
"When God saw what [the Ninevites] did and how they turned from their evil ways, he had compassion and did not bring upon them the destruction he had threatened. But it displeased Jonah exceedingly, and he was angry. [And God said] 'should not I pity Nineveh, that great city, in which there are more than 120,000 persons who do not know their right hand from their left, and also much cattle?'"

Matthew 20:11-16
"When [the hired men] received their wages, they began to grumble against the landowner. 'These men who were hired last worked only one hour,' they said, 'and you have made them equal to us who have borne the burden of the work and the heat of the day.' But he answered one of them, 'Friend, I am not being unfair to you. Didn't you agree to work for a denarius? Take your pay and go. I want to give the man who was hired last the same as I gave you. Don't I have the right

to do what I want with my own money? Or are you envious because I am generous?' So the last will be first, and the first will be last."

SETTING THE TABLE

Have *you ever hosted a party in your home?* Even if you haven't, you know how it goes: you greet people at the door, take coats, shake hands, give hugs. The vegetable trays with Ranch dip are out. Music is on. And when everyone arrives, the party begins. Unless….

One guest is late to the party. Everyone's patiently (or *not* so patiently) waiting for them to arrive. There's uncomfortable chatter. Muttered questions like, 'I wonder where he is?' circle the room. And then, just about the moment when everyone is ready to get started without them – the doorbell rings. Our 'fashionably late' guest is at the door with a smile on their face. No explanation. Just a 'sorry I'm late!' and on they go into the kitchen to enjoy the party.

If you're at that party – and especially if you're the host – it's kind of hard not to get a little offended, especially if they're acting like everything is okay. After all, you've been working hard all day long, getting food prepared, buying extra ice and paper napkins, right on down to vacuuming the carpet and making the kids swear not to walk in the house with their shoes on. The least they could have done, if they were going to be late, was to call. Or at the very least, explain what happened. At least that would in some way acknowledge the trouble you went through to get everyone together. I once knew a lady who held on to her resentment and anger over a habitual 'late-comer' for months and then at a party, blew her top at that person.

Resentment, anger and wrath – three things that never end well in a relationship.

It reminds me of some things Jesus said, when it came to our neighbors. He didn't say, "You must *like* your neighbor as yourself", but "*love* your neighbor as yourself". That kind of love is special – it's sharing *Christ's* love with other people – even when you don't *want* to. Especially when someone has been rude towards you in their actions or words. Or worse, have been hostile to you and hurt you. It's hard to live, love and forgive that way. But if we are called to love like Christ in our *world*, then we are also called to *love* our neighbor – even at those times when we don't *like* our neighbor. Even if they're late to the party.

Prayer: *Heavenly Father, it's very easy to get caught up in anger or jealousy towards my neighbor. To think that I know what's best and how everyone should behave in this life. Humble me with Your Spirit, so that I echo Your words of welcome and Your forgiving heart. Amen.*

TABLE TALK

Take a moment to discuss the following together:

1) How does our world teach us to behave towards those who have hurt us? Disappointed us? 'Owe us' for something they've done to us?

2) How do we know when someone has 'done enough' to make up for what they've done in our society?

3) How do we determine when someone has 'done enough' to make up for what they've done in our hearts?

REFLECTION

If anyone didn't like his neighbor, it was Jonah. In fact, Jonah *hated* his neighbor! His neighbors, the Ninevites, were a ruthless people from Assyria. Assyrians didn't just conquer their neighbors – they wiped them out! They were known for putting fishhooks in people's noses and dragging them hundreds of miles on foot before killing them. Jonah's family, friends, and his nation had all suffered at the hands of their 'Ninevite neighbors'. And it is these people that God asks Jonah to love, even though he didn't want to.

So Jonah, justified in his anger, decides to love *himself* and flees to Tarshish. But after a horrible sea storm and three days inside a *really* big fish, Jonah finally mumbles to the Lord - "sorry". And the Lord tells him to 'mean it' by going to Nineveh and preach His Word to them. So, he does – reluctantly, walking to the heart of the city and proclaiming, "Forty more days and Nineveh will be overturned!" (Jonah 3:4)

And then the Ninevites do the unthinkable – they *repent* – from the king on down. The whole city mourns in sackcloth and ashes (an Eastern way to show repentance) and they collectively say 'sorry' to God. And God turns from His anger. Nineveh is saved! And Jonah *pouts*. He sets himself up as judge and jury on the highest hill of Nineveh and shouts to God, 'I KNEW it! I knew that You were a merciful God and you'd forgive these miserable wretches if they repented! I want those sorry dogs to pay me what they *owe* me!!' Jonah didn't want to share God's love and forgiveness with people he hated, because he knew they just might repent, and God just might forgive them – and *rob* Jonah of his hate.

We've all played that game, haven't we? 'I *can't* love my neighbor as myself. Not this time! I *hate* that guy who deliberately hurt me so much! And Jesus wants *me* to love *him*!?!? I'll love him when he pays me what he owes me!' When we talk that way, we confuse the 'world's love' with Christ's love. 'Loving our neighbor' isn't about feelings – it's a <u>GIFT</u>. 'We love because God first loved us.' And that means forgiving someone with the same measure of forgiveness that *we* have received - and to let go of our hate.

4) **Read James 4:11, James 5:9 and 1 Corinthians 6:7.** How might these verses apply towards one another? Towards our neighbor?

5) **Read Psalm 15:1-5 and Matt 5:23-24**. What does our relationship with one another have to do with our relationship to God?

6) What does the Scripture above imply about the timing of reconciliation and the attitude of the one who has something against someone else?

Letting go of hate, anger and resentment is a challenge in itself to people that hurt us personally. But what about the people in our society we believe don't *deserve* forgiveness or to go to heaven? Don't think you know someone like that? Think about this person: Jeffrey Dahmer.

That name alone will forever be associated with evil and the scum of humanity. His crimes are horrific enough, and if you've got the stomach for it, Google it, some time. There are no words to describe a person who, after luring his victims to his apartment, would kill them, eat parts of them and store the skulls in his freezer.

As horrific as Dahmer's crimes were, it was just as horrific to see the expression on his face during the court trial – emotionless, no sign of remorse, whatsoever. How do you punish someone who's taken seventeen lives? Is life without the possibility of parole enough? We can debate that part all day, but none of that is what bothers me the most. Want to know what does bother me about Jeffrey Dahmer?

The possibility that he came to faith in Jesus.

A few months before another inmate beat him to death, reports were that Dahmer became a Christian. Like the Ninevites, Dahmer said 'sorry' to God in repentance, claiming he put his faith in Christ. He would later say in an interview that when a world believes Darwinism to be the correct worldview and philosophy—then there is no real value to human life. That apart from God there can be no checks and balances and therefore, Dahmer was a huge advocate for including God in the public square.

Here's a guy who's not just late to the party—he's so late, the door has been locked and bolted with no hope of entering!

And yet...

I can't fathom it – his repentance. Sins cleansed. Eternal life, granted. God's Grace available to a *cannibal*?! That disgusts me. I know, I know, I'm a follower of Jesus and I should be thankful he repented. And there's a small part of me that is thankful. But there's a way bigger part of me that is *resentful*.

Maybe you can relate to how I feel. If not for Dahmer, maybe another situation you know. How many times have we heard of a "good for nothing" jerk suddenly becoming a Christian on his deathbed? How many "11th hour" pleas from horrible people to the Son of God? These people *deserved* what was coming to them – *and more*. We've judged them all - maybe not in court, but definitely in our *hearts*. So, thinking we're justified in our hatred, we wipe our hands of them and move on. And just when we think it's all said and done, they do the impossible.

They...*repent*.

We see it happening before our eyes, and in our disbelief, we cross our arms, shake our heads and say, 'There's no *way* God's gonna let you off the hook *that* easy! Not after what *you've* done. Grace is reserved for the *average* sinner like *me* – not people like *you*.' Or more personally, when someone directly hurts us in our lives, we wave our fist at God and say in our hearts, 'I *can't* love my neighbor as myself. Not this time! That person was hateful to me and hurt me so deeply! And Jesus wants *me* to love *them*?! I'll love them when they pay me what they *owe* me! THEN, we'll talk about it!'

And that works. For a while.

Until we read the words of Jesus and the Parable of the Workers in the Vineyard.

7) **Read Matthew 20:1-16.** Who are the cast of characters? What

things stick out for you? What groups of workers are there? How does the owner of the vineyard behave?

The Kingdom of Heaven is very much like this parable, according to Jesus. But the primary thing to take away from this parable isn't so much about being in the vineyard. The takeaway is how Jesus describes what *getting to heaven* is really about.

In the Judean world, if you didn't own a business, there was rarely steady employment. So, you took what you could get – often on a daily basis. In Jesus' day, if you needed someone to work for you, you'd go to the marketplace and look for people standing around. People standing around usually indicated that they were looking for work. You'd negotiate a wage and they'd work the day for you. In the same way, if you needed work, you'd go to the marketplace and stand and wait for the wealthier neighbors to come and hire people for whatever chores they needed done that day.

In the parable, the landowner goes first thing in the morning and hires workers right away, offering a day's wage for their work. But apparently, there's lots of work to do, so the landowner keeps returning to the marketplace throughout the day. When he finds more people standing around, he just hires them on the spot. It's important to note, that when the landowner hires people for the rest of the day, he *doesn't* come to a contract agreement. He just agrees to pay the workers 'whatever is right.' Hold on to that statement.

The day ends and everyone lines up to get paid. The landowner tells the paymaster to pay those he hired *last* - first. Already we see the last words of the parable coming true: The last are first, and the first are last. (Matthew 20:16) Then comes a plot twist to the parable - those hired just *an hour* before quitting time come to the paymaster and they each get a *full* day's wages - *exactly* the amount that the first ones hired had agreed to in their contract. This was done in front of everyone else, so those hired first saw it. So, what would you assume, if you're them? A BIG payday is coming your way - wages were going to be *much* more than they thought. But when they come to receive their pay, they get the exact same amount as those who had just started, *a denarius* – a normal day's pay. That didn't sit too well! They figured that their entire day's work in the heat of the day was worth *way more* than the short time those fellas had worked, just an hour or so ago.

But... it *wasn't*.

However, they hadn't been cheated - they had contracted with the landowner at the beginning of the day - they had agreed to a specific sum for their day's labor - the typical day's pay. They just allowed themselves to get distracted by what *others* received for *far less work in the vineyard*. These guys came very late to the party – but the wages they got were the same.

So, those who'd worked all day cried, "Not fair!" But the landowner reminded them of their contract and pointed out that he wasn't being *unfair* with them, but rather *generous* with all the others. The first hired had received *exactly* what they had agreed to be paid. Then the landowner asks two pointed questions, "Don't I have the right to do what I want with my own money? Or are you envious because I am generous?" Only, Jesus isn't talking about a landowner. He's talking about His Father. And Jesus isn't talking about money here. He's talking about Grace. And that question of Grace is ultimately aimed—at *you and me*.

8) **Read Ephesians 2:8-9.** How does God define Grace? What are the requirements?

9) How do you and I often measure Grace and the right to receive Grace?

The Kingdom of Heaven is not about what *you've done* – it's about what's been done *for you*! The Kingdom of Heaven isn't about how good you were, or the time spent in God's kingdom – it's about the merit of Christ and *His time* spent on the Cross. So, whether you were a baptized child of God as an infant or you were *really* late to the party and came to faith on your death bed, the miracle of God's Grace is, both situations receive the *same thing* – mercy and forgiveness through God's One and Only Son. So, the tough questions to ask *ourselves* are the same questions the landowner asked the workers in his vineyard – "Does Jesus have the right to do what He wants with His <u>mercy</u>?" "Or are you envious because He is generous?" Tough questions for sinful people to swallow.

Because as sinful human beings, when it comes right down to it - we don't want what's *right* – we want what's *<u>fair</u>*! It's not *fair* that the serial killer who comes to faith in Jesus gets to bypass hell! Where's the justice in that? What about that "little weasel" you know, who thinks he can live however he wants, and then get away with it all, by coming late to the party and saying he believes in Jesus at the end - skipping the "smoking section" of eternity?!

That's not fair!

Where's the justice?!

Just one problem with you and me sitting in the judgment seat of God, weighing scales against the people who were late to the party—we think we know what's *fair* - <u>in matters of eternity</u>.

And we would be…

wrong.

Jesus Christ is the only One Who *truly* knows the meaning of the phrase, "It's just not fair!" It wasn't fair that people spit into the eyes that had wept for them. It wasn't fair that people rejected Him, cursed Him and ultimately condemned Him, for what <u>we</u> did. It wasn't fair that soldiers ripped chunks of flesh out of the back that would bear their sins. It wasn't fair that God abandoned the Savior of the world on a cross. Was it *fair* what was done to Jesus that great and terrible day on the hill of Calvary? *No*. Was it *love*? …Yes!

10) **Read Romans 5:6-11.** How did God view our hearts before He saved us? How did you measure up on the scales of eternity?

11) *Note:* People doing sinful, hurtful behaviors is not acceptable, nor excusable. But should they repent – it *is forgivable.* See previous chapters on the subject.

12) What do we do with criminals who have gone to prison or on death row for horrible crimes, if they repent and come to faith in Jesus? **Read Genesis 9:5-7** and **Romans 13:1-5**

Maybe you've been a Christian all your life, from the moment your parents brought you to the Baptismal font. You've been working in the Lord's vineyard and you've never known anything else. That's why it can be very easy to cast judgment on the workers who are late to the party – the ones *just now* hired to be in the vineyard – and now they're getting *the same pay* as you.

But while you're casting all your attention on the new workers, you're missing a rock-solid, unchanging truth:

Who has *always* been with you during your years of labor? *The Owner* of the vineyard.

Your Lord, Who has *never* left your side.

No matter what, He has *always* taken care of you.

And you've *never known* anything else.

Even in the low moments, even through the hard times, it's always been good working in His vineyard. Because when you work in His vineyard, you have Jesus – Who makes your yoke easy and your burden light. (Matthew 11:28-30) If you doubt me, just ask those new vineyard workers – the ones who came late to the party – the ones with a permanent smile of joy and relief on their faces.

Ask the ones who came to work at the 11th hour. They'll tell you what it feels like to live a life *outside* the vineyard. How those men and women *wish* they could have *always* been in the vineyard, like *you*! And how grateful they are to be working in the vineyard, today! So, don't worry about how long someone *else* has been in the vineyard – don't be upset about how late they were to the party - because that's not the point. The point is: rejoice that they *are* in the vineyard! Rejoice that they made it to the party!

And rejoice that you've *never* known what it's like to be *apart* from it.

Be thankful that by God's Grace, in Christ – you *never* will.

So, give God back His judgment seat. He's the only one big enough to sit there.

He knows real faith - and He alone knows if someone is trying to con Him with a "fake plea" for mercy. We leave the judging of *both* - up to Him. As St. Paul says, "Do not judge before the right time; wait until the Lord comes" (1 Cor. 4:5). In the meantime, quit worrying about *who* is in the Kingdom of Heaven. Simply "rejoice that <u>*your*</u> names are written in heaven"! (Luke 10:20) Because if you and I demand to get what's *fair* in matters of eternity, we'd all deserve death and hell. Instead, we receive something we *don't* deserve – the nail-scarred hands of a Savior Who loved us enough to receive the punishment we *do* deserve.

Grace for a *cannibal*?

<u>There'd better be</u>.

Otherwise, there would be no grace left for you and me.

So, we simply fall at Jesus' feet, and ask for His undeserved mercy and forgiveness. And incredibly, we receive it.

13) **Read Ephesians 4:25-32.** How is God calling us to treat those who are in the vineyard? Those who are 'late to the party'?

14) **Look at Ephesians 4:25-32 again.** What things is God calling us to rid ourselves of so that we can enjoy the kind of relationships He wishes for us?

BRINGING IT HOME

An editorial appeared in the Chicago Tribune a few years ago entitled, "Have We Lost the Language of Forgiveness?" The writer told a story of her visits to her grandmother's church - a Finnish Lutheran Church - in Pennsylvania on 'communion Sundays', an event that happened infrequently, as it was the congregation's habit to celebrate Communion only four times a year. But on communion Sundays, there was another practice, equally infrequent, but nonetheless significant. It was the confession and forgiveness of sins.

The worship service began as a Lutheran liturgy typically begins, with general confession. But then it all changed. The pastor stepped down out of the chancel. There was silence throughout the cavernous sanctuary. Then a quiet shuffling of feet could be heard. The creaking of pews added to the muted sound. Movement began as people quietly got up out of their seats and began to move around the sanctuary to meet with others. A few whispers grew into a quiet hum of muffled voices. One person would stop and bend over to speak quietly to another still sitting. Another met a fellow member in the aisle, standing, face to face. Scattered around the sanctuary, in pews and standing, one even kneeling before a friend, multiple conversations were going on, quietly. "I was wrong to…" "I hurt your feelings when I…and I am sorry." "I mis-spoke when I… will you forgive me?" "Do you remember when…? Can we start over again?" And words like "I am sorry too, will you forgive me?" "Let's forget about it, OK." "I forgive you." This went on for several minutes.

As quietly and softly as it had started, the whispers and shuffling feet and creaking pews quieted again as everyone returned to their seat. Just as quiet as before, but you could feel the difference those few moments made in peoples' lives, and in the life of the congregation. The pastor walked back up the steps into the chancel and spoke the general words of forgiveness, "As a called and ordained minister of the church of Jesus Christ I now announce to you the forgiveness of all of your sins." It was a powerful word. But they had already heard it. They already knew. *They were forgiven.*

Agape love – Christ's love – love that is not a feeling, but a *gift*. A *gift* that Jonah finally gave when he preached repentance to his enemies. The *gift* that Christ gave on a cross to truly love us to the point of death for our sins. To cancel *our* debt – a debt we could never repay. There will likely always be people in our lives that we won't particularly like or trust. But - we can love them – with *Christ's* love. A love that we can share even when we don't *want* to. Even when they're late to the party.

Through Jesus, we can celebrate – that we are there.

With Him.

Forever.

> Beautiful Savior,
> King of Creation,
> Son of God and Son of Man!
> Truly I'd love Thee,
> Truly I'd serve Thee,
> Light of my soul, my Joy, my Crown.
>
> Fair are the meadows,
> Fair are the woodlands,
> Robed in flowers of blooming spring;
> Jesus is fairer,
> Jesus is purer;
> He makes our sorrowing spirit sing.
>
> Fair is the sunshine,
> Fair is the moonlight,

Bright the sparkling stars on high;
Jesus shines brighter,
Jesus shines purer,
Than all the angels in the sky.

Beautiful Savior,
Lord of the nations,
Son of God and Son of Man!
Glory and honor,
Praise, adoration,
Now and forevermore be Thine!

—Lutheran Service Book
537, public domain

Closing Prayer: *Jesus, lead us to live in Your forgiveness and make peace with our past. For those who have wounded us, we pray Your Holy Spirit would give us the strength to 'forgive those who've trespassed against us'. May we learn to rejoice that we are in Your vineyard – and You lovingly continue to bring others into Your vineyard. May we live <u>Christ's</u> love - let it go – and let the healing begin. Amen.*

CHAPTER 12
The Hospitable Host and the Welcome Guest

Luke 10:39-42

"[Martha] had a sister called Mary, who sat at the Lord's feet and listened to his teaching. But Martha was distracted with much serving. And she went up to [Jesus] and said, 'Lord, do you not care that my sister has left me to serve alone? Tell her then to help me.' But the Lord answered her, 'Martha, Martha, you are anxious and troubled about many things, but one thing is necessary. Mary has chosen the good portion, which will not be taken away from her.'"

SETTING THE TABLE

In a previous chapter, we looked at the parable of the Good Samaritan. And if you remember, we saw just how easy it was to turn that parable in to *one more* Law that tells us to, "Be a good neighbor." If you recall, the Law tells us to 'do something' and that is not to be confused with the Gospel, which is the work of God to save us.

As we discovered, we'll never be saved by doing *more* Law, and learning that truth led us to the true Gospel in that parable - that *Jesus is the 'Good Samaritan'* – the One Who *truly* loves His neighbor as Himself. Even though He is despised and rejected—Someone we considered our enemy—He comes to us *anyway*, binds up our wounds, carries our burdens and pays our debt *for* us.

This is sweet Gospel truth!

But since we are hard-wired to think that we *must* do *something* to earn our salvation, it's *very easy* to stumble right back into the Law, all over again, in the story of Mary, and her sister, Martha.

So, let's set the scene: Jesus has just told the Old Testament lawyer that if he wants to save *himself* – he must 'go and do likewise' by 'loving his neighbor as himself' – *perfectly, all the time*. Jesus has made it really clear that <u>He</u> is the only One Who can do this – we *can't*.

But that *doesn't* mean that Martha isn't gonna *try*!

Martha is a real 'trooper' – and a fantastic host, by any standard – including the standard of Jesus' day.

She invites Jesus into her home, and right away, she gets to work: scrubbing toilets with a toothbrush, two pots on the stove and one in the microwave, three cutting boards going at once - and don't forget the scented candles!

And then, in the midst of this whirlwind of activity, Martha happens to peek through the kitchen window, where she sees – *(GASP)* her sister in the living room doing absolutely – *nothing*. Just sitting there at Jesus' feet, listening to Him talk! The *nerve* of some people! And her own sister, at that!

And this is the part of the story, where things take an interesting turn. A turn that has a truth to teach you and me, today, about what giving a wholehearted welcome to someone is all about.

Prayer: *Jesus, this story is kind of familiar to me, because I do a lot of familiar things: rushing to and fro, business to be done each and every day, only to come home to a waiting kitchen and the dreaded question, "What's for dinner?" Help me take a deeper look at this story, to see where I, too, can find a welcome that not only lasts - but fills my soul. Amen*

TABLE TALK

Take a moment to answer the following together:

1) What do you do to prepare for a special guest coming over to your house?

2) What would you do if you saw a family member goofing off, instead of helping get the house ready?

3) What would *you* do in Martha's situation, after working so hard for guests?

REFLECTION

In a huff, Martha marches up to Jesus and says, "Lord, do you not care that my sister has left me *to serve* alone? Tell her to *help* me!" (Luke 10:40) If her own family won't do the obvious and help her, perhaps the honored guest in her home would be able to call Mary to the mat on what should have been proper protocol.

The key word, here, in Martha's request to Jesus, is the Greek word, '*diakonia*', which means, 'to serve' but it can also be translated as, 'doing good works'. And 'doing good works' is a kissing cousin to 'loving your neighbor as yourself.'

UH-OH...

There's a flag on the play!

Jesus just told us in the parable of the Good Samaritan, that sinful people *can't* love their neighbors as themselves. What's going on here? Well, to help us better understand what Martha's really asking of Jesus - let's try looking at her request *another* way.

Imagine Martha says *this* to Jesus, instead: "Jesus, don't you care that my sister, Mary, is *not* 'loving her neighbor as herself' right now? Didn't you just spend *ten whole verses* on a parable that will *forever* be misunderstood as a command to 'go and be a Good Samaritan to serve your neighbor'? You're even going to have pastors for *centuries* telling us the *real* Gospel is to 'do nice things' for people, *(crying)* and here I can't even get my own flesh and blood sister to 'go and do likewise' in my *own kitchen*, because she's sitting there like a bump on a log, listening to *You!!*"

Yes, I'm being melodramatic – but do you see how much Martha and the lawyer from the parable of the Good Samaritan have *in common* with each other, in their understanding of the Law? The lawyer denied his *need* for Jesus by trying to *justify himself* – thinking he could love God and his neighbor - *perfectly, if he just had a little guidance from Jesus.*

Martha welcomes Jesus into her home, but then she turns right around and uses Jesus as an *excuse* to *justify herself* - thinking that she could 'love her neighbor' and her Lord – *if she just had a little more help from Mary*!

The same fruitless *attempts* from *both.*

The same sinful *results* from *both.*

But before we shake our heads and wag our fingers at Martha – we need to remember that Martha is doing *exactly* what *we*, as Christians, are *tempted* to do – and *often* do, ourselves.

Every. Single. Day.

We gladly welcome Jesus into our homes, only to miss out on Him altogether. Instead of doing family devotions or night prayers together, we waste countless hours updating our Facebook status, 'pinning' on Pinterest, tweeting on Twitter or 'graming' on Instagram.

We gladly welcome Jesus into our homes but *only* when He fits in to *our* schedules or doesn't impose on our free time – choosing, instead, to run through life like chickens with our heads cut off, to the point that even giving God just *one hour* on Sunday seems like *a burden.*

Yes, people get sick on Sundays. Accidents and catastrophes happen on Sundays. Our jobs sometimes require us to be 'on call' on Sundays. That's just what happens in our world and that part can't be helped. But let's be honest—is an *un*avoidable emergency really the reason that *most* people miss out on Jesus? How many people miss out on Him just because it's easier to get a 'tee time' at the golf course on Sundays? How many people miss out just because it was a good day for swimming, boating, or going to the cabin? How many people miss out on Sunday *morning* because they stayed out too late on Saturday *night*? How many people miss out because they have guests in town and are *literally* in the kitchen, like Martha was?

What lesson do we teach our children, when we show them that baseball and soccer tournaments, band, and countless other activities are *more important* than Jesus?

Folks, if you're living your Christianity like 'Martha in the kitchen' *right now*, don't be shocked and shaken when your children grow up to be 'Marthas', *later* - just too busy with their lives, to be in Church, to be in prayer or to even bother with Jesus.

TABLE TALK

4) Think of your weekly schedule. Make two columns: things that *need* to be done and things that *could* be done. What column does prayer fit in? Weekly worship? Social media time? T.V.? Sports? Extracurricular activities?

5) How has having the 'perfect place setting' for a meal taken away from your time to be with your guests? When guests are coming over, is the whole family involved in preparing or are only one or two people helping? What might change if everyone pitched in?

6) Discuss this statement: When worship with Jesus and prayer life is presented as a multiple-choice question to children, their parents shouldn't be surprised that their children grow up to choose *anything* but Jesus.

REFLECTION

The struggles we have of welcoming Jesus into our lives isn't limited to just our *homes*. We Christians can even wrestle with that problem, in church. Because who are the people that we 'worship' in Christianity? We bow before the supposed 'super-saints' who are busy trying to 'out-mega-church' one other. The "Kardashians of Christianity", who, at least on the surface, have their lives together and tons of free time to volunteer for just about anything. What's worse, we somehow get it in our heads that God must have a 'heavenly honor roll' for the 'Super-Christians'—so we'd better get busy trying to *impress* Him.

After all, Jesus is *watching*. He's *counting*. He's waiting to be *'wowed'* by us.

And that means pushing our lives to the point of burnout and completely *missing out* on the Lord of Life.

How many people miss out on Jesus—even when they're *in church*—because they're so obsessed with Easter breakfast or whether or not there are donuts, homemade goodies and coffee available?

I once had a 'come to Jesus' with a group of ladies who were upset that a single mom brought a store-bought Bundt cake to a social function, instead of it being homemade. I told them, in no uncertain terms, that their near-sightedness caused them to miss out on the beauty of a single mom, who had no time to bake, show up and bring something, even risking ridicule - simply because she wanted to be a part of their lives. At least, she *thought* she could be a part of their lives, until she found out the price of admission was a homemade Bundt cake.

When *food* in the *kitchen* trumps *Jesus* at the *altar*, we got a problem!

All these things can so distract us – both at church, and at home, that *those* things become *more* important than simply listening to Jesus and receiving His gifts. God never said, "Be *busy* and know that I am *impressed*". He said, "Be *still*, and know that I am *God*." (Psa. 46:10)

But we often can't hear His Words, because we're just *too busy* working in the kitchen, while Jesus is preaching in the *other room*.

And we are missing out.

TABLE TALK

7) Why do we attend worship at church? What is the point?

8) What is the point of our time in fellowship as a church family?

9) What welcome do we give others, when we scrutinize *how* they are serving at church, instead of rejoicing that they *are* serving at church?

10) What welcome is waiting for the newer members of our church family, when they bring a store-bought Bundt cake, instead of one that is homemade?

11) **Read Psalm 46:10**. The rough Hebrew translation reads, "Lay down your arms/drop your hands." How might this be used to discuss 'letting go' and 'letting God'?

REFLECTION

Martha was missing out, too.

While she was busy running around, the King of Kings and Lord of Lords was standing *right there* in her midst. Breathing everlasting salvation with every Word that came from His mouth. That's why Jesus stops this frantic woman from trying *in vain* to 'love her neighbor as herself' and He tells her, "Martha, Martha, you are anxious and troubled about many things, but *one thing is necessary*. Mary has chosen *the good portion*, which will not be taken away from her." (Luke 10:42)

Now, it wasn't that Mary had *better* faith than Martha. Not at all. They *both* loved Jesus very much and they both had faith in Him. Martha would later give a tremendous confession of faith in Jesus, at the passing of her brother, Lazarus. She would confess her belief in the promise of the Resurrection and Jesus being the Christ (see John 11:17-27). She had great faith.

The difference between these two sisters was - Mary knew something special: she and her sister, Martha, were *not* the hosts in their house that day – they were the *guests*!

All they were called to do by faith was – *be still*, and listen to the Host, and be His welcome guest.

Jesus is our 'good portion', as well.

And when compared to Him, all the 'going and doing likewise' in the world, doesn't amount to a hill of beans.

'The one thing that's necessary', is Jesus – crucified, died, buried and risen again - for the forgiveness of your sins. Claiming you in your baptism, feeding you with His true body and true blood, by the power of the Holy Spirit - placing His forgiveness upon you. Nothing else required. You simply *sit still* and by faith – receive what the Host has come to give you – *the good portion* – which will *never* be taken away from you, for all eternity.

TABLE TALK

12) How have you 'missed out' on Jesus in the other room, while you've 'been busy in the kitchen'?

13) Brainstorm ways you and your family can be intentional in 'not missing out' on being Jesus' welcome guests.

BRINGING IT HOME

And *yet...* since you and I are hard-wired that 'we have to do *something*', that sweet Gospel truth—of Jesus being our Hospitable Host and we the Welcome Guests—nothing more required— just seems *too easy.*

We can't accept it!

In our heart of hearts, we *still* think we need to do *something* to contribute to our salvation or to *prove* we love Jesus. And so, the questions in our hearts begin:

"So, I'm free because of Jesus?"

YES! Absolutely!

"But don't I still need to go and love my neighbor as myself, to contribute <u>something</u>?"

NO! You don't *need* to go and love your neighbor as yourself. That wasn't the point of Jesus' words. Jesus took care of 'loving your neighbor' on the cross and paying for your sins.

"I'm so confused! I <u>shouldn't</u> do something, but I <u>should</u> welcome my neighbor, too. What on earth am I supposed to do now?!"

Well, there are *many, many things* to worry about and to waste your time running around like a chicken with your head cut off over - but why do that *right now*? Why do that when the Hospitable Host is in your presence?

I'm willing to bet, you will have *no problem* embracing the Law again whole-heartedly and start worrying about all the things you're *not* doing - the moment you say, 'amen' to your prayer, the moment you close your Bible or the moment your pastor gives the Benediction and the last hymn has been sung at church.

But why worry about what you are *supposed* to be doing?

Why worry about that *right now*?

I guarantee you'll have no problem being 'up to your ears' in worry without any effort. You'll do it just fine without *anyone* telling you to do it from a pulpit. Because *that* – my fellow 'Martha's of the world' – is called 'the Law'. It's hard-wired into us. And doing *more* Law *never* saves anyone.

So, instead of doing that—how about you hit the pause button and hear – *really hear* - Jesus' words, "Christian, Christian, *you* are anxious and troubled about many things – but only one thing is necessary". Right now, it's *Sunday morning*. Or maybe it's nearing night time, where you are. Or maybe it's the beginning of a new day. Regardless of the day or the time, God Himself, through His Son, Jesus has invited you to *His* house - to *His* heart - to be your *Host*.

You are His welcome guest – *all the time, any time.*

You are forgiven—and that is *enough.* Not only to *be welcomed* by the Lord, but to *be welcoming* to others.

In a world that screams at you all the time, "Don't just *sit* there – *do* something!"—Jesus tells you, "Don't just *do* something – *sit there.*"

"*Be still* and know that I am God" (Psalm 46)

"Have a seat, *Mary*. Have a seat, *Martha*. Have a seat - *Child of God*.

Take. Eat. This is My Body, given for you.

Take. Drink. This is My Blood, shed for you.

This is My Word, as a gift to you.

Don't serve at this moment.

That moment will come.

For now – Be *still*. Be *served* by Me, Whole-heartedly."

Served as the Welcome Guest of our great, forgiving, Hospitable Host.

TABLE TALK

14) **Read Matthew 25:40**. How might this verse refer to welcoming others?

15) What does it look like to welcome the lonely? The hungry? The homeless? People far away from home? A refugee? An international student?

16) In what ways can you provide an opportunity to 'be still' for others? For that family down the street with a new baby? A person who needs someone to listen to them?

17) Have a family meeting. Brainstorm ways you can build 'quiet time' in your home, to be with Jesus.

18) Discuss setting aside a space in your home for a family altar, as a sacred space.

19) Put up a 'prayer board' in your kitchen, to keep the petitions of your family and others in front of you.

> Be thou my vision, O Lord of my heart;
> Naught be all else to me, save that thou art--
> Thou my best thought by day or by night,
> Waking or sleeping, thy presence my light.
>
> Be thou my wisdom, and thou my true word;
> I ever with thee and thou with me, Lord;
> Thou my great Father, I thy true son;
> Thou in me dwelling, and I with thee one.
>
> Be thou my battle shield, sword for my fight;
> Be thou my dignity, thou my delight,
> Thou my soul's shelter, thou my high tow'r:
> Raise thou me heav'n-ward, O Pow'r of my pow'r.
>
> Riches I heed not, nor man's empty praise,
> Thou mine inheritance, now and always:

Thou and thou only, first in my heart,
High King of heaven, my treasure thou art.

High King of heaven, my victory won,
May I reach heaven's joys, O bright heav'n's Sun!
Heart of my own heart, whatever befall,
Still be my vision, O Ruler of all.

Closing Prayer: *Lord, how often do I miss Your invitation to me, because I'm just too busy in the kitchen of life. Help me to slow down, be still, and sit at Your feet for a while. Help me model, not busyness to my family, but trust in You. Help me, by Your Holy Spirit, to embrace Your rest in my home, where You are the Host and I am Your most welcome guest. Amen*

CHAPTER 13
Welcome, Barriers and Boundaries

Romans 12:1-2
"I appeal to you therefore, brothers,
by the mercies of God, to present your bodies as a living
sacrifice, holy and acceptable to God, which is your
spiritual worship. Do not be conformed to this world,
but be transformed by the renewal of your mind,
that by testing you may discern what is the will of God,
what is good and acceptable and perfect.

Philippians 4:8
"Finally, brothers, whatever is true, whatever
is honorable, whatever is just, whatever is pure,
whatever is lovely, whatever is commendable,
if there is any excellence, if there is anything worthy
of praise, think about these things."

1 Peter 4:7-11
"The end of all things is at hand; therefore be self-

controlled and sober-minded for the sake of your prayers. Above all, keep loving one another earnestly, since love covers a multitude of sins. Show hospitality to one another without grumbling. As each has received a gift, use it to serve one another, as good stewards of God's varied grace: whoever speaks, as one who speaks oracles of God; whoever serves, as one who serves by the strength that God supplies—in order that in everything God may be glorified through Jesus Christ. To him belong glory and dominion forever and ever. Amen."

SETTING THE TABLE

B*oundaries have been around, since the beginning of time.* At the dawn of creation, God puts in place boundaries in our world: "And God said, "Let there be light," and there was light. And God saw that the light was good. And God *separated* the light from the darkness. God called the light Day, and the darkness he called Night. And there was evening and there was morning, the first day. And God said, "Let there be an expanse in the midst of the waters, and let it *separate* the waters from the waters." And God made the expanse and *separated* the waters that were under the expanse from the waters that were above the expanse. And it was so. And God called the expanse Heaven. And there was evening and there was morning, the second day." (Gen 1:3-8)

The English word for 'separate' doesn't fully give us the deeper Hebrew meaning of this word. In Hebrew, the word 'separate' is *badhal*. It means more than just separating one thing from another. The Hebrew word 'to separate' can also be translated as, 'to *consecrate*'. When something has been consecrated, it has been set apart *by* God

Himself – and set apart *for* God Himself. It is a sacred act that God does to create a holy boundary and set apart for a holy purpose.

We see this when God consecrates the Garden of Eden: "And the LORD God commanded the man, saying, "You may surely eat of every tree of the garden, but of the tree of the knowledge of good and evil you shall not eat, for in the day that you eat of it you shall surely die." (Gen 2:16-17) This tree had a *boundary* around it – something that God had set apart. That boundary was created by God's Word, spoken to the first man, Adam. This boundary was not created as a form of temptation but as a form of *protection*. That made this particular tree as something set apart in the Garden of Eden to be a means for *worshipping* the Almighty God.

The underlying questions that God wants us to think about when He consecrates the tree of the knowledge of good and evil is - will man trust that God alone provides all he needs to support this body and life - including all things that needed to be known and are worth knowing? Will man respect the boundaries He has put in place, for his good? Or would man trust *himself*, try to become his own god and suffer the consequences? We all know the sad choice that Adam made. "[God] drove out the man, and at the east of the garden of Eden he placed the cherubim and a flaming sword that turned every way to guard the way to the tree of life." (Gen 3:24) Through Adam and Eve's fall into sin, the boundary of protection becomes a *barrier of separation*, that forbids Adam and Eve from having access to the Garden of Eden, ever again.

In a world where pluralism, tolerance and acceptance has become the creed of society, it's hard for people to comprehend the purpose of *boundaries*. When the world around us has no tolerance for boundaries, it is difficult for God's people to understand how boundaries fit in to our *welcome*.

In this lesson, we'll explore what God means when He 'consecrates' something, compare His 'holy boundaries' to 'unhealthy barriers' and discuss how God's Church can honor the *boundaries* He created, while still extending a *warmhearted welcome* to others.

Prayer: *Lord, You alone determined the boundary of our salvation – that's why we can trust that You have fulfilled exactly what You promised in Jesus. Help us to honor the boundaries You put in place—boundaries that exist, because you love us. Help us to remove all barriers to the Gospel, to receive others with joy, and share Your hospitality as Your people. Amen*

AT THE TABLE

1) What do you think is the difference between 'boundaries' and 'barriers'?

2) How can boundaries in life be a *good* thing?

3) What do you think of when you envision a 'barrier'?

4) How are barriers *harmful*?

REFLECTION

Caroline Westerhoff is an author who wrote an article for Baylor University, called, "Boundary and Hospitality"[90] who describes a time when she took a three-day silent retreat in a Trappist monastery. She claims that the monks' hospitality was very warm and inviting and she sensed God's grace in the quietness of their community.

However, there were *boundaries*:

"Upon arrival and checking in, I easily found my sparsely furnished, pleasant room. A single sheet of information on the small desk told me where I could go and provided the schedule for meals and times of prayer. A graciously worded paragraph reminded me that while I was welcome to attend daily community masses, as a non-Roman Catholic, I could not receive communion; prayer for the unity of the Church would be appropriate. I spent the rest of the time before vespers at 5:30 p.m. exploring my surroundings, soon discovering that signs on doors and fences gave me all the directions I needed: 'Women's Toilet,' 'Women's Shower Room,' 'To the Church,' 'Silent Area,' 'Please Do Not Enter—Cloistered Area.' I began to feel more at ease: paradoxically welcomed, greeted hospitably, as I became aware of the boundaries"[91].

As Americans, we live with the idea of 'rugged individualism,' 'pulling ourselves up by our bootstraps,' and the freedom to do whatever we want. Because of this, we often confuse *welcoming* strangers with *including* them in every aspect of our faith community. Westerhoff helps us see the distinction between the two. Boundaries are everywhere and they define the family, the group, or church family into which we welcome people. In fact, *genuine hospitality* requires *proper boundaries*.

In a world that screams the mantra of tolerance and acceptance, for Trappist monks to have a statement that doesn't allow communion for everyone is pretty countercultural. To some, it could cause offense. Perhaps the reason why Westerhoff wasn't offended, was because the monks genuinely welcomed her and took the time to explain *why* such boundaries were in place. She grew comfortable with them because she knew that the rules and restrictions were *boundaries* to establish the monastic community, *not barriers* to keep her away. The monks made her feel welcome, even though she was not included in every aspect of their community.

She writes, "One of the things my visit to the monastery stirred up in me was my long fascination with boundaries" – boundaries which, as she claims, define *identity*: "Neither good nor bad in its own right, a *boundary* determines something that can be pointed to and named: a person, a family, a geographical region, a city, a town, a nation, a parish church, a denomination, a faith. A *boundary* provides essential limits - for what is not limited, bounded, merges with its context and ceases to exist in its own particular way."

TABLE TALK

5) Can you think of any *boundaries* that your family has?

6) How can *boundaries* in your church family be misunderstood as a '*barrier*'?

7) How can rules, schedules and activities within a church become unintended *barriers* that keep guests and new members out?

Barriers form when we (intentionally or unintentionally) design our walk together as Christians to only welcome those who look, live, think, and even vote like we do—to join us, because they make us comfortable. All others need not apply.

8) How might God's people have subtle ways of making the *unwanted* feel *unwelcome*?

9) How was Caroline Westerhoff *welcomed* but not *included* in the life of the Trappist monastery?

10) What would it mean in the life of your church family to *welcome* but not *include* someone? Who would you not include?

11) What boundaries should be put in place when you welcome a guest into your home?

12) Discuss the difference between a *barrier* to hospitality and a *boundary* to hospitality.

REFLECTION

The rhythms, rules and guidelines of praying together, reading Scripture, attending worship—all these things are 'consecrated'—set apart by God in an order—a carefully designed boundary that defines us as a community of faith, set apart from the world. According to Westerfhoff, the monks proclaimed in their daily routine, "This is who we are; this is what we do and don't do." Yet outsiders were graciously welcomed and cared for, provided they honor the monastic boundaries.

Barriers oppose the practice of hospitality and welcome. *Boundaries* are *essential* for it. "We must have something into which we can extend authentic invitations," notes Westerhoff. That is why "the concept of boundary, put in a theological framework, can give us guideposts for faithful participation in God's reign."

TABLE TALK

13) **Read 1 Peter 4:7-11**. How are the boundaries for the Church described, even as it calls for love and hospitality?

14) Discuss this statement by Westerhoff, "Like Jesus, we are to welcome strangers and sinners into our midst, just as we ourselves have been welcomed into God's hospitable company. But we first must have the baptismal identity and its boundaries intact before we can genuinely welcome all those who choose to come."

15) Discuss the privileges and responsibilities of *members* as opposed to short- or long-term *guests* of the congregation. Are the boundaries between the two well-defined?

16) Describe the expectations and requirements of *members* in regard to:

   a. Our confession of faith
   b. Baptism
   c. Attendance

d. The Lord's Supper
   e. Financial stewardship
   f. Participation in worship
   g. Bible Study
   h. Practice of Prayer

17) Read **Ephesians 4:11-16, 1 Peter 5:1-4 and Titus 1:5-9**. What roles are restricted to members? To Elders? To Pastors? Why these distinctions? Why does God consecrate/give different role assignments for men and women?

18) **Read Ephesians 5:21-33** Why does God put in place boundaries and roles that are distinct, yet complementary, for men and women?

19) Discuss how a *guest* could participate in and benefit from the life of the congregation.

20) What beliefs and practices would the congregation accept in a *guest*, but not in a *member*? Discuss why the boundaries are drawn in these places.

REFLECTION

Once, when I was serving at another congregation, a man in a super-loud Harley-Davidson motorcycle pulled up to my office. He lumbered in, all 6'5", 320 pounds of him, leather jacket, tattoos and all and plopped down in a chair. I was scared to death. This was a guy I wouldn't normally have hung out with—in fact, I'd have likely crossed to the other side of the street, if he was walking my way! I had no idea what was going to happen next!

That's when he started crying.

When he regained his composure, he said his name was Jake. He told me he'd been baptized when he was a baby, but only came to church every so often, and only when his grandmother took him. He left home at sixteen. He was in jail by eighteen. He got out, joined a biker club and put the 'hell' in 'hellraiser'. But he said, "No matter how hard I tried, I couldn't run away from God. He kept talkin' to me over the years, no matter how I tried to shut Him up. I kept readin' my Bible. He kept tellin' me what I was doin' wasn't right. Tellin' me I needed to come home. So, I saw your church sign and I just pulled in. And I'd like you to baptize me again."

I told him, "Jake, you don't need to be baptized again. Sounds like your baptism worked just fine the first time. When you were a baby, God claimed you with the forgiveness of Jesus Christ and put His Holy Spirit in you. Even though you walked away from Him, *He hasn't gone anywhere*. The fact that you're sitting here with me now, proves it. He never gave up on you. He never will."

And so, in my office we went through Confession & Absolution together. Jake started going to church and before long took adult instruction classes. Jake later joined the church, and he became one of the best members of - the *altar guild* - that I've ever known. What made this so unique was the altar guild, more often than not, consists of kind, gentle women, who take care of the set up and removal of the elements of communion, the altar linens and banners (sometimes called paraments). And here was a guy who could have been a stand-in for the Brawny Towel Guy, wanting to be in the altar guild! He insisted that's where he wanted to serve, and I didn't stop him. No one *else* did, either!

TABLE TALK

21) **Read Ephesians 4:4-6**. How might St. Paul's words apply to my situation with Jake, the 'Brawny Towel Guy'?

22) What *boundaries* were put in place to help Jake in his walk of faith?

23) What *perceived barriers* were torn down in the altar guild membership when Jake showed up?

24) What *barriers* do we wrongly put in place regarding:

   a. Ethnicity
   b. Race
   c. Economic and social class
   d. Political ideas
   e. Gender
      - Note: This is not referring to the Godly boundary of men serving in the Pastoral office or serving as Elders. (see 1 Pet. 5:1-3; Titus 1:6; 1 Tim 3:2)
   f. Physical or mental ability
   g. Educational background
   h. Past grudges
   i. Unhealed hurts
   j. Painful memories

25) **Read Philippians 4:8**. What actions is St. Paul telling us to 'consecrate' or to 'keep holy' in our daily lives?

26) How might these consecrated actions look different than the actions of the world around us?

27) How do the Creeds (Apostles', Nicene, Athanasian) also serve as *boundaries*?

REFLECTION

Another *boundary* that people often confuse with a *barrier* in Christian circles is the practice of Holy Communion. In our American 'I did it my way' mentality, we think that we can open the table to anyone when we celebrate the Lord's Supper and that somehow this will create unity. Ironically, when I tell people that the Lord's Supper is reserved to be received by those who share in our common confession of faith, it is typically *Lutherans*, not our *guests*, who wrestle with that boundary.

I think it is because we Lutherans, and most Christians, believe that 'opening the rail' is somehow more welcoming. But this way of thinking goes completely against the *boundaries* in place in the Holy Sacrament. Even the word, "communion", speaks to a boundary. Communion is a compound word from, "common union." That means, when I gather at the rail, I am gathered with the people of God who confess the same thing as I do about the Lord's Supper – that it is Christ's true Body and Blood, in, with and under the form of the bread and wine, for the forgiveness of my sins (Matt. 26:26–29; 1 Cor. 11:23-32) and is not merely a symbolic representation. This is such an important part of what we believe that, in my congregation, we confess this boundary every Sunday, in the words below, before receiving the Lord's Supper:

Pastor: The Lord's Supper is God's gift for Christians who are properly instructed. (1 Cor. 10:17; Act 2:42) In communing, we want people to receive Christ's body and blood for their good. (1 Cor. 11:23-32) This means that as you come to the Lord's Table you affirm with each communicant that Jesus is your Savior and Lord; and with Lutheran Christians you confess:

Congregation: **I recognize and confess that I am a sinner. I repent of my sin and ask God's forgiveness.**

Congregation: **I believe that Jesus Christ is my only Lord and Savior from sin, Satan and death.**

Congregation: **I believe that the risen Christ is really present in the Sacrament and, under the form of the bread and wine, I receive His true body and blood for the forgiveness of my sin and the strengthening of my faith and life. (Augsburg Confession – Article X)**

Simply put, Communion doesn't *create* unity – it is a holy boundary that *celebrates* the unity that's *already there*. To do otherwise doesn't take into account those who don't understand what they're receiving or even confess the same thing as those who do, creating harm and confusion.

Think of it like a prescription the doctor gave you – not just anyone can take your prescription. And to do otherwise would be harmful. The doctor has explained to you what the prescription is, given you instructions on how to receive it and when the doctor is sure that you fully understand it, you rightly receive it.

St. Paul makes a similar claim in 1 Corinthians 10 and 11:

"The cup of blessing that we bless, is it not a participation in the blood of Christ? The bread that we break, is it not a participation in the body of Christ? Because there is one bread, we who are many are one body, for we all partake of the one bread. (1 Cor. 10:16-17)

"For I received from the Lord what I also delivered to you, that the Lord Jesus on the night when he was betrayed took bread, and when he had given thanks, he broke it, and said, "This is my body, which is for you. Do this in remembrance of me." In the same way also he took the cup, after supper, saying, "This cup is the new covenant in my blood. Do this, as often as you drink it, in remembrance of me." For as often as you eat this bread and drink the cup, you proclaim the Lord's death until he comes. Whoever, therefore, eats the bread or drinks the cup of the Lord in an unworthy manner will be guilty concerning the body and blood of the Lord. Let a person examine himself, then, and so eat of the bread and drink of the cup. For anyone who eats and drinks without discerning the body eats and drinks judgment on himself." (1 Cor. 11:23-29)

Are there other Christian denominations around that do *not* believe the Lord's Supper carries with it the forgiveness of sins and Christ's Presence in the bread and wine? Yes, there are. And I respect that they confess something different from me. I would also know *not* to receive Communion with them, were I to gather with them at worship in their house. That doesn't make me *intolerant* – it makes me respectful of their *boundary*.

Like going to a Trappist monastery, I know that their boundaries regarding Communion are not *excluding* me from their community.

If anything, it shows me that I'm in the presence of a community of faith that *stands for something*.

In my faith tradition, while we have *boundaries* with the distribution of Communion, we do not have *barriers* to the Communion rail. For those who are of a different Christian faith tradition, we ask that they come forward and cross their arms with an "X"—not to show they've been 'crossed-out'—but to show they carry with them the seal of the Name of Christ – where "X" is the first letter in the Greek word for "Χριστός", meaning "Christ." The Pastor distributing Communion then knows to give a blessing to the person, continuing to distribute Christ's body and blood to other Christians with the same confession of faith as the congregation.

Just as I would expect to respect the practices and beliefs of the community of faith I enter, I pray that same courtesy be extended to me, when others are welcomed to worship in my community of faith.

These are healthy *boundaries*, that define communities of faith in Christ – a community of faith that *stands for something*.

Boundaries don't need to be a means of exclusion – only *consecration*. God's People set apart for a common confession and purpose, while remaining a warm and inviting community of faith to others, regardless of our differences.

TABLE TALK

28) What work do you think needs to take place to explain *boundaries* that could be misconstrued as *barriers*? What methods did the Trappist monks use to instruct their guests about their boundaries?

29) **Read John 17:20-23.** How do we reconcile Jesus' words with

barriers and *boundaries*?

30) **Read Galatians 1:6-10**. How does St. Paul see boundaries and unity with regard to what we confess as believers?

31) This is where often believers misconstrue Jesus' words in John 17:20-23 to mean, "Let's come together where we do agree and set aside the areas we don't agree on." Christian unity does *not* mean denominational unity above all else. It does *not* mean we set aside doctrine and confession 'just to say we're united.' Denominations that have tried, fail miserably. Christian unity is based on our salvation in Jesus and glorifying Him. While we pray for the day when divisions will cease, we also must stand firm in the truth of the Gospel and not water it down for the sake of a false unity.

32) How might different denominations unite around a single purpose? When would it be best *not* to unite different denominations?

33) **Read Romans 14:13-23**. Also look at the study notes of your Bible related to these verses. What was going on in St. Paul's world regarding food and drink? How might new Christians misunderstand the removal of food and drink boundaries? How did St. Paul determine when to cross boundaries that didn't harm the Christian confession of faith?

34) Read through my congregation's Welcome and Communion Statement below. Highlight the parts you see as a *welcome* or a *boundary*. Highlight the parts you think will take work to explain the boundary in place:

CONGREGATION WELCOME AND COMMUNION STATEMENT

Welcome to all who are joining us for worship this day, especially to any guests who are among us.

We are so glad you are here and want to get to know you!

Please fill out one of the sheets in the red booklet at the end of each pew.

If you wish to join or to have a Pastor call, please indicate that in the red booklet as well.

As you enter the Sanctuary…

Before the service, Speak to God; During the service, Let God Speak to You; After the service, Speak to One another

If you are a Guest visiting with us this morning…

If you want to know more about us, talk to an usher, an elder, or visit our Information Desk outside and take home a Visitor Welcome Bag. You'll also find info about our Sunday School and/or Adult Bible classes there.

For assistance, please ask an usher at the entrance of the Sanctuary.

To the Parents of Our Young Children, May We Suggest…

Relax! God put the 'wiggle' in children; don't feel you have to suppress it in God's House. This house of worship is their HOME. There's Children Worship Bags for the kids in the back of Church, too.

Quietly explain the parts of the Service and actions of the Pastor, Ushers, the Choir, etc. to your children.

Sing the Hymns, Pray and Say the responses. Children learn Liturgical behavior by copying you.

If you have to leave the Service with your child, feel free to do so. We have a Family Room in back with sound and windows to allow you to worship while calming or feeding your children – but please come back. No one will care if you come and go. As Jesus said, 'Let the little children come to Me.'

The way we welcome children in Church directly affects the way they respond to Church, to God and one another.

What We Believe About the Lord's Supper:

Receiving the Sacrament is not merely a matter between God and the person, but a 'communion' - something done in 'community' and a public confession of a 'common union'.

We believe in the real presence, that the body and blood of Jesus is truly present—in, with, and under the bread and wine (Matt. 26:26–29) and is not merely a symbolic representation.

If there are communicant members of a congregation of The Lutheran Church—Missouri Synod or of congregations which are part of a church body which is in altar and pulpit fellowship with the LCMS, we welcome them to come to the Altar to receive the Sacrament of Christ's Body and Blood.

If there are members of other Christian denominations or those who have questions/doubts about the Sacrament, we also welcome them to come to the Altar, crossing their arms over their chest. Then the elders who distribute Communion will pass by and our Pastor will speak a blessing over those persons.

Scripture teaches that Holy Communion is to be a confession of a common faith (1 Cor. 10:17; Acts 2:42) and that those who are unprepared may do themselves spiritual harm (1 Cor. 11:23–32). We do not thereby presume to question another's faith in Christ but hold this historic position out of love for God's Word and in care for souls. Even as we try to respect the practices of other Christian denominations, so we ask others to please respect our practice.

If there are those who wish to remain in their pews during Holy Communion, we ask that they join us in praying for the great day when all in Christ may be one, as He is with the Father (John 17:21). Any who would like to discuss this practice at more length may make an appointment with our Pastor to do so.

For further preparation and study concerning this precious meal you may wish to turn to pages 326 and 327 in the hymnal and read over the section titled, 'The Sacrament of the Altar.' In addition, on pages 329 and 330 there are questions Dr. Martin Luther wrote to assist people in their preparation for this blessed meal.

The following prayer may be helpful during your time of self-examination: Lord, search my heart - Have mercy on me and forgive me all my sins. Thank You for the gift of Your son, Jesus Christ, whose body was broken and blood was shed on the cross for me. As I come to Your Supper grant me faith to recognize the gifts You give to me in this sacrament – Your own body and blood for the forgiveness of my sins. Thank You for coming to me in this holy sacrament to forgive me and strengthen my faith in You. Amen

> The gifts Christ freely gives He gives to you and me
> To be His Church, His Bride, His chosen, saved and free!
> Saints blest with these rich gifts are children who proclaim
> That they were won by Christ and cling to His strong name.
>
> The gifts flow from the font where He calls us to His own;
> New life He gives that makes us His and His alone.
> Here He forgives our sins with water and His Word;
> The triune God Himself gives power to call Him Lord.
>
> The gifts of grace and peace from absolution flow;
> The pastor's words are Christ's for us to trust and know,
> Forgiveness that we need is granted to us there;
> The Lord of mercy sends us forth in His blest care.
> The gifts are there each day the Holy Word is read;
> God's children listen, hear, receive, and they are fed.
> Christ fills them with Himself, blest words that give them life,
> Restoring and refreshing them for this world's strife.

The gifts are in the feast, gifts far more than we see;
Beneath the bread and wine
Is food from Calvary.
The body and the blood remove our every sin;
We leave His presence in His peace, renewed again.

All glory to the One who lavishes such love;
The triune God in love assures our life above.
His means of grace for us are gifts He loves to give;
All thanks and praise for His Great Love by which we live!

—Lutheran Service Book
602, public domain

Closing Prayer: *Father, even though our first parents, Adam and Eve, violated the boundaries You put in place, You still chose in love to break down the barriers of sin and death by sending Your Son, Jesus, to save us. By Your Spirit, keep us in the boundaries of Your love and forgiveness, living in a way that is always thankful for Your welcoming us as daughters and sons, through the shed blood of Your Only Son. Amen*

CHAPTER 14
Welcome Refreshment

Philippians 4:4-9
"Rejoice in the Lord always; again I will say, rejoice.
Let your reasonableness be known to everyone.
The Lord is at hand; do not be anxious about anything,
but in everything by prayer and supplication with
thanksgiving let your requests be made known to God.
And the peace of God, which surpasses all understanding,
will guard your hearts and your minds in Christ Jesus.
Finally, brothers, whatever is true, whatever is honorable,
whatever is just, whatever is pure, whatever is lovely,
whatever is commendable, if there is any excellence,
if there is anything worthy of praise, think about these
things. What you have learned and received and heard
and seen in me—practice these things,
and the God of peace will be with you."

Philemon 1:4-7
"I always thank my God as I remember you in my prayers,
because I hear about your faith in the Lord Jesus and your
love for all the saints. I pray that you may be active

in sharing your faith, so that you will have a full understanding of every good thing we have in Christ. Your love has given me great joy and encouragement, because you, brother, have refreshed the hearts of the saints."

SETTING THE TABLE

When I was a kid, I can remember my mom announcing to the family that we had to attend a wedding on Saturday. And when I heard that, I'd break out in a "big ol' grin". Why? Because even though I *hated* having to sit through a wedding ceremony, I knew what was coming *after* it – the wedding reception!

That meant wedding cake and cookies, those cool little mints shaped like hearts and punch bowls holding a sugary concoction with ice cream floating on top! Maybe you can relate to how I felt as a kid. Even if you've been at a social function that was a *total bore*, at least you could say at the end of it, "The coconut shrimp and the pastries - sure were great!"

Refreshments are one of the best parts of any party or get-together. Think about it - how often do you get together with folks and *not* have some sort of refreshments? There's almost always something to eat or drink where people are gathered. I've even overheard the occasional kid at Sunday School time say, "I sure hope we have doughnuts today!" We all enjoy refreshments, because they do just what they say - they 're-fresh' us - making us "fresh" again. They renew our energy so we can continue our visits, or Sunday School or party - and keep enjoying our time together.

In a letter he once wrote, St. Paul talks about refreshment - but he's not talking about cookies and punch. He's talking about *Philemon*. According to Paul, *Philemon himself* had served as a "refreshment" for God's people. Philemon's *love* is what provides *special* refreshment – a refreshment of the *heart*, and especially a refreshing of the *saints of God.*

Prayer: *Lord, refreshment isn't just a vital part of a party – it's a vital part of the human experience. Open my mind and heart to welcome the refreshment of the soul that only You can give. Amen*

TABLE TALK

Take a moment to discuss the following together:

1) Think of a great vacation you or your family experienced. What was special about it?

2) Have you ever taken a vacation where you were *more tired* when you got home? What made the vacation feel that way?

3) Think about someone in your life who makes you feel *more tired* after a visit with them? What about them makes you feel that way?

4) Think about someone in your life who 'refreshes your heart'. What are they like? What about your time with them 'refreshes' you?

REFLECTION

Philemon's love as a Christian – the love that Paul had experienced himself from Philemon – is what prompts Paul to write a letter to him, concerning a man that Philemon once *owned* as a slave – a man named *Onesimus.*

You see, Onesimus had run away from Philemon, and during his many travels, he ran in to Paul. And along the way, Onesimus became a Christian. A Christian that St. Paul loved like family, to the point that he writes Philemon these words, "I appeal to you for my *child*, Onesimus, whose *father* I became in my imprisonment." (vs.10)

In this letter, Paul requests - and *expects* - Philemon to take Onesimus back - but not as a slave—as a *brother in Christ* and out of love. He practically *pleads* with Philemon to do this: "refresh *my heart* in Christ," he says. He calls on Philemon to do this by doing what is *right* – by accepting Onesimus back as his Christian *brother*. And by doing so, he in turn, will refresh *Paul's heart*, too.

It would have been really easy, though, for Philemon to say, "No" to Paul. Onesimus was, by legal right, *still* his slave – and that meant, according to the culture of his day, he could do *anything* he wanted with him.

And no court on earth would stop him.

Philemon's slave wasn't working at the home of his master like he was supposed to, and instead, was hanging out with Paul. The bond between master and slave had been broken. It also would have been really easy for Philemon to just 'play along' with Paul's request: to accept Onesimus back, alright, but then treat him poorly — maybe even *worse* than he had before. Keep things the way they *were*, before he 'up and left' without permission.

Philemon as the master again – Onesimus as the slave again.

Forget all that Christian talk about "love" and "forgiveness" and return to the *status quo*. That would have been the *easy* way to do things.

Just as easy as it is for *you and me* to treat other people poorly today - and ignore all that Christian talk about "love" and "forgiveness".

Bonds have been broken—and it's *really easy* to keep things that way.

TABLE TALK

5) Think of a time when the 'easy thing' to do would have been to keep up the status quo, in a difficult relationship. Why does it feel 'easier' to keep the status quo? What 'hard' decisions

would need to be made to make things better?

6) How easy is it for us to break the bonds of fellowship with people we're supposed to be the closest to?

   a. That neighbor you used to spend so much time with but don't speak to anymore because of an argument.

   b. Your brother or sister in Christ who you haven't seen in years because of something they said a long time ago.

   c. Close friends "breaking ties" and now having nothing to do with each another.

REFLECTION

When you take the easy way, when you remain apart from those you should love, your heart becomes *sour*. It's kind of like drinking poison and expecting the other guy to die! You get *bitter* instead of *better* - and instead of sharing your love, you end up sharing the things you *shouldn't*: your dislike, your angry words, your scorn – even your *hatred*. In all our lives there are relationships that have been broken. And that sinful brokenness brings pain - even heart*ache*. If you haven't experienced it already, at some point, heartache brought on by anger, or betrayal, or thoughtlessness *will* touch your life. And hearts that *ache* are hearts that are in need of *refreshment*.

TABLE TALK

7) **Read Phil. 4:4-7**. What do you think it means to "rejoice in the Lord"?

8) What causes God's people to rejoice?

9) Where do you experience rejoicing in your family? In your church family?

10) How does living in a place of gratitude change the way we *welcome* our world? *Think* about our world? *Live* in our world?

RELATIONSHIPS AND REFRESHED HEARTS

So, can Philemon refresh *your* heart, as St Paul says that Philemon did for the *saints* – that is, the people of God? Can your neighbor, your child, your friend, your spouse or your parent refresh *your* heart?

Here's the truth that a lot of people miss.

On their own, no relationship can truly refresh your heart, like you need.

But that doesn't mean we won't *try*, anyway.

How many people look for a connection to 'make them whole' and after the excitement wears off from a new relationship, they always end up disappointed? Maybe it's a boyfriend or girlfriend. Maybe it's a husband or wife. Maybe it's a friendship. Regardless of the relationship, it's a dangerous place to be when you place such high expectations upon another sinful human being to make *you* happy.

According to Greek tradition, human beings started out with two heads, four arms and four legs. The gods, in their mischief, split humans in two, body and soul, and tossed the halves to the opposites ends of the earth. Humans were then doomed to spend the rest of their lives roaming the earth, trying to find their 'other half' - so they could be happy and whole.

That sounds an awful lot like the words we use in romantic language today, when we refer to our spouses or latest date as our 'other half' or 'soul mate.' Remember the movie, *Jerry Maguire*, when the guy tells the girl, "You complete me"? Our culture eats this stuff up.

But it's a very slippery slope when you believe that you are an *incomplete* person until you've 'found someone' to *complete* you.

Let's stop and think about that reasoning, for a moment.

Logically, if you believe there is only 'one person' out there *just for you* – a 'soul mate', then that means this person's *sole function* in life is to complete *you* and make *you* happy. They exist for no other reason than for *you*.

You can choke on the narcissism behind that reasoning.

And I don't think you'd appreciate it if someone believed that *your* sole function in life was to make *them* happy. Maybe you have a toxic relationship where that is the case.

Relationships where *you* are the only goal or where *someone else* is the point of the relationship – misses the point, entirely.

Martin Luther used to say, "Whatever you put your faith and trust in – that is your god." If our happiness and fulfilment in this life stands or falls on the relationships that we have—or *don't* have—we have made those relationships our 'gods'.

And false gods *always* disappoint.

That's why some marriages end with the phrase, "I just don't *feel* in love anymore." That's a statement from Greek mythology, where love is an emotion equal to passion.

That's not Christian love.

Christian love is a *choice* – not a feeling.

Now, love certainly starts out as a feeling. People write songs and poems about that feeling and the world talks endlessly about it. That's why the world is in love with *Romeo and Juliet* and thinks that's the definition of love. But *Romeo and Juliet* isn't a love story – it's a three-day relationship between a thirteen year-old and seventeen year-old that caused six deaths! That's why Shakespeare called it a 'Tragedy'. If love is going to last, it has to be – it must be, a *daily choice*. Otherwise, when life throws hard times at you, it's really easy to turn an "I do" - in to "I don't," if your love is just a feeling.

It reminds me of the words of C.S. Lewis about a "Christian marriage": "If the old fairy-tale ending, 'They lived happily ever after' is taken to mean, 'They felt for the next fifty years exactly as they felt the day before they were married,' then it says what probably never was nor ever would be true, and would be highly undesirable if it were.

Who could bear to live in that excitement for even five years? What would become of your work, your appetite, your sleep, your friendships? But, of course, ceasing to be 'in love' need not mean ceasing *to love*. Love in this second sense – love as distinct from 'being in love' – is not merely a feeling. It is a deep unity, maintained by the will and deliberately strengthened by habit; reinforced by the grace which both partners ask, and receive, from God. They can have this love for each other even at those moments when they do not like each other; as you love yourself even when you do not like yourself.

'Being in love' first moved [the two] to promise fidelity: this *quieter love* enables them to keep the promise. It is on this love that the engine of marriage is run: being in love was the explosion that started it."

Jesus didn't wait till you got your act together before He would feel you were worthy enough to save. He chose, in true sacrificial love, to love you, *anyway*. To save you, *anyway*.

TABLE TALK

10) What might happen to two people, if the husband displayed actions that 'loved his wife', even when his 'heart wasn't in it'? How might those actions impact the relationship? How might those actions, over time, become heartfelt emotions?

Couples that are celebrating fifty years or more of marriage together often say they are 'soul mates.' But it has very little to do with passion – which is often, 'here today-gone tomorrow.' The reason their marriage has worked is because they stopped looking for the *other* person to 'complete *them*' long ago. And in by doing so - they found *true completion.*

I read a story a few years back about a couple that was celebrating *eighty years* of marriage on this earth. Can you imagine?! Eighty years married to the same person – and *liking it*? Well, this cute little couple from England was being interviewed by a local newspaper about what real love was and how they stayed together, and here's the wisdom they had to share with the reporter: "Love is 99% persistence, and we're the most persistent people we know!"

THE VOCATION OF SINGLEHOOD

As I write this chapter, it's Valentine's Day. Never was a national holiday so focused on all the wrong things about relationships as this one day. All my single friends dread February 14th every year, because it's a reminder that, in the eyes of the world, they are somehow *incomplete*. And not just to the world – there are well-meaning Christians who believe that the only way their Christian friends will be happy is if they 'find a husband/wife'.

These folks mean well, and after all, God says it 'is not good that man be alone.' So, they try to 'ship' their single friends, so that way they'll be happy and complete – at least in *their* eyes.

Just one problem with this.

Relationships for their own sake will *never* complete you.

If it did, why did St. Paul stay single? In 1 Corinthians 7:8-9, he says, "To the unmarried and the widows I say that it is good for them to remain single, as I am. But if they cannot exercise self-control, they should marry. For it is better to marry than to burn with passion."

St. Paul states that living as a single *celibate* (not a *promiscuous* single person – God does *not* approve of that) can be a God-pleasing thing. It is not good for man to be alone. But that does not mean that a single person is a second-class citizen because they aren't married. Living out the vocation of singlehood means surrounding oneself with healthy relationships that don't necessarily involve marriage.

By the way, St. Valentine, the guy we remember with candy hearts,

Hallmark greeting cards, and overpriced flowers - died as a martyr for the faith – and he was *single*.

People get married - and sometimes people stay single.

What is *not* good, no matter your relationship status on Facebook or Instagram - is to be *alone*.

You and I, single or married, are called in to *healthy, God-pleasing* relationships.

Sometimes, God blesses us with a relationship that includes a spouse. Sometimes He blesses us with deep friendships and close family. If we have close relationships with our church family, so much more the blessing.

Regardless, you and I were made for community.

A community of *faith*. Where our relationship with God and with one another refreshes us, heart, mind, body and soul.

That's why the author of Hebrews says, "And let us consider how to stir up one another to love and good works, not neglecting to meet together, as is the habit of some, but encouraging one another, and all the more as you see the Day drawing near." (Heb. 10:24-25)

So, whether you're married or single – whichever path God sets you upon - don't go it *alone*.

And find true *completion* – in Christ and in His People.

My oldest daughter wrote these words to her single girlfriends, today:

"Happy Valentine's Day! On this day when we're all 'single Pringles', I wanted to just remind you of your worth. That even though a boyfriend would be nice, our worth doesn't come in their approval or acknowledgement. Our worth is in the Lord and His love for us. So, don't be depressed today because God is beaming with pride for you, His daughter. Psalm 139:14 says, "You are FEARFULLY and WONDERFULLY made. Your works are wonderful. I know that full well." Remember your worth as a Daughter of the King and be proud of Who and Whose you are. Love ya!"

And I love you, daughter of mine, for the woman and Christlikeness that God is making in you!

A *complete* woman, who has found her worth in *Christ alone*!

TABLE TALK

11) Do you know anyone in your circle of friends who seems to 'bounce' from one dating relationship to another? Have you asked them what it was about each relationship that kept them from pursuing it further?

12) What is the danger of seeking a 'soulmate' while you're dating, instead of seeking a 'mate'?

13) How have you made some of your relationships about how much *you* are getting out of your time with them?

14) Have you made it your mission in life to get your close friends 'married off'? How might God be nudging You to get your close friends connected to *Him* and His People, instead?

15) What might it look like to live a life of celibacy and singleness? (Pro Tip: it doesn't mean you have to join a convent or monastery)

16) How might Mother's Day be a time to celebrate the *single* women in your life who have been 'spiritual mothers/aunts' to others? How about doing the same thing for the *single* men who are 'spiritual fathers/uncles' on Father's Day?

YOUTH AND REAL RELATIONSHIPS

We all know the 'boy crazy' or 'girl crazy' teenager. You can see them heading towards you from a mile away. Studies show that while, yes, hormones are raging from the twelve year to nineteen-year age range, at the same time, equally raging inside the average youth – is a hunger for *deep connection.*

This is why peer pressure carries with it a tremendous amount of influence at this age range. The need to be welcomed and accepted is so overwhelming, that at times, the nice kid you know can, in the blink of an eye - morph into a monster, picking on other kids and making fun of them – just so they can 'fit in'.

What might it look like if youth could gather together in a place where everyone was welcome, and they didn't have to focus on 'shipping' each other or putting up a front to be cool? That can happen in youth group fellowship.

And my church's youth group recently proved it.

Our youth director came up with a great idea called, "Friendsgiving". A week before Thanksgiving, she challenged our youth to invite one friend, bring a dish to share and watch *A Charlie Brown Thanksgiving.*

We had no idea the response we would get, but we hoped for maybe sixty youth to show.

We didn't reach that goal. We had eighty-nine youth show.

In fact, one parent commented, "This table looks like Whoville at the end of *How the Grinch Stole Christmas*!" And he was right – we had long white tables, laid end-to-end from one side of the youth room to the other. And there wasn't a single empty seat.

Most of the youth brought two or more friends. They beamed as they shared with us how they made their dish to share 'all by themselves.' And even if they didn't have time to make something, they brought KFC chicken and *still* felt proud that they were contributing to the bounty before us.

'Table leaders' led discussions about what they were thankful for. They wrote it down on the butcher paper laid over the table. They shared a devotion. And it was *so loud* from all the conversations, we couldn't hear Charlie Brown on the big screen.

Parents that usually would drop their kids off on Wednesday nights, stayed for the food and fellowship. So much so, that we had two separate rooms just for the adults to be able to sit and eat!

And it. Was. *Amazing*.

I had youth come up to me during this event and say it was the first time they'd ever cooked anything. One said he'd never sat down for a meal with his family, before, so he didn't know *what to do*.

Let that sink in for a minute.

In youth group fellowship, it's all too tempting to order pizza and just entertain them. It's quick and easy. But "Friendsgiving" made it abundantly clear that if all we ever feed our youth is 'junk food', then we imply that the Church doesn't really offer them anything different than the junk food the world *already* offers.

What would it look like if we did with our youth the same things that we do when our adults get together to fellowship? Would regular potlucks, gathered around the Word and Prayer reshape our youth and foster meaningful relationships?

St. Paul certainly thought it would have a deep, lasting impact on the Christian Church, which is part of why he focuses on fellowship and meals in 1 Corinthians 10 and 11, along with the deep connections and forgiveness celebrated there.

The Lord's Supper, that sacred meal we celebrate on Sundays as a church family, testifies against the world's claims that there will not be enough food to go around. It is a reflection of the manna in the wilderness the Lord provided—daily bread—from Him to His people. And now, shared by His people to others. A visible raging against this sinful world, that when God shows up – there is *always* enough.

Our youth saw the hidden value in preparing and sharing a meal together, as God's hands and feet, working together to provide for all. Relationships – and food – when brought together, become something sacred.

TABLE TALK

17) How might your youth group plan for preparing meals together as part of their fellowship time?

18) What do we tell our youth when we allow them to contribute to a meal?

BRINGING IT HOME

Ultimately, *only Jesus* can refresh your heart. And that's St. Paul's point. Jesus refreshed Onesimus just as He also refreshed Philemon and Paul. Jesus is the One who can heal the scars of our hurt, remove the pain that remains from betrayal or carelessness. Jesus is the only One Who can truly refresh *your* heart. And through His refreshing and renewing of *your* heart, Jesus then empowers *you* to refresh the hearts of *others*.

When you forgive those in your church family who might have caused you heartache and accept them as Christian brothers and sisters - that's Jesus softening *your* heart and refreshing *theirs*. When you quit holding that grudge against your neighbor, your parent, your sibling or your child - that's Jesus refreshing your heart with His divine love. When you forgive others and try to mend a relationship, that's Jesus pouring refreshment into your heart and into the hearts of those around you, repairing what was broken with the greatest refreshment ever - His love and forgiveness for you. And even if, after *trying* to refresh the heart of the one you've broken bonds with - even if they slap your hand away, you will *still* be refreshed, through the nail-scarred hands of your Savior.

Jesus does all this for us because He knows what it's like to experience heartache. He knows it as well as you and I do.

Even *better* than we do.

He, too, was separated from those He loved, from those He came to save, and even from His own Father. Jesus suffered His own heartache, even heart*break* on the cross when He cried out, "My God, my God, why have you forsaken me?" Jesus felt the heartache of broken relationships, even as He was repairing the very brokenness of this world through His own death.

So, He *knows* what you feel when you think about your neighbor, or your child or your parent – and you *wish* things were better. He knows your heart is aching - and He has refreshment for you. He gives you refreshment by His presence in your life, by His Baptism, by His Supper, by His promise to be with you always, even to the end of the age.

I don't think it's an accident that the word 'hospital' comes from the word, 'hospitality.' Because both provide healing. Imagine the healing God can do through you, when you open your door, and your heart, to others. By the power of the Holy Spirit, Jesus can refresh hearts through *you*, just as He refreshed the hearts of the saints through *Philemon*.

Did Philemon accept Onesimus back as his brother in Christ? We don't know. But what we *do* know is this: God our Father has accepted *us* as His children - because our *brother*, Christ Himself, has refreshed our hearts. And just as Jesus refreshed the hearts of the disciples, appearing to them after the resurrection, He refreshes our hearts today, through His presence and His forgiveness. And just as Paul calls on *Philemon* to refresh *his* heart, Jesus calls on *us* to refresh the hearts of our brothers and sisters with the refreshment He's already given us: forgiveness, eternal life, and most of all – His love. So, come to your brother, your sister, with the love of your Savior. Reach out to your neighbor in need with Christ's love – live out the refreshment in Christ that's freely been given to *you* – and be *refreshed*.

Jesus loves me!
This I know,
For the Bible tells me so.
Little ones to Him belong;
They are weak, but He is strong.

Yes, Jesus loves me!
Yes, Jesus loves me!
Yes, Jesus loves me!
The Bible tells me so.

Jesus loves me!
He who died
Heaven's gates to open wide.
He has washed away my sin,
Let His little child come in.

Yes, Jesus loves me!
Yes, Jesus loves me!
Yes, Jesus loves me!
The Bible tells me so.

—Lutheran Service Book
588, public domain

Closing Prayer: *Heavenly Father, You graciously welcomed me as Your forgiven child when I didn't deserve it. It's so easy in this life to hold grudges, harbor hate, and forego forgiveness. To be bitter, instead of better. It's also easy to think that my relationships – healthy or not*

– are an adequate substitute for you. Which is why sometimes those relationships disappoint. Help me by Your Spirit, to remember that the change You have worked in me through Your Son can also happen in the very people I least suspect. Let me give them a chance to show the change You have also worked in them. And help me, most of all, to keep You as my first love. Amen

BONUS CONTENT

Years ago, I put together a Mother's Day and Father's Day Litany that I share every year on the Sundays closest to those dates. I found a lot of the pieces online for the Mother's Day Litany, but I wrote the majority of the Father's Day Litany.

I'd like to share them with you now, as we honor the men and women in our lives, single and married, who are participating in some way, shape or form, to motherhood and fatherhood.

LITANY OF MOTHERHOOD

P: Father of Glory, Your Son, our Lord Jesus, in His incarnation, took on our created human flesh and was born of the Virgin Mary. He submitted to His mother, honoring and obeying her, so fulfilling the commandment, where we have not.

On this Mothers' Day, we pray that Your Bride, the Church, would be a caring and healing reflection of Your presence to all women throughout the various seasons of motherhood:

P: To those who gave birth this year to their first child…

C: We, the Church, celebrate with you.

P: To those who mourn the loss of a child…

C: We, the Church, mourn with you.

P: To those who are in the trenches with little ones every day, teaching the next generation the fear of the LORD…

C: We, the Church, appreciate you.

P: To those who have experienced loss through miscarriage, failed adoptions, or children who have run away from home…

C: We, the Church, grieve with you.

P: To those who are foster moms, mentor moms, and 'spiritual' moms…

C: We, the Church, need you.

P: To those who have chosen life and given up their child for adoption…

C: We, the Church, honor you.

P: To those who carry the silent pain of infertility, fraught with tests and disappointment…

C: We, the Church, walk with you.

P: To those whose season of motherhood was never meant to be, yet are called to be a 'spiritual mother' to others…

C: We, the Church, are grateful for you.

P: To those who have warm and close relationships with their children…

C: We, the Church, celebrate with you.

P: To those who have disappointment, heart ache, and distance with their children…

C: We, the Church, support you.

P: To those who serve as "Godmothers" and as mothers to children from a previous marriage, loving them as their own…

C: We, the Church, honor you.

P: To those who mourn the loss of their mother…

C: We, the Church, remember you.

P: To those who experienced abuse at the hands of their mother…

C: We, the Church, acknowledge your experience.

P: To those who have opened their homes and hearts to adopt a child…

C: We, the Church, honor you.

P: To those who care for children with special needs, disabilities and chronic illnesses, both seen and unseen…

C: We, the Church, are better for having you in our midst.

P: To those who hurt from the mothers who have abandoned them…

C: We, the Church, hurt with you.

P: To those who are pregnant with new life, both expected and surprising…

C: We, the Church, joyfully anticipate with you.

P: To those who will have emptier nests in the upcoming year…

C: We, the Church, anticipate life's changes, with you.

P: To those with mothers who are mentally ill…

C: We the Church, walk with you.

P: To those who have no memory of their mothers…

C: We, the Church, remember you.

P: To those who grieve the pain of an abortion…

C: We, the Church, grieve with you.

P: To those young women who will be mothers someday…

C: We, the Church, joyfully anticipate with you.

P: We, the Church, lay these litany of prayers at the feet of the One Who loved us to the point of death, even death on a cross – the One Who, from the cross asked John to look at Mary and said, "Behold, your mother."

This Mother's Day, we acknowledge Christ's care for us in all facets of life, having molded us in to a new family, through His own precious blood.

Continue to make us mindful of the joys, pains, sorrows and triumphs of the women among us who have been bound to us as a Church family, continuing to serve one another for the sake of Jesus Christ, Your Son, our Lord, Who lives and reigns with You and the Holy Spirit, One God, now and forever.

C: Amen.

FATHER'S DAY LITANY

P: God our Father, in Your wisdom and love You created all things. On this Father's Day, we ask You to bless all men, that they may be godly and strengthened as Christian fathers. Let their example of faith and love in Christ Jesus shine forth in their lives. Grant that we, their sons and daughters, may honor them always with a spirit of profound respect. We pray for all men throughout the world and in the various seasons of fatherhood:

P: Let us praise those fathers who have striven to balance the demands of work, marriage, and children with an honest awareness of both joy and sacrifice.

C: We, the Church, are grateful for you.

P: Let us praise those fathers who, lacking a good model for a father, have worked to become a good father.

C: We, the Church, support you.

P: Let us praise those fathers who by their own account were not always there for their children, but who continue to offer those children, now grown, their love and support.

C: We, the Church, uplift you.

P: Let us praise those fathers who have been wounded by the neglect and hostility of their children yet remain hopeful and faithful in a fatherly relationship with their children.

C: We, the Church, hurt with you.

P: Let us praise those fathers who, despite divorce, have remained in their children's lives.

C: We, the Church, encourage you.

P: Let us praise those fathers whose children are adopted, and whose love and support has offered healing.

C: We, the Church, honor you.

P: Let us praise those fathers who, as stepfathers, freely choose the obligation of fatherhood and earned their stepchildren's love and respect.

C: We, the Church, are thankful for you.

P: Let us praise those fathers who have lost a child to death and continue to hold the child in their heart.

C: We, the Church, grieve with you.

P: Let us praise those men who have no children but cherish the next generation as if they were their own.

C: We, the Church, need you.

P: Let us praise those men who have "fathered" us in their role as mentors and guides.

C: We, the Church, celebrate you.

P: Let us praise those men who are about to become fathers; may they openly delight in their children.

C: We, the Church, joyfully anticipate with you.

P: Let us praise those men who will become fathers someday; may they continue to model fatherly character and faith to those they encounter.

C: We, the Church, honor you.

P: And let us praise those fathers who have died but live on in our memory and whose love continues to nurture us.

C: We, the Church, remember you.

P: Most gracious God and Father, we thank You for the blessed gift of a father. As we are thankful for our earthly fathers in different ways, we truly are thankful for You, our heavenly Father. For you give us life on earth and, through Your Son Jesus, eternal life in His kingdom. We, Your children, praise You, who attends to all our needs and gathers us safely in Your bosom. In the name of Jesus, we pray.

C: Amen.

CHAPTER 15
A Welcome Opportunity

Psalm 51:15-17
"O Lord, open my lips, and my mouth will declare your praise. For you will not delight in sacrifice, or I would give it; you will not be pleased with a burnt offering. The sacrifices of God are a broken spirit; a broken and contrite heart, O God, you will not despise."

Malachi 3:10
"Bring the full tithe into the storehouse, that there may be food in my house. And thereby put me to the test, says the LORD of hosts, if I will not open the windows of heaven for you and pour down for you a blessing until there is no more need."

Matthew 19:16
"And behold, a man came up to [Jesus], saying, "Teacher, what good deed must I do to have eternal life?"

SETTING THE TABLE

As I mentioned at the beginning of this book, my Dad is an electrical contractor. Since he owned his own business when I was growing up, that meant I got to work with him year-round. We went everywhere: repairing oil wells and irrigation wells, rewiring old houses and wiring in new ones. There was never a dull moment and there was always a change of scenery.

But there was one place that I *never* wanted to go.

In fact, I wouldn't have sent my worst enemy to this place!

And Dad knew it.

He knew I hated this place so much that when we got the call to go there – he *wouldn't* tell me. He'd just drive with an innocent look on his face until we turned on that certain road at FM400. And when he knew I was on to him, he'd turn to me, give a little grin and say, "I'm sorry, son." And then I knew for sure that we were heading to the most disgusting job we did – by working at the commercial swine breeder. Or, as I liked to refer to it: "The most God-forsaken place on earth!"

The local swine breeder housed and cared for over *one million* swine.

That's pigs, to you and me. A *lot of pigs*. Have you ever been downwind from a hog farm after a good rain? It makes being near a cattle pen after a good rain downright pleasant by comparison.

Multiply the scent of a hog farm by about *one billion*, and that's the sweet bouquet that wafted our way from the swine houses. And we weren't driving *away* from the smell, like sensible people. We were the only idiots headed *towards* it.

But the worst part about this place wasn't *the smell*. The most dehumanizing, degrading experience of all – was trying to get *in* the place. Since the walking slabs of bacon inside were supposed to be 'disease-free pigs', it greatly increased their value. That also meant that to keep it that way, everything going into the swine houses needed to be 'disease-free', as well. That included our work truck, which was sprayed down with antiseptic right down to the tires. Our tool pouch and all our tools were cleaned. But that wasn't all.

Trucks and tools not only had to be disease-free. So did all the *people* going inside. So that meant Dad and I needed to be disease-free – by using the swine breeder's public showers. We used their special soap and dried off with their germ-free towels. We dressed in their hypoallergenic, disease-free socks, t-shirts, coveralls and then – for the *coup de grâce* of all experiences – we put on their disease-free underwear. (Thank God all this stuff was washed *before* we put it on!)

Then we dipped our oversized rubber boots in special antiseptic and – having been fully traumatized from the experience of the previous twenty minutes – we trudged outside toward the waiting swine pens, which caused you to go 'nose deaf' from being so close to such an awful stench. But even though you were nose deaf, you still knew the smell was there by the stinging tear drops that occasionally fell from your eyes.

Now, in my teenage mind, by this point we had officially entered Dante's ninth circle of hell. Only, this was darker and more devoid of hope. You can just imagine the expression that was on my face by that point. I'd *glare* daggers at my father, as we trudged to the first swine pen to experience a day comparable to what Mike Rowe would affectionately call, 'a little slice of hell.'

Dad, on the other hand, became more joyful with every step, which caused my temper to boil with the heat of a thousand suns. Occasionally, Dad would just grin, breathe in deep and say, "Ah – smells like money! What a great day to be the 'Lord of the sty'!" Needless to say, I was *not* amused.

'Lord of the sty' – or a 'sty-warden', literally, 'someone who takes care of someone else's pigs'. The Olde English word 'sty-warden' is where we get our modern English word for 'steward'. And that's our focus this chapter – to pause and reflect on how we're doing as God's people – as 'sty-wardens' of God's blessings. I know what you're thinking, "Hold up! I thought this was a book on welcoming, not on stewardship!" That's true. And what could be more welcoming than to invite God into your pocketbook? Even better, to acknowledge that *your* pocketbook has really been *His*, all along.

Prayer:

Lord, this is a tough one, because I'm so busy worrying about how I'm going to have enough to pay bills, afford the kids' doctor visits and the random car breakdown, that just the thought of giving much-needed funds back to You scares me. Help me to lean into You more, as the Great Giver of Every Good and Perfect Gift. Help me to trust You more - the Only One Who held nothing back from me – and gave everything You had on the cross to pay my debt. Amen

REFLECTION

I think we all get why the government wants our money. We get why restaurants, our bank and our kids want our money. But why does our *church*? Usually, when people hear of "stewardship" in church, their reaction isn't a good one, because they think being a "steward" means to "give money". Furthermore, people complain that all the church *ever* talks about is money.

Many people think that money and religion shouldn't even mix. Maybe it's because they see money as corrupting everything. That they've been burned one too many times by T.V. preachers who have stolen money from little old ladies so they can get a brand-new private jet. And – after all, the Bible tells us that money is the root of all evil.

Only – the Bible *doesn't* say that.

It says, "For the love of money is a root *of all kinds of evils*. It is through this craving that some have wandered away from the faith and pierced themselves with many pangs." (1 Timothy 6:10)

Giving money to your church is not evil – it's *practical*.

It's how the church keeps the lights on, pays the bills and enjoys the blessings of a ministry team whose heart serves Jesus and equips us in our walk of faith.

It's also part and parcel of how mercy ministry was supported throughout the ages, all over the world.

When was the last time you drove by a "St. Atheist Hospital" or "Agnostic Elementary"? There's a reason for that. Hospitals, education, support for single mothers, widows and orphans – the Christian Church, for a couple thousand years and counting, has cornered the market on mercy and relief ministries, development of society and support of the weakest among us. That kind of ministry simply doesn't happen adequately or faithfully, apart from the support and work of God's people.

Money's *part* of stewardship – but it's not *all* of stewardship. Because God doesn't own *money*.

He owns *everything*!

Psalm 24 says, "The earth is the Lord's, and everything in it, the world, and all who live in it…" (Psa 24:1) In pig farming language, that means the things in our "sty": our money, our possessions, our husbands, our wives, our kids, even our talents and abilities, aren't really ours. We're just the 'warden' of those things. Every blessing we have is on loan to us. We simply manage it. <u>*Our*</u> "sty" is really <u>GOD'S</u> "sty" – He expects us to use these gifts to honor Him, not just at our church, but in our everyday lives.

TABLE TALK

Take a moment to discuss the following together:

1) **Read *The First Article of The Apostles' Creed*,** found in Luther's Small Catechism (text below):

The First Article: Creation
I believe in God, the Father Almighty, Maker of heaven and earth.

What does this mean? I believe that God has made me and all creatures; that He has given me my body and soul, eyes, ears, and all my members, my reason and all my senses, and still takes care of them. He also gives me clothing and shoes, food and drink, house and home, wife and children, land, animals, and all I have. He richly and daily provides me with all that I need to support this body and life. He defends me against all danger and guards and protects me from all evil. All this He does only out of fatherly, divine goodness and mercy, without any merit or worthiness in me. For all this it is my duty to thank and praise, serve and obey Him.

This is most certainly true.

2) Go back through The First Article above and circle all the things listed that God gives us.

3) Is there anything else you can think of that could be added to the list?

REFLECTION

Now, in *theory*, God being the owner of everything sounds really good. God owns all things. God it. *Check*.

But as sinful people, it's *scary* to put the *theory* in to *practice* – because that's when the rubber meets the road in our faith lives. I admit that at one time, I was a *bad* example of a Christian 'sty-ward'. I had no excuses: I grew up around parents who tithed of their time, their talents and their treasure. But the world got in the way by the time I was in college, convincing me that I couldn't *afford* to give up anything in my 'sty'. Besides, I was just a poor college student. I'd get around to it when I graduated and then I could 'afford it'. Only problem was, my *income* changed after graduation, but my *heart* didn't. I got a job with a computer company in Houston, but by that point, I felt I needed to 'climb the ladder' for a while before I could afford to give from my 'sty'.

My giving (or lack thereof) to God tells me just how far my heart was from God.

Just as how you spend your (*God's*) money tells you a lot about who you are on the inside. Where your hope and trust really are. So, if I, as a pastor, care at all about the people God has asked me to shepherd, I need to – I *must* – talk about money and the priority it has in the lives of God's people. Because, whether you want to believe it or not – welcoming God into your pocketbook is a huge indicator of wealth – *true* wealth. And a welcome opportunity to grow rich towards God.

Financial experts claim that the average American *minimum* wage is worth *fifty* times <u>more</u> than the world's *average* wage. Over one third of the world survives on an income of about one dollar a day. Americans 'survive' on the equivalent of one-hundred fifty dollars a day.

The *poorest* Americans live better than the *wealthiest* people in a third world country.

Yes, it's a blessing to live in America - and it also means we're better off than we think we are. So, according to Jesus' financial spreadsheet, we have far more than we think we do and far more opportunities to bless others with what He's gifted us.

The disciples in Jesus' day would have loved to have welcomed wealthy people into their fold, because they believed from Jewish tradition that to be rich was a sign of God's blessings. That a 'strong portfolio' meant God was on your side and that it even got you a special place in heaven. Then, along comes a rich man seeking out Jesus and His wisdom (Matthew 19:16-30). A rich man possibly becoming a disciple was very appealing to them. Just think of what they could do with his wealth, power and position! And maybe that outward sign of God's favor on this guy would trickle down to *them*, too!

The devil is still using that old trick on Christians today. When a wealthy and powerful person walks into our church, the temptation is to give them more attention than other folks, even 'court' them because of what they can give to the church. St. James warns against that kind of thinking, when he says, "if a man wearing a gold ring and fine clothing comes into your assembly, and a poor man in shabby clothing also comes in, and if you pay attention to the one who wears the fine clothing and say, "You sit here in a good place," while you say to the poor man, "You stand over there," or, "Sit down at my feet," have you not then made distinctions among yourselves and become judges with evil thoughts?" (James 2:2-4). Making distinctions between the rich and the poor had become a big problem in the Jewish world – things haven't changed all that much today.

TABLE TALK

4) Discuss the challenge of *not* giving special preference to someone because of their wealth, influence or fame.

5) Discuss the challenge of harboring envy against those who have more money, privilege or influence than you.

6) Take an internal inventory of your wealth, privilege and influence. How has God gifted you in ways that you may have taken for granted? How might they be used for His Glory?

7) Take an internal inventory of your *spiritual* wealth, privilege and influence. How has God gifted you in ways that you may have taken for granted? How might they be used for His Glory?

REFLECTION

Jesus said to him, "If you would be perfect, go, sell what you possess and give to the poor, and you will have treasure in heaven; and come, follow me." (Matt. 19:21) Jesus' words to the rich man go to the heart of the problem. The problem wasn't that this guy had money. Because Abraham, David and Solomon all had money and they still had salvation.

The real problem with the rich man was his *riches* owned *him*.

If possessions and money own *you*, instead of the other way around, then you'll fool yourself in to thinking they'll *save* you, too. And with that mindset, the more you have, the more likely you'll be tempted by the devil to ignore God altogether and *rely* on yourself - and you'll be far less likely to *give* of yourself. And end up spiritually bankrupt.

There once was a businessman who came to a chaplain with a concern he had about tithing. He said: "I've been tithing for some time. It wasn't too bad when I was making $20,000 a year. I could afford to give $2,000. But now I'm making $500,000, and there's just no way I can afford to give $50,000 a year." The chaplain thought about it and said: "I can see your problem. I think we should pray about it." So, the chaplain bowed his head and prayed, "Dear Lord, this man has a problem, and I pray that you will help him. Please reduce his salary, back to the place where he can *afford* to tithe to You again."[92]

If we rely on our riches for security and comfort, we'll never really get either one. We'll waste our lives not just keeping up with the Joneses but trying to *be* the Joneses. And if your heart sees rich people as having God's special favor and you spend all your time 'courting' their pocketbooks – you will have sold your soul to gain the approval of men. None of this brings us any closer to the kingdom of God. You might as well be a camel trying to squeeze through the eye of a needle. Which is why, with that kind of spiritual bankruptcy, Jesus could say, "Again I tell you, it is easier for a camel to go through the eye of a needle than for a rich person to enter the kingdom of God." (Matt. 19:24)

TABLE TALK

8) Reflect on this question: How would you know when you 'had enough' money and possessions?

9) If, God forbid, your house was to catch on fire, what three things would you take with you (apart from your family)?

REFLECTION

After graduating college and even after having a good career in Houston, my money matters with God didn't change much. Not even after I left Houston to enter the seminary. There always seemed to be bills to pay, loans to <u>re</u>pay and when I entered seminary, I argued that my tuition towards studying to be a pastor was more than fair to fulfill my 'obligation' to be a good 'steward'.

Obligation?...

As if 'obligation' was even the issue! As if the Law could motivate *anyone* to give to God! We've already talked about how the Law never works to motivate people with God – doing more or being coerced in to doing something will *not* bring you peace.

Stewardship isn't about *force*, where we *give* to God out of *guilt* and say, "Okay, if I *have* to – here you go!" Some gift *that* is! The Psalmist says that we can't praise God with our offerings, until we first have this: "a broken spirit; a broken and contrite heart."(51:17) Thankfulness and humility for all that He's given us, that calls us to give God our "first-fruits", not our "sloppy-seconds".

My first year at the seminary, I was talking with my advisor about my struggles to give to God. I rationalized it – I was a poor seminary student, I had books to buy, rent to pay. I just couldn't afford to give to God. I was fully expecting my advisor to back me up, pat me on the head and say, "I understand, and God understands, too." But instead, he looked at me and said, "Rance, if you aren't *giving* to God – you're *robbing* Him instead." He opened up the Bible to Malachi, chapter 3 and read, "Will a man rob God? Yet you rob *me*. 'But you ask, 'How do we rob you?' 'In [your] tithes and offerings, you rob me. Bring the whole tithe into the storehouse, that there may be food in my house. Test me in this,' says the LORD Almighty, 'and see if I will not throw open the floodgates of heaven and pour out so much blessing that you will not have room enough for it.'"

Then my advisor said, "For example: God's given you the means to clothe yourself. If you don't thank Him for that, you're wearing *stolen merchandise*! You say that you trust God, but by not giving Him what's rightfully His, you're telling Him you don't trust Him to meet your needs and that you don't trust Him to be faithful. You know God is faithful, so why are you so nervous about giving God what's *His*, anyway?"

So, I stepped out in faith, and as a seminary student, at my lowest possible income ever I started tithing again.

And I've *never* been so scared.

TABLE TALK

10) On a piece of paper (or in this book), write down your income. Now, without doing the math in your head, write down a number of what you think you already give back to God. Now write down a number that would make you *uncomfortable* to give. *That* number – the uncomfortable one – is where the Holy Spirit may be tapping you on the shoulder to give. Because He knows *that* number is where real trust and growth with His children takes place.

REFLECTION

In my mind, we didn't have the extra funds to give.

And I was pretty close to telling the truth about that.

Our savings was wiped out from the move to St. Louis to attend seminary in 2001. The national tragedy of 9/11 had happened one month before, so the job market collapsed, and people weren't hiring. We had bills that totaled $152. And we simply couldn't pay it. Falling to our knees, Leslie and I prayed, "We trust You, Lord. You brought us here for a reason. Please help us!"

Two days before the bills were due, a letter from a small Lutheran church in South Texas arrived. They had received our name from a friend that we were going to the seminary and they decided to have a bake sale for us. In the envelope was a check – for $156 dollars. God *had* provided – and He gave us a $4 surplus, too! And since that day, I've continued to step out in faith of God's care for me and give – because I know He's got my back. And if *God's* got my back – what on earth do I have to be afraid of? The *least* I can do is show Him I trust Him, by giving Him back a portion of all He's given to me.

You see, stewardship *isn't* about *ownership*, asking, 'what's mine?', 'what's God's?', 'how much should I give?', 'how much should I keep?', because it's *all* God's anyway.

Stewardship is about a *relationship*!

Welcoming the relationship between *you* and your *Heavenly Father*. Jesus Christ came to restore that relationship, and He went as low as He could go – He became flesh in a feeding trough, where the animal spit and dirt and dung collected. He wallowed in the 'pig sty' of a world that we had ruined for Him. In His love for us, He bore it all – the punishment and judgment and death we deserved – this much and more was piled on Jesus until the stink and filth was so bad, His Father couldn't recognize Him anymore and turned His back on His Son, so He could *always* turn His face to you. Jesus' sacrifice has given us robes washed clean in His blood and set us free. As His 'wardens', He has placed us in His world to engage it – to welcome the opportunity to give *freely* - and from *the heart*.

Look at it this way: Let's say God has ten pies and He gives you nine of them to use how you like. He's keeping one. Just one. But you immediately say, "That's a raw deal! I had ten pies before God took one! Now I've only got nine!"

Newsflash: you didn't have *any pie at all*, before Almighty God showed up, to give them to you. Who got the *better* deal in this transaction?

That's why stewardship – *real stewardship* - is not about the Law, and all about our *heart response* to the Gospel – the privilege of being a 'sty warden' of all the Lord's blessings in our lives and returning a portion to Him for His work on earth.

TABLE TALK

11) Challenge: The next paycheck you receive, give God 'His cut', *first*. Then use the remainder to live on. Contemplate the spiritual impact this makes, when God gets 'His pie' first thing, from you.

BRINGING IT HOME

One of my favorite John Wayne movies is "McClintock!", a western about the Duke playing a rich cattle baron with a lot of land to his name. His daughter, Becky, had just come back from charm school up North, and she's a little snobby. So, in an open field, the Duke has a heart-to-heart talk with his daughter. He says, "Becky, you're going to have every young buck west of the Missouri tryin' to marry you - mostly because you're a handsome filly, but partly because I own everything in this country from here to there. They'll think you're going to inherit it. Well, you're not. I'm going to leave most of it to the nation for a park. What I'm going to give you is a 500-cow spread on the Upper Green River. Now that may not seem like much, but it's more than we had, your mother and I. Some folks are gonna say I'm doin' all this so I can sit up in the hereafter and look down on a park named after me, or that I was disappointed in you - didn't want you to get all that money. But the real reason, Becky, is because I love you, and I want you and some young man to have what I had, because all the gold in the United States Treasury and all the harp music in heaven can't <u>equal</u> what happens between a man and a woman with all that growin' together. I can't explain it any better than that."

And that, brothers and sisters, is similar to how God deals with us.

God doesn't give us *everything* we want – but He does bless us with everything we *need*. And it looks like a cross and an empty tomb. God even uses our *wants* to help us learn how to *want* Him above all things. Which leads to us *giving* in ways we never dreamed possible.

I've never seen a church give *so much*, then at those times when it felt they had so *little* to give. Because it's at times like that, that our priorities get straight with God. Jesus has paid it all and cancelled our debt, and in those lean times, *especially* in lean times, God allows it - because He *loves* us, and He will use it to grow our faith and have us lean on Him more. Because all the gold in the United States Treasury and all the harp music in heaven can't equal what happens between Christ and His Church, with all that growin' together. I can't explain it any better than that.

As 'wardens' of God's blessings, we don't 'give 'till it *hurts*', we 'give 'till it *feels good*', by 'going the whole hog' and offering our lives to God, knowing He offered His life to us, to give us exactly what we need: the eternal treasure of forgiveness, life and salvation.

Folks, it's true that 'you can't take it with you' – but you can *send it on ahead*.

If we live as a 'sty-ward' of Jesus, it makes life a sweet aroma, where each day we are free to breathe in deep and say, "Ah – smells like *forgiveness*! What a great day to be a 'ward of the Lord's sty'!"

What a truly *welcome opportunity* that is!

We give Thee but Thine own,
whate'er the gift may be;
All that we have is Thine alone,
A trust, O Lord, from Thee.
May we Thy bounties thus
As stewards true receive
And gladly, as Thou blessest us,
To Thee our first-fruits give!

—Lutheran Service Book
781, public domain

Closing Prayer: *God, You are so generous with me. When I take the time to stop the distractions of life and think about it – I can't begin to count the blessings You have richly lavished upon me. Help me to never be so busy with life, that I forget to be about 'Your business' in this world. Create in me a generous heart, God, that longs to give of the gifts You have given me in all that I say and do. Let me never forget the eternal riches I have gained through the payment of Your Son's blood. Amen*

CHAPTER 16
Welcoming Ties That Bind

Hebrews 10:24-25
"And let us consider how to stir up one another to love and good works, not neglecting to meet together, as is the habit of some, but encouraging one another, and all the more as you see the Day drawing near."

1 Corinthians 12:12
"For just as the body is one and has many members, and all the members of the body, though many, are one body, so it is with Christ."

SETTING THE TABLE

Have you ever heard of something called 'Google Reviews'? Maybe you've written one, yourself, a time or two. Many people write Google Reviews to publicly put in their 'two cents' about what a business was like when they visited. And then people have the option of rating that business, giving them anywhere from one to five stars – five stars for 'Excellent' and one star for 'I will NEVER go to that place again!' Well, believe it or not, Google

Reviews now let you review *churches*. I ran a Google search, once, of the church where I currently serve, and I found tons of people's thoughts about what their experience was like here.

Most of their thoughts were very encouraging and uplifting. But every so often you read one that makes you go, 'What were they thinking?' Take this review, for instance: This lady gives my church '1 star': "While the layout was great, I was really disappointed in the service. It took the waiter at least 15 minutes to give us a menu and another hour before we were served. Ambiance is nice but: worst service, ever." Now, unless there's a buffet and maître d on our ministry team that I don't know about (and shame on you, church family, if you've been holding out on me), there's no way this lady is reviewing my church - or the kind of *service* we offer!

Here's another '1-star' review that made me chuckle. And this one was actually about my church: "Service was beautiful, and the music was great. People were very friendly. But it was the coldest Air Conditioning I've ever experienced! FREEZING Cold!! Probably won't be coming back." Seriously, we got a 1-star review because the deal-breaker—the unforgiveable sin—was COLD A/C at church?! Personally, I'd give '5-stars' for cold a/c!

Just goes to show how much the consumer culture has influenced people, even among the church-going crowd. Sadly, in our modern-day culture, correct preaching and teaching at a church doesn't seem to be as important as the *coffee bar* they might find at a church! But are coffee bars, plush pew seats, cold a/c and '5-star' Google reviews the point of the Church? Why do we come to church on Sundays? What would be the harm of just staying home and catching the latest worship service on T.V? Let's find out, together.

Prayer: *Lord, You have formed us into one fellowship of faith. Help us to keep in our minds and hearts the true reason for our fellowship and never forget how much we need it. In Jesus' Name. Amen.*

TABLE TALK
Take a moment to discuss the following together:

1) What childhood memories do you have about going to church?

2) How often did your family worship together at church? Go to Bible study? Attend fellowship events?

3) How did the regularity (or irregularity) of your church activity impact your life? Your perception of 'the Church'?

4) How do you feel after missing a couple of weeks of church fellowship? Has there been a time when you were away from the church for lengthy periods? How did that make you feel?

REFLECTION

A few years back, a dear friend of mine sent me an email, because she was really concerned about a blog post that her friend had written. In this blog post, her friend wrote about how she was fed up with the Christian Church and she was going to stop participating in the life of the Church. Here's what her friend wrote, "It's not Jesus that I'm giving up. But I'm giving up my supposed white robes and taking the Israeli-dirt-covered one instead. I'm spending time with the unclean ones instead of the ones that whisper. And I'm picking up the lame ones that the Church has hobbled one too many times. Because I feel like the Church is locked in this childish game. From now on it's just 'me and Jesus.'"

Hey - I get it. She's obviously upset with the Christian Church. And I can even relate to her frustration. Maybe you can, too. Christians can be very 'un-Christian' in their behavior, at times. She's not the first and she won't be the last to cry out, "I'm fed up with the un-Christian behavior of Christian people!" But is the solution to her problem – to go it alone? Is she going to be better off by saying, "It's just me and Jesus"?

Seems a lot of Christians are making that their choice, as well. In fact, there are many Christians in the Church who model their faith after that great American hero, "The Lone Ranger". The Lone Ranger is as American as apple pie, right? He's an independent, self-made man, who pulled himself up by his own bootstraps – he's alone and self-sufficient. In fact, Christians who think like the Lone Ranger will even argue that it is Biblical to go it alone, with 'Just me and Jesus' as the real goal of the Christian faith.

AT THE TABLE

5) **Read 1 Corinthians 12:12-27.** How does St. Paul connect us to Christ? To each other?

6) Look through the above verses, again. How are Christian people like the parts of the body?

7) How does the metaphor of the body celebrate the different talents and gifts of Christian people? Has your bad history with another Christian possibly been connected to their having different gifts and perspectives? Have differences with Christian people sometimes been simply rooted in different personalities?

8) If we're all a part of one another in Christ, how does Jesus call us to 'bear with one another', not just *put up* with one another?

9) Reflect on this statement: Christianity is the most unusual organization on earth. We don't join because we have common interests, backgrounds, races, preferences or dispositions. We are connected to one another because we are first connected to Christ.

REFLECTION

The struggle to attend worship together with God's people was something that the Hebrew Christians were wrestling with, too, not long after Jesus ascended into heaven. But their struggle wasn't from living in a *consumer* culture - it was from living in a *Hebrew* culture. You see, the Hebrew Christians were converts to Christianity. They'd been shunned by family members who didn't believe Jesus was the Messiah. These families would even hold a funeral for their Hebrew Christian relatives – where they were declared *dead*.

They risked persecution at every turn, with only a cave or a house as a place of worship. They lived in fear that a friend or relative would turn them in to Roman authorities for being followers of 'The Way'. They feared being fed to lions in Roman arenas or being set on fire to serve as torches in the streets at night. Some Hebrew Christians thought it would be best to worship *on their own*, in secret. Others felt pressure to reject Christ publicly – so that they could be welcomed back home again to their Hebrew family.

That's why the author of Hebrews tells them this, "And let us consider how to stir up one another to love and good works, *not neglecting to meet together*, as is the habit of some, but encouraging one another, and all the more as you see the Day drawing near." The writer of Hebrews knew how easy it was to walk away from a Christian Community, from the life of the Church, especially in the face of such hardships. He also knew that when you give up Church - you give up Christ – and all the blessings that He gives – that are found *only* in His Church.

10) **Read Genesis 2:18.** How might God's words apply to the Christian life?

11) If someone told you, "I don't need to go to church. I worship God in my own way." How might you tell them what good

things they're missing out on?

12) Thinking of what the person said in question 11 – what might be going on at worship that we can get nowhere else on earth?

13) Reflect on this statement: You can find God out on a fishing boat, a golf course and among His creation – but you *won't* find His forgiveness there.

REFLECTION

Have you ever attended a service where the Rite of Confirmation was done? In the Lutheran Church, Confirmation is a special time when we recognize our youth (usually somewhere between 7th and 9th grade) publicly as adult Christians, who have walked through the Bible and the Small Catechism, where Martin Luther and other Christians put together questions and answers related to our faith and God's Word. We lay hands on these 'confirmands,' praying God's blessing upon them and often pray a Scripture verse over them – a verse that the confirmand has chosen. This is usually done with Godparents (sometimes called 'sponsors') present with the parents and grandparents. It is a beautiful celebration of faith being owned as adults by these young people.

But before the laying of hands, before the Scriptures are read, the confirmands make some serious vows related to their faith in Christ. They also will make some radical claims. They come forward, stand at the altar rail and say that they believe God's Word is absolutely true. That Jesus Christ is the only way to salvation. That they will live a life that is a witness of their faith in Christ. That they would rather face *death*, then deny Jesus Christ.

But there are also some vows they will *not* be making: They will *not* vow to behave like The Lone Ranger. They will *not* vow to 'go it alone'. They will *not* vow to come to Church only when Grandma is in town or to faithfully attend church - every leap year. They will *not* vow to whisper behind other Christians' backs and *not* attempt to clear the air with their fellow Christians. They will *not* vow to pitch a fit and whine and carry on when people who claim to be Christian sometimes act very 'un-Christian' towards one another.

Why won't they be making those vows? Because the Rite of Confirmation is *bigger* than them. That day is not only for the confirmands. It is about the *Body of Christ* and what Jesus continues to do for all of us in His Presence, gathered together for worship and sharing life together.

If as Christians, we ignore the Body of Christ and try to go it alone, what do you think will happen to us? I'll tell you what will happen: *nothing*. To go it alone tells our young people that the Rite of Confirmation was nothing more than the *end* of a journey, rather than a rite of passage to *continue* on our journey as adult Christians – and nothing happens to grow *our* faith. We'll see Christians sinning against one another and see it as a failure of the Christian Church, rather than just what happens when you put a bunch of *sinful failures* together – and in our bitterness, *nothing* happens to strengthen our faith.

14) Take a moment to reflect on how your body participates in worship. If you are a part of the Body of Christ, how do your hands worship? Your tongue? Your feet? Your eyes? Your ears?

15) How does God redeeming us – *body* and *soul* – cause us to celebrate His forgiveness with our bodies, today?

16) Why do Christians sometimes 'share God's Peace' just before Communion is shared? What is the significance of shaking hands and greeting one another in the Name of the Lord?

Alone, you'll convince yourself that sure, you have your problems, but at least you 'aren't like those other sinners out there' – and *nothing* happens to keep you in the faith. If you go it alone, you convince yourself that nobody has the answers, and so you start making up your own answers. That you're doing okay and not *that* bad of a person. You'll write blog posts about how it's gonna be 'Just me and Jesus now'. Because the devil knows, the quickest way to keep you from Christ is to convince you - to go it alone. After all, it's a whole lot easier to be an 'awesome Christian' - if you convince yourself that you're the *only* awesome Christian on the planet. In fact, you may end up thinking you're doing so well, that you don't need Jesus - *at all*. And that, my friends, is nothing short of a one-way ticket to disaster.

> 17) Reflect on this statement: You were not created to be The Lone Ranger. You were created to be *Tonto*. Through the forgiveness of Christ, you instantly because a part of a 'holy tribe'.

Yes, The Church is a place filled with problems - because it's filled with *sinners*! That's why you and I fit in - *perfectly*! If you've got it all together, have no struggles, have a life that's always happy and completely free of sin - then the Church is *not* for you. But if you struggle with selfishness, greed, lust, addiction, fear, loneliness, or anything else that plagues our humanity, then the Church was custom-built for you! God has tied you to a community of faith, through Jesus. *Without* a community, you can't be enriched by <u>others</u>, and you can't enrich <u>them</u>.

The Church is a *messy* place for *messed up* people - who are in dire need of a God who *cares*. And incredibly – He *Does*. Right here. In This Place. In the Church you'll encounter the God who takes all His *'beautiful'* and exchanges it for your *'ugly'*. That's why you and I *need* to be here and to *keep coming* here. That's why you and I need *each other*. And most of all, why we need *Jesus*. Jesus binds Himself to you through His forgiveness. And He ties you to *one another* as the Body of Christ. Because of Jesus – He has made absolutely sure, that you don't *ever* go it alone. You are *Tonto*. You are part of a *holy tribe*. You are forgiven in Christ. And that is truly a blessed thing.

18) Think about the following people you might encounter at you church. How might God be calling you to interact with them?

    a. The widower who is missing his loved one so badly he can't even sing a hymn.

    b. The teenage who never says a word to you – but is watching you.

    c. The grumpy old man who has a grumpy perspective about everything.

    d. Your wife and children who worship with you each week.

    e. The single mom who bravely attends with her children each week.

    f. For the babies who are crying during worship.

    g. For the parents trying to comfort their crying babies.

    h. For the special needs child who sings off-key – loud and proud.

19) Read the following Scripture. "Let us hold fast the confession of our hope without wavering, for he who promised is faithful. And let us consider how to stir up one another to love and good works, not neglecting to meet together, as is the habit of some,

but encouraging one another, and all the more as you see the Day drawing near." (Hebrews 10:23-25) What things stand out for you?

20) Reflect on this statement: "I don't need to go to church this week because my life has been going great, and I truly don't have any struggles, right now. I've been blessed."

21) Ponder how this statement, that we say at my church at every service, might be applied to the statement in question 19: "Thank You, Lord, for Blessing us, so that we may be a Blessing to others."

BRINGING IT HOME

Jesus never said, "Thou shalt go to church on Sunday morning." But He did create communities of faith for a reason. Just ask a Celebrate Recovery group, who regularly meet at churches all over the country. Ask them how awesome it is to keep meeting together as a community of faith – to walk together as broken people, who are getting through life *together*, with Jesus. Their life as a community of faith – *our* life as a community of faith – echoes why the author of Hebrews speaks about the importance of continuing to meet together. (Hebrews 10:25).

I don't know about you, but since Christ promises blessings like that in His house, among His people, there's *no* place I'd rather be - than *here* - basking in the forgiveness and peace and love of the God Who merges heaven and earth within the four walls of His sanctuary, to fill us with gifts of Grace. No, the Church was never about 'consumer cultures' and 'creature comforts' – but it's *always* been about Christ. About His *Church*. About you and me – a 'holy tribe' gathered with a forgiving God - as His forgiven people. A *real* people, with a *real* need – finding *real* peace as a community of faith

– walking together as broken people, who are getting through life *together*, with Jesus leading the way.

Here's the Good News. God isn't asking for *perfection*. That's already been handled by Jesus. He is, however, asking for your *participation*. That is the point of serving our neighbor. That is the point of growing in Christ, ourselves. That is the point of stay connected to the Body of Christ. It's a connection worth fighting for.

When you tell your buddies, "Hey, I'm looking forward to meeting you at the lake on Sunday – *right after church*", they will know you worship a *different* God than 'fishing' or 'waterskiing'. When your language and jokes are noticeably *cleaner*. When you tactfully change the subject when one guy is bad-mouthing the other guy in your department, people will *know* you're somehow different. When you decide to speak *good* things about your spouse and children instead of joining in with the other 'sheep' and saying, "Yeah you know how spouses and kids are these days", people will see there's *a lot of loving* going on in your family. When you bow your heads at a restaurant to pray together as a family, you show the world Who has provided you with 'daily bread' - and Who to thank for it. Will what you do in this life be *perfection*? No, not on this side of Glory. But it will be *participation*. Participation in the Body of Christ. Participation in God's work in the world. St. Paul tells us this, "Do not be conformed to this world, but be transformed by the renewal of your mind, so that by testing you may discern what is the will of God, what is good and acceptable and perfect." (Romans 12:2)

This is the decision before you—*now*—*today*. This is the decision that confronts the saints who gather in the pews as the Body of Christ. And it is the decision that confronts the Christian you see, when you look in the mirror. This is a decision that confronts every generation of Christians – and it confronts you, *now*. So – you who are forgiven in Christ, it's time to renew your Confirmation vows: Will you refuse to be conformed to the pattern of this world? Will you put down your smartphones and pick up God's Word? Do you intend to hear the Word of God and receive the Lord's Supper faithfully? Will you pursue a life of faith and discipleship for your children with the same passion that you have when you bring your kids to sports and to band contests? Do you intend to continue steadfast in this confession and Church and to suffer all, even death, rather than fall away from it?

Will you choose *life* – will you choose Jesus and deepen your walk with Him - so that you and your children and all the generations to come, may truly *live*? What say you, Church? I, for one, have decided to say, "AMEN!" What we do will not be *perfection*—but it will be *participation*. What say *you*, Church? Will you join me by faith and say, "AMEN!" with me? Will you decide to stand and be counted with the saints who have gone before us? Will you strive towards committing your hearts to something better than the pattern of this world? Confirmation vows are not dead words – they are alive in Christ – and alive in YOU by the Holy Spirit! Through the forgiveness we have received in Christ, there is work left to do. May we all prayerfully decide to quit *talking* about it – and *do* it – and choose *life*!

22) Do an honest 'spiritual inventory': How might you have 'crushed the bruised reed' or 'snuffed the smoldering wick' when you've seen someone come back to church who's been missing for a while?

23) Write down the names of five people or families that you've missed at worship, lately. Where are they? Can you find out? How might you reconnect with them?

24) If God allows you an opportunity to reconnect with these people, what difference would it make to say, "I miss you" instead of, "where have you been?"

Blest be the tie that binds
Our hearts in Christian love;
The fellowship of kindred minds
Is like to that above.

Before our Father's throne
We pour our ardent prayers;
Our fears, our hopes, our aims are one,
Our comforts and our cares.

We share our mutual woes,
Our mutual burdens bear,
And often for each other flows
The sympathizing tear.

When here our pathways part,
We suffer bitter pain;
Yet, one in Christ and one in heart,
We hope to meet again.

From sorrow, toil, and pain,
And sin we shall be free
And perfect love and friendship reign
Through all eternity.

—**Lutheran Service Book**
649, public domain

Closing Prayer: *Lord God, Your Son, Jesus calls us in to His Body, warts and all. Help us to remember that on the cross, You took our warts and all – to add us to Your Body. Help us to celebrate each and every person You have welcomed into Your kingdom. Help us to embrace the strains and struggles of the parts of the Body in Christian love, praying that the Body will extend to us that same grace. Help us to be charitable with one another and say everything in the kindest way. Help us most of all, to live – not as perfect people, but as forgiven people. Welcoming the people in Your Body - as You have welcomed us. In Jesus' Name. Amen.*

CHAPTER 17
The Uncomfortable 'Yes' - When Welcome Is a Challenge

John 13:34–35
"A new commandment I give to you, that you love one another: just as I have loved you, you also are to love one another. By this all people will know that you are my disciples, if you have love for one another."

SETTING THE TABLE

T*he aggressive in-law.* The grouchy neighbor. The preschool parent who second-guesses our parenting skills. The cocky coworker. The whiny church member.

Difficult people. They're everywhere, and they're a key reason why people recoil at the idea of sharing hospitality, opening their home - much less, their lives - to other people. People are difficult sometimes. But, then again, so am *I*. And if we are honest with each other – so are *you*. Because it's a sinful world and none of us will be perfect, this side of glory. But still, that does not make it easy to be welcoming to people like the ones listed above.

The primary reason people give for recoiling at hospitality is they are either *uncomfortable* with people or they do not have the *time* for people. That certainly reflects the discomfort we have with building relationships in our society and the lack of time we have for others today.

Even as our society becomes more 'plugged in' than at any other point in history through advancements in technology and social media, we are also more disconnected from people than ever before. That is certainly reflected in today's youth and the consequences of social media:

'Today's young generation (often called Millennials, GenY, or Generation Me) are the first to grow up with the Internet and social networking websites. Have these experiences led to more and better social connections or fewer and atrophied ones? Social media builds shallow, 'weak' ties, increases self-focus (including narcissism), and may lead to mental health issues for some individuals. Over the time social media became popular, young people's empathy for others, civic engagement, and political involvement declined.'[93]

And yet, despite these sobering observations, we still have a generation of people who crave relationships and deep connection. To their detriment, those places of deep connection and conversations are in short supply, because the practice of building relationships in a person-to-person context is hard to find. Richard Foster, a contemporary of the 1970s, foresaw how society's disconnection, lack of time for others and the loss of people who foster connection could potentially have severe ramifications for relationships within our culture:

'Superficiality is the curse of our age. The doctrine of instant satisfaction is a primary spiritual problem. The desperate need today is not for a greater number of intelligent people, or gifted people, but for *deep people*.'[94]

This struggle continues in society and bleeds over into the welcoming (or lack thereof) found in the home setting. Our culture has arrived at a place where it is not only difficult for people to welcome others into their homes; it is just as difficult for people to be guests at *another person's* home. People today have just as much difficulty *hosting* as they do *being hosted* by others, which makes extending or receiving hospitality challenging in a disconnected world:

'The other half of hospitality is harder. The other half of hospitality takes place when I'm invited into someone else's life. <u>The other half is when I'm receiving</u>. When I'm receiving, I have less control. There are more unknowns. Instead of playing host I become the guest (and my kids become guests too - which can be a little unnerving for any parent). But the other half of hospitality also goes so much further. It carries friendships further. It deepens relationships. I think this half of hospitality is powerful for one reason: vulnerability.'[95]

In this session, we'll take a look at the ways that God's Word guides us to expand our worldview from welcoming our families with the heart of God to engaging others with the hospitality of the Gospel.

Prayer: *Lord, as we enter our world, we pray that our love for You would be reflected in the love we share among our families. We also pray that Your love would go out into our everyday lives, lived through us, welcoming others as You have welcomed us. Amen.*

TABLE TALK

Take a moment to discuss the following together:

1) Complete this thought: When I think of inviting others into my home, I feel _____.

2) Why do you believe you feel that way?

3) Complete this thought: When I think of staying over at someone's home, I feel _____.

4) Why do you believe you feel that way?

5) When the doorbell rings, what's your natural reaction? If you know it's a friend, are you comfortable inviting them in without notice? Why or why not?

REFLECTION

She was the most uncomfortable that I'd ever seen her.

Leslie and I had been married just a few short years. We were visiting her grandfather in his home and had planned to stay the night, which we'd done a few times before. All was going according to plan.

Until it wasn't.

A couple of different things happened (you know how that goes; best laid plans…) that was going to keep us from being able to stay there that night. The problem was, we were several hours from home and it was already getting dark. We were both tired and just needed some sleep.

But there was hope!

Leslie's aunt and uncle lived just a few blocks from her grandfather. So, I suggested, "Hey, why don't we stay at your aunt and uncle's place overnight?"

I didn't expect the look of horror I received.

"What?!" she replied with a mixture of shock and fear. "I've *never* been overnight at their place. I don't even know what they'd do on such short notice." Me, I was a little surprised, for a different reason. All I knew, growing up was an 'open door policy': if someone needed a place to sleep, we gave it. If *we* needed one, we knew it was okay to ask family or close friends in a pinch.

I soon learned not everybody did that sort of thing. "Rance, this is SO out of my comfort zone!", Leslie whispered under her breath, as we gathered up our things and loaded them back in the car for the several block trek to her aunt and uncle's place – who'd graciously told us without hesitation, that we could stay. "I've *never* don't this before," she continued to repeat the refrain the entire ride there.

We got to her aunt and uncle's door and rang the bell. We were quickly welcomed with a big bear hug from them both, who took our things and showed us the spare bedroom they'd prepared. We pitched in to prepare dinner, visiting the entire time. We had a great dinner together and spent the rest of the evening sitting around the kitchen, reminiscing and laughing.

As we prepared for bed, Leslie turned to me with a smile and said, "This was fun. I haven't been over here like this since I was a little girl." And we went to sleep with a smile on our faces.

I think the struggle most people have with hospitality, isn't in giving it – it's in *receiving* it! We feel like, if we go over to someone's home, especially on short notice, that we're not just imposing – we're *invading*!

Our modern culture hasn't helped.

In our world, homes are more than just a place to hang your hat – they are considered private sanctuaries, open only to a select few – a couple of family members, maybe several close friends – and *only* by appointment.

TABLE TALK

6) When it comes to staying in other people's homes, how does that make you feel – excited or nervous?

7) If a family member or friend 'drops by' with little to no notice, how do you feel about letting them stay a while? How about overnight?

8) What possible challenges are there by staying overnight in someone's home? How about for a few days? What are the possible joys?

9) What possible challenges are there by letting someone stay

overnight in your home? How about few days? What are the possible joys?

10) I've heard it said: "Guests are like eggs – after three days, they *all* stink." What makes that statement somewhat true? What mind/heart shift might we need to combat that way of thinking?

A RADICAL HOSPITALITY

What might it look like if our world had an 'open-door policy' to people? Where drop-ins weren't an inconvenience but an opportunity to welcome others?

One such man lived this radical lifestyle.

A man by the name of Martin Luther.

While we have no *direct* records of Luther's thoughts on the subject of welcoming others and how it was woven into the Christian life, we do have formal statements that he made, which give us great insight into the man's beliefs on hospitality. For instance:

"That extraordinary praise of hospitality which appears in the Letter to the Hebrews (13:2) had its origin in this passage. 'Do not neglect to show hospitality to strangers, for thereby some have entertained angels unawares.' There is hospitality wherever the church is. For the church, if I may say so, always has a common treasury, inasmuch as it has the command (Matt. 5:42): 'Give to him who begs from you.' And we must all serve the church and take care of it, not only by teaching but also by showing kindness and giving assistance, so that at the same time both the spirit and the flesh may find refreshment in the church."[96]

One cannot gain full insight into Luther's views on much of anything without also taking in to account his high regard for Holy Scripture and the implications that regard held for Christian living. Luther made a theological connection in God's Word between welcoming those in his midst and doing God's work on this earth. For Luther, the home offered a 'rich opportunity for faithful exercise of loving service to one's relatives and neighbors.'[97] Therefore, the Christian vocational service of the home was an integral part of expressing love for the neighbor. According to his view, one's private residence was not closed, that is, where one believed their home belonged to *them alone*. If all creation belonged *to God*, then it followed that all creation was to be used in service to God and our neighbor, including the home, where 'faith can be put to work for the benefit of others.'[98]

Luther's zeal for welcoming the neighbor into the home became legendary, as it became common knowledge that if one were traveling, Luther's house would be open to them. As his generosity and hospitality became known, Luther would often find himself at a loss for space to accommodate more people. In a letter from Martin Luther to Kaspar Muller, a dear friend to him and even a godfather to his first son, Johannes, he conveys the news that he will not be able to take him in, saying, 'The table is full',[99] mainly because he had too many guests already living there and could not, in good conscience, 'expel' any other guest. Luther concludes his letter that if a vacancy should open up, he would 'gladly notify' him and welcome him.[100]

Luther's hospitality was different from the taverns and inns of the day that made a good living from weary travelers. Luther is referring to welcoming others in the home where he lived, known as the Black Cloister Monastery, in Wittenberg, Germany. Luther spent most of his life there, from 1508 until his passing in 1546. In all that time, the only other time we know that he had to turn someone away from extending hospitality to someone was when a friend asked him to host a wedding reception. Even this reception would likely have come to pass in the Luther household, had not his spouse, the indomitable Katharina von Bora denied him. In anger, Luther wrote in response to this denial, 'If I were to court a girl again, I would chisel myself an obedient wife from a rock.'[101] In truth, Luther deeply loved his 'Kitty,' and were it not for her restraining Luther's hospitable ways, they'd have likely given away all they owned and died homeless paupers.

The answer to Luther's zeal for loving the neighbor from the location of the home can be traced to his commentaries on God's Word and its day to day impact on Christian living. As is typical of Luther, he spares no feelings in his writings that call to the carpet the Christian who would not welcome their neighbor, saying that 'nothing is more hideous that inhospitality', since 'By it you shut out from your house, not a human being but the Son of God, who suffered and died for you on the cross.'[102]

Luther saw hospitality, not as a 'good work' but as a state of *being* in Christ. True faith in Christ, as Luther saw it, made 'a good life an ordinary one,'[103] where we did the things God called us to do, including hospitality. So, Luther viewed offering hospitality to our neighbor, along with receiving it, as merely part and parcel of Christian existence, where the Christian was free from the curse of the law by faith, and yet, was bound to the law in the love of Christ that served the neighbor.[104] Therefore, it made complete sense to Luther that, with this law of love alive in the Christian heart, that when one welcomes their neighbor, 'Those who are hospitable are not receiving a human being, but are receiving the Son of God Himself.'[105]

TABLE TALK

11) What impact would it make on our perspective if we received every person as Luther did: as 'receiving the Son of God Himself'? Who might God be 'tapping you on the shoulder' to see differently in your life?

12) **Read Luke 19:1-10.** Write down some key moments in this story.

13) Reflect on this statement: "Anyone engaging in such trades [tax collector] could never be a judge, and his inadmissibility as a witness put him on the same footing as a Gentile slave... In other words, he was deprived of civil and political rights to which every Israelite had claim...This makes us realize the enormity of Jesus' act in calling a publican to be one of His intimate disciples...and announcing the Good News to publicans and 'sinners' by sitting down to eat with them."[106]

14) Looking at verse 7 of Luke 19. What do you think was the people's deeper reasons for complaining about Zacchaeus?

15) **Read Exodus 22:1** – When Zacchaeus promises to restore the wealth, what is he doing according to this verse? What is Zacchaeus admitting about himself?

REFLECTION

As Martin Luther saw it, hospitality is a state of 'being' in Christ and not entertaining – a state of the soul, not a state of personal taste. With this rediscovered life in Christ, our homes may, once again, be a place where the broken are welcomed, and the hurting are helped.

Our worldview in Jesus has a direct correlation to how we live out a life of welcome.

Through our worldview, we decide to either be *a host* or *a hostage*. This means setting aside the attempts at the perfect place setting, scented candles, and artesian food design and focusing on being God's 'imperfectly perfect' people as we do 'life on life' in Christ.

16) As we have journeyed through relational hospitality together, what have you learned about what God's view of hospitality is? How the world's view of hospitality is?

17) How has your perspective possibly changed on living out hospitality in the home?

AT THE TABLE
Read John 6:1-13

If you read this text and think it's a Sunday picnic – think again! This is more like a rock concert where the organizers are told that there are no toilet facilities. Thousands of people who have come and they have left the comfort of their homes and they have traveled from far and wide to see Jesus.

One part of the story that is often overlooked is 6:8-9 "One of His disciples, Andrew, Simon Peter's brother, said to [Jesus], "There is a boy here who has five barley loaves and two fish, but what are these for so many people?"

Andrew was the brother of Simon Peter. If Peter was the one who acted as the head disciple, Andrew seems to have served as their minister of outreach. In John Chapter 1, he brings his brother Simon to the Lord. In John Chapter 12, he will be bringing some Greeks to Jesus. Here he brings a young boy with his lunch pail to Jesus.

There are some key things to note:

- Five barley loaves - Like Bagels without the holes in the middle. They were not even whole wheat bread, but barley, made of the cheapest available ingredients.

- Two fish - The typical Greek word for "fish" is *icthus*, but the Greek word used here is two *opsaria*. These are fish about the size of sardines. They were cooked and dried, then used as a paste to spread over the bread to make a fish sandwich.

This boy did something special. He had planned ahead (unlike the disciples), but willingly gave his lunch (everything he had) to Jesus. It was very little, but Jesus made up for the difference. If he had kept the lunch to himself, he never would have been so blessed by Jesus. The boy relinquished control - gave it to Jesus. And God provided in abundance!

Think also of the boy's mother. How many times had she packed her son an ordinary sack lunch of sardine sandwiches? Who could have imagined that her simple, mundane, everyday task of providing a meal – and her son's simple gift to Jesus – could have been used as a miracle to feed so many?

The hospitality of God, as expressed through His people, has little to do with the food we serve, our home décor, house cleanliness or a ton of other factors that are often out of our control. But God can take the mundane, the simple, the everyday – offered up by His people – to do extraordinary miracles of welcome to others.

God's hospitality lives in the mundane - in those unexpected moments that rarely fit into our plans.

It is when we release our agenda to the One Who orders the universe, that God works His welcome to others in our homes. Lay aside your worries about a perfect table. Embrace your five loaves and two fish!

TABLE TALK

18) Thinking back on the miracle of the loaves and fish from John 6: What new insights have you gained from looking at this story from a different perspective?

19) How might you 'embrace the mundane' in your life as an offering to God for His use?

20) What 'loaves and fish' i.e. resources might be available to you in your community to utilize for the Glory of God?

21) Think back to a special meal experience that you had. What made it so special? What things might you do in your home to allow more experiences like that?

22) How might you create a space to give your time and attention to your children? To the youth in your neighborhood?

23) How could you pass along what you know to the next generation in your own kitchen? In your garage? At your dinner table?

RISKING HOSPITALITY, SHARING THE KINGDOM

Now that we've seen how the world's view of hospitality is very different from God's, we can see that the Kingdom of God breaks into our homes when we live out God's mercy and grace first with our own families and then with the people God places in our path.

We began this session with the words of Jesus:

John 13:34-35 "A new commandment I give to you, that you love one another: just as I have loved you, you also are to love one another. By this all people will know that you are my disciples, if you have love for one another."

This commandment goes back to the Old Testament command from Leviticus 19:18. The focus in that verse was on 'loving your neighbor as yourself'. What the Jews had done over the centuries was to massage the verse to mean that a 'neighbor' was whomever *they* decided their neighbor was. That way, they could love or hate whoever they liked, without it pricking their conscience.

Jesus masterfully changes the focus from 'neighbor' to 'one another.' This new commandment now has a new object.[107] 'One another' denotes *proximity* – the people you come in contact with. That means *we* do not get to choose who we will love with the love of Christ. *Christ* does. And He chooses – everyone. He also calls on us to make the *time* to be with everyone He places in our path. You never know how God might use you through His 'heavenly appointments'.

I remember a time when I was sharing my troubles with Rev. Chris Gorshe. Chris is a dear friend and one of the kindest men I've ever met. I greatly value his listening ear and words of wisdom. I was sharing with him how some days it felt like, no matter how much I needed to get things, every time I tried, I was getting interrupted. Just as I'd sit down to work on something, someone would interrupt me and need something. After Chris heard my litany of complaints, he turned to me and with a gentle smile, said, "Buddy – ministry happens in the *interruptions*." I don't think I have ever looked at the so-called 'interruptions' in my day the same way, again.

TABLE TALK

24) What might it look like if we put aside our comfort and security and engaged people, expecting nothing in return?

25) What might it look like if we were willing to risk 'bearing one another's burdens', engaging other people's pain, sitting with people amid their grief?

26) What might it look like if we were simply present with people, instead of worrying about what we should say when they're hurting?

27) How might 'interruptions' in your day, your plans, and your agenda actually be an opportunity to do ministry in your world?

28) **Read Matt 25:35-40** How might God be calling us to live in relation to the 'inconvenient drop-in' to our homes?

29) If Jesus was the ultimate 'drop-by' guest (think Luke 19:1-10 and Zacchaeus), how might you be called to welcome people who drop by?

30) **Read Roman 15:7** How is St. Paul calling us to welcome people? What are the spiritual implications of this?

31) **Read Luke 14:15-24** Who was on Jesus' invitation list?

32) Compare His list to yours: who might you add to the 'invitation list of your life'?

Engaging people who are in the orbit that God places us in is part of the Gospel call. It is only when we develop genuine interactions and service to others that we can prove the world wrong about what Christianity truly is and what His People stand for. It gives us the unique opportunity to truly *listen* to people, to hear their stories, and learn their hurts.

Welcoming others has very little to do with us 'liking' someone or not. As the people who follow the Prince of Peace, we do our best to pursue peace with others – even the most difficult people in our lives. That includes our loving those who follow Jesus – and loving those who do not.

When we lay aside our agendas and simply welcome *people*, we show others that we are free in Christ – and are better able to love our neighbor as ourselves. To listen, more than we speak. And be a genuine reflection of God's hospitality to other people. C.S. Lewis said it best, "The rule for all of us is pretty simple. Do not waste time bothering whether or not you 'love' your neighbor; act as if you did."[108] This view of relational hospitality is radically countercultural – and just the thing our culture needs.

It's time to risk – to give an uncomfortable 'yes' to God's call to love our neighbor.

Maybe you do not feel you are ready. If that is the case - Great! Opening the door to others when you are not prepared is exactly the place where God does His best work in His people. And best of all, He promises to walk through the door with us (Matthew 28:20b).

So, what are you waiting for? Put out the welcome mat of your heart – and say 'yes' to the adventure of welcoming people!

BRINGING IT HOME

33) Take some time and ponder one conversation you could have, one act of kindness, one moment to take time for another or one opportunity to connect. Pray for the Lord to lead you to that one thing.

34) Pray about the person who the Lord might be leading you to show one gesture of kindness towards this week. A handwritten note, a thank you card, a bunch of flowers, a verbal affirmation – small gestures to others make a deep impact.

35) Pray for the chance to invite one person into your home, your faith community or your small group. Then – take the leap and invite them!

> **Hark, the voice of Jesus crying,**
> **"Who will go and work today?**
> **Fields are white and harvests waiting,**
> **Who will bear the sheaves away?"**
> **Loud and long the master calls you;**
> **Rich reward he offers free.**
> **Who will answer, gladly saying,**
> **"Here am I. Send me, send me"?**

If you cannot speak like angels,
If you cannot preach like Paul,
You can tell the love of Jesus;
You can say he died for all.
If you cannot rouse the wicked
With the judgment's dread alarms,
You can lead the little children
To the Savior's waiting arms.

If you cannot be a watchman,
Standing high on Zion's wall,
Pointing out the path to heaven,
Offering life and peace to all,
With your prayers and with your bounties
You can do what God demands;
You can be life faithful Aaron,
Holding up the prophet's hands.

Let none hear you idly saying,
"There is nothing I can do,"
While the multitudes are dying
And the master calls for you.
Take the task he gives you gladly;
Let his work your pleasure be.
Answer quickly when he calls you,
"Here am I. Send me, send me!"

—Lutheran Service Book
826, public domain

Closing Prayer:

Lord of my life, I know that my life is not my own. By Your death and resurrection, You made me Your own.

Help me to live under Your direction, always ready to hear the call, "Follow Me"; always aware of Your presence; always knowing that I have received the gift of Your Spirit; always living so that others may receive Your love and mercy through me.

It is not easy to ask for these things, Lord, because I know I have much to give up. I can no longer pretend that my life is my own. My prayer is my surrender to Your care and direction. I want to follow, Lord, but it is very hard. I will get very tired. I will make selfish mistakes. I will fail time and time again. I will fall.

Show me again that there is love and forgiveness and mercy in Your hand. Use me in spite of my reluctance, doubt, and disobedience.

Pour into me Your good Spirit, so that I am not afraid to follow – and fall – and follow again. Amen[109]

CHAPTER 18
The Welcome Discipline of a 'Two-Question' God

Proverbs 3:12
"…for the LORD reproves him whom he loves, as a father the son in whom he delights."

Isaiah 40:21-31
"Have you not known? Have you not heard?
The LORD is the everlasting God, the Creator of the ends of the earth. He does not faint or grow weary; his understanding is unsearchable. He gives power to the faint, and to him who has no might he increases strength. but they who wait for the LORD shall renew their strength; they shall mount up with wings like eagles; they shall run and not be weary; they shall walk and not faint."

Hebrews 12:5-11
"And have you forgotten the exhortation that addresses you as sons? "My son, do not regard lightly the discipline of the Lord, nor be weary when reproved by him. For the Lord disciplines the one he loves, and chastises every son

whom he receives." It is for discipline that you have to endure. God is treating you as sons. For what son is there whom his father does not discipline?
If you are left without discipline, in which all have participated, then you are illegitimate children and not sons. Besides this, we have had earthly fathers who disciplined us and we respected them.
Shall we not much more be subject to the Father of spirits and live? For they disciplined us for a short time as it seemed best to them, but he disciplines us for our good, that we may share his holiness.
For the moment all discipline seems painful rather than pleasant, but later it yields the peaceful fruit of righteousness to those who have been trained by it."

SETTING THE TABLE

Baseball was my first love, from an early age. My Dad coached me from the time I could play tee ball, all the way up to my high school years. Our house had a sandlot lot right across the street, which was where I first learned how to hold a mitt, throw a cross-seamed slider and stretch a double into a triple. Practice times for my team were also held there, among the dust devils, the tumbleweeds and the chain-link backstop that Dad had put up for us.

Before each practice, Dad would take our little Ford Courier pickup, attach a chain to the bumper, and from that chain, attach a metal grid, that looked like a giant barbeque grill. With the pickup, he would drag that metal grill in circles around the sandlot, smoothing over the land as best he could, so we wouldn't get 'bad hops' from the ground balls or twist an ankle going for a double-play.

I remember one time, my assistant coach told me to 'knock the cover off the ball', before throwing me an inside fastball. It was on that sandlot, that I *literally* did just that – I perfectly hit the seam of the cover and blew that baseball to bits – string and cork flying everywhere. My assistant coach and I couldn't stop cheering. I felt like Babe Ruth, 'calling my shot.'

Great memories on that sandlot.

All except for *one*.

I was in the 5th grade and playing in the local VFW little league at the time. Me and my team were hanging out in my front yard, waiting for Dad to arrive home from work to start practice at the sandlot. But he was running late.

You know the saying, 'Idle hands are the devil's workshop'?

Well, the devil got to using *mine*.

For some idiotic reason, I thought it'd be a great idea to load up my team in the tailgate of my Dad's Ford Courier pickup and *drive them* the half-block walk to the sandlot, so we could start warming up for practice. I'm in the 5th grade. I can't drive. The Ford Courier was a stick-shift transmission. I'd never driven before but I'd watched it done enough that I thought I could do it.

Did I mention I'm in the 5th grade?

I found the keys to the Courier hanging in the key rack, loaded up the team, and started up the pickup. So far, so good. I put it in gear, popped the clutch and off we went – for about twenty-five feet. Then, I popped the clutch too quickly going in to second gear. The engine choked and died, and the Courier rolled to a stop, kitty-cornered at the intersection of the road beside my house.

As I was trying to get the pickup started again…Dad rolled up in his work truck.

I saw the expression on his face through the windshield.

It wasn't a look of joy.

Without saying a word, Dad's coworker, who was riding with him, excused himself from the cab and walked away, not even looking back. Kind of like how Lot did when God was about to smite Sodom and Gomorrah. He might have turned in to a pillar of salt, by fixing his eyes on the destruction that was about to take place.

Stepping out of the truck, Dad bellowed in anger, *"What were you thinking?!"*, his words booming loud enough for my baseball team and the entire block to hear. He marched over to me, grabbed me by the arm, and began dragging me into the house. They say your life flashes before your eyes, when you die. My adrenaline was giving me a horrific preview, as I dug my blue *FastBak* sneakers into the ground, with visions of a life that was going to end, far too soon.

Back in the day, Dad wore a custom leather belt with his name, "DON", in bold black letters on the back. It was the instrument of punishment chosen for me that day, as he bent me over his knee.

Dad's hands were shaking as he gave me what I deserved, over my high-pitched pleas of, "Daddy, don't kill me!" When the punitive action ended and the wailings of my impending death subsided, Dad came over to me, hands still shaking. He then spoke in a tone that was so soft, I had to concentrate to hear his voice - words that came from a man who loved me - and was scared to death.

"What were you thinking?! Can you imagine what would have happened if one of those boys fell out of the truck? What would have happened if you'd have gotten hurt or killed? What would your mother and I have done, having lost our oldest son?!"

Suddenly, it dawned on me, that Dad's words were taking on an entirely different meaning than when he had first said them in anger outside. This time, his words were filled with fear…worry…*love*. Dad pulled me to him, holding me so tight, that my ribs ached. Then he started to cry. At that moment, my tears changed from those of a boy who was recovering from a punishment he'd deserved, to a boy overwhelmed by a father's love that he didn't deserve.

We walked out of the house together, not saying a word but with a new understanding of each other.

Actually, *he* walked – I *limped*.

For a few days I had whelps on my hind end that spelled, "NOD", from Dad's custom leather belt. I knew that I deserved every single one—and I didn't touch the Courier again, until I got my driver's license. But what was burned into my mind and heart, far longer than the punishment, was the memory of a father who would have died inside, if anything had happened to me during such a reckless stunt, that day…

"*What were you thinking?!*"

Maybe you've been asked that question a time or two, when you were a kid. Maybe the question came from a parent, a friend or a teacher. And the moment they asked it, you *already* knew the answer: There was *no* thinking involved, at all! No one *thinks* about driving a pickup truck in the 5th grade, because their brain has already left the station. No one *thinks* about how they will probably choke their baby sister to death while dumping Johnson & Johnson's baby powder down their throat. (Yes, that was also me) No one *thinks* about the consequences of jumping off a roof trying to fly like a superhero, only to skip like a rock off the trampoline below and land in the picket fence. (That one was my brother). So, when your friend or loved one bellows, "*What were you thinking?!*" – they don't really want an answer, it's just *their own* reaction of anger and frustration out of your idiotic decision that could have gotten you killed.

But that question can take on a *whole new meaning* if a child needs to be reassured that their mother or father loves them. When you know you've disappointed your parents and when you're afraid you'll lose their love, your mother or father have probably said to you, "*What were you thinking?* We would *never* stop loving you! *What were you thinking?* You mean more to me than anything on this earth! *What were you thinking?* We are *always* proud of you, no matter what!"

Depending on how your parents used that question, it carried with it a message of anger *or* love – frustration *or* reassurance.

In those moments when we hear exasperation and anger from those in authority over us, more often than not, we would later hear words of love and reassurance from them, because regardless of our idiotic behavior, we could trust that they would always love us.

How much *more*, our Heavenly Father! The One Who welcomes us into a daily relationship with Him, using *one* question, *two* different ways - to discipline us in His love, as His sons and daughters. The One Who calls us to do the same with those He has entrusted to us.

Prayer: *Father in heaven, there are so many things I've done in this life that could have gotten me in to so much trouble, gotten me badly hurt or worse. Some of those things did hurt me, physically or emotionally. Help me to remember that You have never left my side and will use all of the chapters of my life to be a written testament to Your never-ending patience and never-ending love to me. Help me use the story of my life to welcome others with Your Grace. Amen*

TABLE TALK

1) Discuss a time in your childhood when you had a loved one who was angry at you for the *right* reasons? How was that a time of fear? Of shame?

2) Discuss a time when you received reassurance from someone that they loved you, no matter what? How was that a time of relief? Of hope?

REFLECTION

In Isaiah, chapter 40, God's words are a lot like a parent's words to his child. He uses one question that can have two different meanings. God first asks a question to the children of Israel, like my Dad would have asked them after taking their 5th grade friends for a ride in his Ford Courier: "*Do you not know? Do you not hear?*" God is speaking to Israel out of anger and frustration. Anger and hurt over His people constantly chasing after false gods. Their constant need to sin and walk away from His covenant with them. This is an *exasperated Heavenly Father*, asking in anger of His children, "*Do you not know? Do you not hear?*" "Israel, stop for a minute and think about all I've done for you – can't you recall? What were you thinking?! Israel, shouldn't you remember better than anyone else Who I Am for you and what I've told you…who sits above the circle of the earth, and its inhabitants are like grasshoppers; who stretches out the heavens like a curtain, and spreads them like a tent to dwell in; who brings princes to nothing, and makes the rulers of the earth as emptiness."

"Israel, *what were you thinking?!*"

But after God speaks to Israel His anger and frustration, He later uses the *same question* to speak with love and reassurance - as a loving Heavenly Father.

"Have you not known? Have you not heard? The LORD is the everlasting God…He gives power to the faint, and to him who has no might He increases strength…they who wait for the LORD shall renew their strength; they shall mount up with wings like eagles…they shall run and not be weary; they shall walk and not be faint."

Like me at the sandlot, at some point in your childhood it dawns on you – just because your father punishes you, doesn't mean you *stop* being his child. Discipline is one of the greatest loves. And God the Father disciplines His children, Israel out of His love for them – letting them know how much He treasures them and lifts them up when they are "weary" or "faint." A God Who calls on His children to follow His Word – but also a God Who shows unconditional, unrelenting love for His children.

Just like with you and me.

TABLE TALK

3) **Read Hebrews 12:5-11**. What does God have to say about discipline, fathers and children? How does that echo God and His heavenly discipline to His children?

4) If you have good memories of your father disciplining you, what about those memories made them 'good'?

5) Were they any others in your life who stepped up to play the role of a good father for you? What made their actions 'good'?

6) What does your Heavenly Father have in common with the 'good fathers' in your life?

7) **Read Proverbs 3:7**. What do you think it means to 'fear' God?

8) **Read 1 John 4:16-18**. What do you think it means to 'love' God?

REFLECTION

When we talk about "fearing God," we're not talking about being afraid like when you watch a horror movie. We're talking about the kind of "fear" that you had for your *own* earthly father: the deep respect and understanding that he was your authority and you were to do what he said. God's people live in *holy fear*—but they also live *in love*. When we disobey Him, we will hear God say, in discipline, *"Do you not know? Do you not hear? What were you thinking?"* When we are beaten down and in need of being comforted and lifted up, we also will hear God say, in love, *"Have you not known? Have you not heard? What were you thinking? You are My child."*

God says both questions to us because as His children, we *do* know and we *have* heard His Words. We *should* know better! But we often don't. No matter how we try, our sinful nature keeps us from keeping His Words. Even when we are mothers and fathers, ourselves. That's why we desperately need our Father's voice of mercy, too. This is why we also need to hear words of *love* and forgiveness from our Father when we fail. It's also why *our children* need to hear those *same* words of love and forgiveness, from *us*. It's also why *we* need to hear those same words of discipline and love and forgiveness from *them*…

****

"*Daddy will you please talk to me?*"

That was the question my youngest daughter asked me, one day, while I was looking at my phone at the dinner table.

Again.

I'd gotten into the habit of coming home from work, changing clothes, coming downstairs to the kitchen for dinner to be with the family. Only, I wasn't really *present* with them. I was a body taking up space, as I used my phone to check my Facebook feed, reply to emails or read an article or two. This time, my daughter, Tressa, had pulled up her little kitchen stool right next to me, so close our arms were touching, as she began to tell me about her day and wanting to ask me a thing or two.

At least, I *think* that's what she was trying to do.

I don't really remember – I was using my phone.

Then came her innocent question, "*Daddy, will you please talk to me?*"

That stopped me, cold.

Ashamed, I put my phone in my pocket. It took me putting my phone away before I could really 'tune in' to her, listen to her and talk to her.

My daughter's question to me got me thinking about how *much* attention I was paying to my *phone* and how *little* attention I was paying to my *kids*. Even when they're in the same room.

You see it all the time: people pushing shopping carts, driving on the highway, walking in the park: glued to their phones. Kids trying to have a conversation with their parents, while mom and dad are giving the obligatory 'uh-huh' and 'yeah', while they text or check their social media. And the problem is reaching *epidemic* proportions.

I was shocked to learn that Americans check their phone on an average of once every twelve minutes – that factors out to about *80 times a day*. A study by a global tech protection and support company, Asurion, found that the average person *struggles* to go little more than *10 minutes* without checking their phone. According to research from RescueTime, one of several apps for iOS and Android created to monitor phone use, people generally spend an average of three hours and fifteen minutes on their phones every day, with the top 20% of smartphone users spending upwards of *four and a half hours*.

At the end of our time together at the dinner table, I said, "Tressa, I'm so sorry I was ignoring you."

Without missing a beat, she said, "It's okay, Daddy, I forgive you." Then, she gave me a little squeeze with her tiny arms and ran off to play.

Sometimes, not only do dads need to *extend* forgiveness—we also need to *ask* for forgiveness.

And hear the words of absolution, too.

TABLE TALK

9) How easy is it for you to ask someone for forgiveness? What makes it difficult? What makes it easier?

10) How easy is it for you to ask your children for forgiveness? What makes it difficult? What makes it easier?

11) What difference does it make to verbally tell someone, "I forgive you" after they have asked for your forgiveness? What difference does it make to hear the words, "I forgive you" after you have wronged someone?

12) How much of a challenge would it be to leave your phone in your bedroom at dinner time? If you already do this, was it an easy transition, at first? If not, what made it difficult?

REFLECTION

In our constantly plugged-in world, while we're busy looking at phones and not people, we miss a lot of information that you just can't get through texts, emails and status updates. Since most of the information we receive in our interactions are *nonverbal*, we lose a lot: facial expressions, tone of voice, even eye dilations. All important aspects of communication that you can't include in an email attachment. Even if you Skype or Facetime, it's still no substitute for a face-to-face discussion with people. Especially in matters of forgiveness and reconciliation.

13) **Read 2 John 1:12**. How important did St. John think face-to-face communication was? How important is it to the Church, today?

14) **Read Matthew 18:15-20**. How important is face-to-face communication in matters of reconciliation?

15) **Look again at Matthew 18:17**. How did Jesus treat Gentiles and tax collectors? How does His treatment of them inform your treatment of people who refuse to repent?

16) How does Matthew 18:15-20 help us understand Jesus' meaning behind "For where two or three are gathered in My Name, there am I among them"?

Challenge: Remove all social media apps from your smartphone for one week. If you must check social media, log in with your browser, instead. At the end of the week, see what difference it makes not to have 'instant access' to social media. What impact did the extra step of logging in through a browser make to access social media?

REFLECTION

When our kids were very little, every night we would tuck the kids in, tell jokes and stories, and maybe watch a YouTube video of "The Gummy Bear" song. Then we would say our night prayers as a family, closing in Luther's Evening Prayer. Our children *lived* for that evening ritual – and so did Mom and Dad.

If you're old enough, you may remember "The Waltons" T.V. show. There was a moment in every episode that stood out, for me. As they turned out the lights, the camera would pan back from the old farmhouse, as each family member told one another goodnight. I learned a routine like that, early on, from my parents, who would read books, tell stories and say night prayers as a family. And the last thing I heard from them, before closing my eyes, was, "Goodnight. I love you. See you in the morning."

That tradition lives on in my family, today.

The very last thing we do, as we turn out the lights is give a hug and tell each other, "Goodnight. I love you. See you in the morning".

And as our kids grow, while the pre-prayer routine has changed (no more "Gummy Bear" song), the night prayers and the goodnights have not. And our littlest one still wants Mom to tuck her in before she can go to sleep.

Now, I know that my children have heard me speak harshly to them in our day-to-day world, and I've apologized to them for saying things I've regretted. But that nightly ritual reminds me that my children *want* to forget the words I've said in the heat of the moment – they don't *want* to remember me that way. They *need* to hear words of *love* and *forgiveness* from their father. And *those* words are the words their hearts will remember from me. They want the last words they hear from their father to be, "Goodnight. I love you. See you in the morning."

TABLE TALK

17) Discuss the following statement: "Our first mission field – is to our families."

18) Is there a bedtime routine for you and your family? What parts make it special?

19) Have you followed the practice of night prayers in your family? For yourself? For you and your spouse?

20) Who do you know in your church family who could use some prayer? In your family? In your neighborhood?

BRINGING IT HOME

That's why a child of God needs to hear *words of love* and *forgiveness* from our heavenly Father. Words like, "Do you not know? Do you not hear? You are My child." Words like, "Almighty God in His mercy has given His Son to die for you, and for His sake forgives you all your sins." Words like, "Take and eat, this is My body given for you…Take and drink, this is My blood, shed for you for the forgiveness of sins." Jesus comes to show you a God of Love – a God of Welcome - a Heavenly Father Who greatly desires to share His love and forgiveness with you. A Father Who delights in relieving you of your burdens. A Father Who takes the weight of your sorrows and sins and puts them on His only Son, so that you "shall mount up with wings like eagles."

Our 'Two-Question' God asks us, "Do you not know? Do you not hear?" We *do* know and we *have* heard but we also know how often we fail to measure up to God's commands. We've done some pretty idiotic things in our lives and we know we deserve punishment. And yet, just when it seems like all hope is lost, our 'Two-Question' God asks us, "Have you not known? Have you not heard?" We hear of God's Fatherly love, shown to us through His Son, Jesus. We hear His words of forgiveness to us. And we walk away in freedom and forgiveness, with a better understanding of Him, of ourselves and of His eternal welcome to us.

We hear His words of love – "What were you *thinking*? You are more precious to Me than you could ever imagine! You are My child. You are *forgiven* in Christ. You are baptized into My Name. Rest your head, knowing you are My child. Goodnight. I love you. See you in the morning."

A God of love and forgiveness – *no questions asked.*

> I hear the Savior say,
> "Thy strength indeed is small,
> Child of weakness, watch and pray,
> Find in Me thine all in all."
>
> Jesus paid it all,
> All to Him I owe;
> Sin had left a crimson stain,
> He washed it white as snow.
>
> Lord, now indeed I find
> Thy pow'r and Thine alone,
> Can change the leper's spots
> And melt the heart of stone.

Jesus paid it all,
All to Him I owe;
Sin had left a crimson stain,
He washed it white as snow.

For nothing good have I
Where-by Thy grace to claim;
I'll wash my garments white
In the blood of Calv'ry's Lamb.

Jesus paid it all,
All to Him I owe;
Sin had left a crimson stain,
He washed it white as snow.

And when, before the throne,
I stand in Him complete,
"Jesus died my soul to save,"
My lips shall still repeat.

Jesus paid it all,
All to Him I owe;
Sin had left a crimson stain,
He washed it white as snow.

Jesus Paid It All
public domain

Closing Prayer: *I thank You, my heavenly Father, through Jesus Christ, Your dear Son, that You have graciously kept me this day; and I pray that You would forgive me all my sins where I have done wrong, and graciously keep me this night. For into Your hands I commend myself, my body and soul, and all things. Let Your holy angel be with me, that the evil foe may have no power over me. Amen.*

Then go to sleep at once and in good cheer.

(Martin Luther's Small Catechism, Luther's Evening Prayer)

CHAPTER 19
God's Warm Welcome -
To His People, *Through* His People

Matthew 25:21
"His master replied, 'Well done, good and faithful servant! You have been faithful with a few things; I will put you in charge of many things. Come and share your master's joy!'"

SETTING THE TABLE

You might be surprised to learn this, but the 'parable of the talents' has a 'love/hate' relationship with the United States. In fact, in the beginning of our nation's history, this parable was used to speak out *against* America. Preachers in England thought the Puritans who first migrated to America were lazy, unprofitable servants who matched this parable, and so, in their minds, they weren't going to the 'land of plenty', they were being cast out by God, into the darkness, where there would be 'weeping and gnashing of teeth'.

But as time went on, instead of this parable being used *against* America, it was later used *to promote* America. Revival preachers in the 1920's declared America to be the 'land of opportunity', and whoever served the cause of opportunity would be blessed. Now, I don't know many Americans who interpret this parable *either way* anymore. But I do think we still *struggle* with this parable, as Christians.

Somehow, over the years, we've gotten it in our heads that the real meaning of the 'parable of the talents' is about using the 'talents and gifts' God has given us, and if we don't use them – God will come, *take them away, and give them to someone else who deserves them!* I've heard that sermon preached in many pulpits growing up. Maybe you have, too.

But that's not right.

If you've been paying attention at all in this book, you know the Law can't save us. And a parable telling us to *do* more or *be* more for God sets us up to fail, before we even begin. To think God works that way with us causes us to lose sight of the *real* gifts that He gives to His people.

In this parable, Jesus is talking about way more than '*not* using your gifts' – He's talking about the *real* gifts of the Kingdom of Heaven. The Kingdom of Heaven, that is driven by generous, Divine love, where faith responds in joyful service for what God has done for us. "For we are God's workmanship, created in Christ Jesus to do good works, which God has prepared in advance, so that we might walk in them." (Eph. 2:10)

When the master returns to settle accounts in His kingdom on the Last Day, Jesus wants *you* to hear, "Well done, good and faithful servant! Come and live in your master's *joy*!"

Prayer: *Lord, I long to hear the words, "Well done, good and faithful servant!" from Your lips. I long to please You with the life I live. But there's a difference between the life I live to honor You and the life I live to earn Your favor. Help me, by Your Spirit, not to get the two confused. Help me continue to cling to the work You did for me on the cross, as I look for the Day when You call me to Yourself. Amen*

TABLE TALK

1) **Read Matthew 25:14-30**. Who are the cast of characters? What parts would you expect to happen in this parable? What parts surprised you?

2) How have you heard this parable explained? Any good or bad explanations? Were there any explanations that didn't make sense to you? What parts of the parable make sense?

3) What character traits does the parable reveal about the 'man going on a journey' (25:14)?

4) What character traits does the parable reveal about the three servants?

REFLECTION

It's an odd-sounding phrase to our ears: to *live in our master's joy*. So, what does this mean (always a good Lutheran question to ask)? Let's find out, together.

In the 'parable of the talents', *two* servants react to their master's command with *joy*, but *one* reacts with *fear*. The reason the 'fearful servant' gets into so much trouble with the talents he was given, *isn't* because of his master. And it's not even because of what he did with the talents that were given to him.

It's because of his own *imagination*.

The first thing Jesus does in this parable, is to reveal a *generous* master: someone who gives all He has into the hands of His servants. To show you just how generous this master really is, we first need to understand what a 'talent' is. One talent, by modern-day economics, adds up to about *twenty years' worth of wages*. So, some simple math tells us that the last servant received *twenty* years' worth of wages, the second servant, *forty* years' worth and the first servant *one hundred* years' worth!

I don't know about you, but I wouldn't say 'no' to *twenty years'* worth of wages!

No matter how you slice it, whether you were the first servant to receive wages or the last one - that's *incredibly* generous!

But there's *more*. At one point in this parable, the master says that the talents He gave to the servants was only *a little*, and to those *faithful* servants he would be putting them in charge of *much more*. (Matt. 25:29) This master's generosity knows *no limits*!

That's why the 'fearful servant' serves a master he *doesn't know*.

A master he has invented from his *own imagination*.

A "hard man, reaping where [he] did not sow, and gathering where [he] scattered no seed" (v 24). The servant's imagination and fears have paralyzed him so much, that he buries his master's talents in the ground. So, when the master returns to 'settle accounts', he judges the 'fearful servant' – not by what he has *done*.

He is judged by what he has *believed*.

And as he *believes*, so it is *done* to him. Because he didn't trust the loving generosity of his master, the 'fearful servant' is cast out into darkness, where there will be weeping and gnashing of teeth.

TABLE TALK

5) What kind of master is described in this parable? Who might Jesus be telling us that this master is, in real life?

6) What does this parable show us about generosity, not only with money but with *our lives*?

7) How do our fears paralyze us, to keep us from doing what is right?

8) How do our fears cause us to avoid God? Lie to Him? Re-make

Him in *our* image?

9) What difference would it make to know we serve a generous master that we don't need to fear? What difference would it make in our daily lives?

REFLECTION

The 'fearful servant' describes a lot of people in our world today. But instead of imagining a hard, demanding god, who is to be *feared*, they imagine an impotent god that *they* can *handle*. In a world that lives by the mantra of *tolerance* and *acceptance*, it only makes sense to create a god that is the same. An all-loving, kind-hearted grandpa, with a long, white beard, who sits in a rocking chair up in the clouds - too *weak* to do any harm to them but still *strong* enough to love them. A god who calls for *tolerance*, instead of *repentance*. A god who offers *acceptance*, instead of *forgiveness*. A god whose slogan is 'nobody's perfect' and 'god is love'. A god they can imagine standing before, with all their sins, and be *accepted* for who they are and *tolerated* for what they have done.

They bury God's *real gifts* of love and forgiveness in the ground – planning on one day to dig them back up, hand them back, and like the 'fearful servant', say, "See, here is what belongs to you." The tragedy is, they will find out that the joy they *thought* they had in serving a god of their own imagination was a *lie*.

The reality of their situation will be revealed to them and their *false joy* taken from them.

Like the fearful servant, they have been judged, not by what they have *done*, but by what they have *believed*.

And as they *believed*, so it is *done* to them.

Thrown into the darkness, where there will be weeping and gnashing of teeth.

TABLE TALK

10) Discuss the struggle of dealing with tolerance and acceptance in our world, today.

11) How does the Church struggle with tolerance and acceptance?

12) Can you think of a time when the mantra of tolerance and acceptance was forced upon you?

13) Can you think of a time when you stood for the truth of God, rather than bend to the world?

14) **Read Matthew 10:16-22**. How does Jesus' words address our world's views on tolerance and acceptance? What promises does Jesus give to His people, in these words? Have you faced any consequences by the world for following Jesus' words, here?

REFLECTION

As brothers and sisters in Christ, we know a tremendous truth—that God doesn't save us by *our imagination*, but by *His action*!

We don't need to imagine a kind God – we have one! And He is kind in all the ways that truly matter.

In Jesus, God becomes flesh, dwells among us and loves us so much that He wouldn't flinch at the terrible cost of sin. A generous love that would suffer death and damnation so our debt could be paid, and sins forgiven before God. This love is brutal, violent, uncivilized – *real*. He saves us, not by becoming what *we* want Him to be, but by being the God we *need* Him to be - our Savior!

Our Savior Who knows the *real* dangers of sin and calls us to repent. Our Savior Who knows the eternal cost of sin and dies under *our* eternal punishment. Our Savior Who knows the *eternal joy* of *salvation* and rises again—not to *tolerate* sin and *accept* sinners—but to generously *pay* for sin and *forgive* sinners! Living in the forgiveness and joy of our Heavenly Father, means turning away from the gods of our *imagination* and trusting the generous God of our *salvation*: Jesus Christ, the Son of God, so we might live in *eternal joy.*

In the 'parable of the talents', one servant feared a master he had *imagined.*

But the other servants trusted the master they *knew.*

TABLE TALK

15) In what ways have you created a god of your imagination?

16) How does a god of our imagination cause fear?

17) How does the true God of our salvation differ from the god of our imagination?

18) **Read Psalm 120:3-4**. How does the true God cause 'holy fear'? What's the difference between 'holy fear' and 'fear'?

REFLECTION

The servants who truly knew their master, knew that he was a gracious and generous man. A master who welcomed them into his kingdom – and a master who called upon them to welcome the opportunity he gives them, to use his riches in the world.

Instead of ruling *over* them with an iron fist, the master graciously rules *through them* - giving them his great wealth for service in the world. Each servant is loved, each one a part of the master's household. Yet, each servant is *differently* gifted: one receives *five* talents, one *two*, and one, *one*. He generously divides his possessions according to their *abilities* (v.15) and sends them forth as servants – living in the joy of their master - *differently* gifted – but *equally* loved.

In the past, Christians have misunderstood this parable to think God is a harsh judge who will take our talents away if we don't use them. And if you're like me, you may have heard this way of thinking preached from pulpits and taught in Bible study classes.

But we've also misunderstood this parable to mean God doesn't love everyone - or their service, equally. We live with the idea that 'more is better', so the servant who got five talents must be *better* than the other two. Some churches do this with members, too: a member who teaches Sunday School and sings in the Choir is honored as *faithful*, but another member who works as a single mother <u>and</u> raises her children <u>in the faith</u> is seen as *less committed* as a Christian.

And to that, I will say the time-honored theological phrase, "BALONEY!"

TABLE TALK

19) If your church family 'installs' Sunday School teachers at the beginning of the year, what impact might it make to pray God's blessings over all the parents who teach their children the faith, as well?

20) What might we be telling our church family, if we only recognize the people who are serving in our church? What might we be telling them about the character of God?

21) How would you respond to the following: "I wish I could volunteer at church, but I'm a single mom working two jobs. I barely make it to church most Sundays. I just wish I could do more."

REFLECTION

God does *not* see Christian service in your *congregation* as *more* important than Christian service in your *vocation*. God's love for us rejoices in our differences and rejoices in the many ways He has created us for service! God asks to welcome the opportunity to work through us, by His Spirit, into the world.

As St. Paul once said, "If the whole body were an eye, where would the sense of hearing be? If the whole body were an ear, where would the sense of smell be?" (1 Cor 12:17). The Master receives both the servant who teaches their Sunday School children about Jesus *and* the servant who teaches *their* children about Jesus the same way – with joy. Both *differently* gifted – both *equally* loved. Both one day hearing their master say, "Well done, good and faithful servant. Come, and share your master's joy!" (vv 21, 23). Service in God's kingdom will often look *very* different, from one person to the next. And that's on purpose. Because if God only used *you and your personality type*, He would only be reaching people like *you*.

Several years ago, I was walking around a neighborhood with a man named Frank. Frank and I were going door to door, handing out Vacation Bible School fliers and telling people about our church. I'd never done anything like that before, so I was pretty nervous! But, as least I knew I was safe with Frank, because Frank was almost six feet tall, two-hundred twenty pounds and a retired Navy S.E.A.L.

Frank was a new Christian, still 'ironing out the kinks' and working on controlling his colorful language. Anyway, we knocked on this one door, and a man came out of the house. You could tell he was *not* happy we had darkened his doorstep! I handed him the VBS flier, told him about our church and turned to leave, but Frank just stood there, not moving - and blocking my exit. He kept staring at this man and after giving him a visual inspection, said to him, "You alright, man?"

And that man… *erupted*!

He railed at us for five minutes about how pitiful the Christian Church was, about how we're all a bunch of hypocrites, yadda, yadda, yadda. At that point, I was *really* ready to leave, when the man yelled one more parting shot at us, "And one more thing – I used to be a Christian, until my church told me I was going to hell for being a smoker!!"

Without missing a beat, Frank reached into his pocket, pulled out a pack of Lucky Strikes and said, "Light up, brother—you're forgiven in Christ!"

Now, after I picked my jaw up off the floor from what Frank just said, I turned to look at that man…

… and he was *sobbing*.

Sobbing tears that he'd been holding back *for years*.

Tears of hurt and pain. Rejection and judgment.

Tears of relief.

Tears that had heard the *true* Gospel.

Now, I'd have never in a *million years* said what Frank said that day, because using Lucky Strikes as an inroad to share the Gospel wasn't exactly in my *repertoire*.

But that was kind of *the point*.

God had chosen to use the unique words of His *servant, Frank* – and that man, who shared a cigarette with Frank on his front porch - started coming to our church – and back into the arms of Jesus, again.

TABLE TALK

22) **Read 1 Corinthians 12:12-27**. How does St. Paul describe the body of Christ?

23) What parts of the body are more important than the others? What does that knowledge teach us about *honoring one another* and the gifts God has uniquely given to each of us?

BRINGING IT HOME

Just like Frank, sitting on a front porch and sharing a cigarette with a stranger, God has work for us to do in His Kingdom – and it rarely looks how we would expect.

What is important is that God has extended to us His warm welcome, through the forgiveness of Christ. And that warm welcome calls for us to extend it to others. A warm welcome, given *to* His People and now, *through* His people - to a hurting world. No matter the talents given us, we celebrate the different gifts within our church family and are called to extend the grace to others, to be a 'hand or foot or eye' in His kingdom—and let God determine the harvest.

We're different – in who we are and what gifts we have and how we serve our Master.

But what makes us equal, is what we *believe*.

We believe in Jesus.

And as we *believe*, so it is *done* to us – sins forgiven, eternal life, eternal joy. Differently gifted, but equally loved. And one great day, hearing our Master say, "Well done, good and faithful servant. Come, and share in your master's joy!" (vv 21, 23). Amen

> A mighty fortress is our God,
> A trusty shield and weapon;
> He helps us free from ev'ry need
> That has us now o'ertaken.
> The old evil foe
> Now means deadly woe;
> Deep guile and great might
> Are his dread arms in fight;
> On earth is not his equal.
>
> With might of ours can naught be done;
> Soon were our loss effected.
> But for us fights the valiant One

Whom God Himself elected.
You ask, "Who is this?"
Jesus Christ it is,
Of Sabaoth Lord,
And there's none other God;
He holds the field forever.

Though devils all the world should fill,
All eager to devour us,
We tremble not, we fear no ill:
They shall not overpow'r us.
This world's prince may still
Scowl fierce as he will,
He can harm us none.
He's judged; the deed is done!
One little word can fell him.

The Word they still shall let remain,
Nor any thanks have for it;
He's by our side upon the plain
With His good gifts and Spirit.
And take they our life,
Goods, fame, child, and wife;
Though these all be gone,
Our vict'ry has been won;
The Kingdom ours remaineth!

—Lutheran Service Book
656, public domain

Closing Prayer: *God, how I've tried to make this parable about me, instead of about what You have done for me. Forgive me for holding on too tight to the blessings You've given me. Forgive me for burying Your Grace, afraid of what You'll do. Help me, by Your Spirit, to focus on what You have done – sending Your priceless treasure, Jesus, to give the riches of His Grace to me, a poor, miserable sinner. Help me to embrace that this lavish Grace extends to all people – people who I have nothing in common with, have different abilities than mine and different heart stories. Help me to rejoice in the One Story You are writing in us all, as the Body of Christ, in every time and every place - using the kaleidoscope of gifts You have gifted to Your people – for Your Kingdom, and for Your Glory. Amen*

CHAPTER 20
God's Welcoming Embrace

Luke 15:11
"[Jesus] said, "There was a man who had two sons..."

SETTING THE TABLE

I *hate math.* Ask my wife or children and they'll tell you I'm *not* the guy to ask to do times tables or to balance the check book. So, my go-to line, when people ask me to crunch numbers is, "Sorry guys – I don't do math." And, it would seem, from what Scripture tells us – that the Almighty God doesn't do math, either.

I'm willing to bet, that out of all the parables in the Bible, the one that people are most familiar with is the parable of the Prodigal Son. To be a 'prodigal' means, to be 'wasteful or reckless' with your life and the *younger* son in this parable certainly fits the bill: he does some pretty despicable things to himself and to his family. Now, this parable originally didn't have a title but since we've been calling it 'the parable of the Prodigal Son' for so long, we tend to think this parable is *only* about that son. Well, that's part of the story, but there is so *much* more to it than that. Because the parable actually *isn't* about repentant or unrepentant sons. The parable is about two sons who are *good* at math, and their Father who definitely *isn't*. Figuring out what's the deal with the two sons and their use of math, tells us the meaning of the parable and shows us the heart of the Father.

Prayer: *Lord, as we look at Your words about fathers, sons and welcoming embraces, help it to call to mind the embrace You have welcomed us with, while we were wandering from You. Help us to never take for granted the lavish, untamed love You so graciously give to us in Christ. Amen*

TABLE TALK

Take a moment to discuss the following together:

1) **Read Luke 15:11-32**. Who are the main characters? What events take place?

2) Is there anything in this parable you would expect to happen? Anything that surprises you?

3) How might Jesus be using the culture of His day to convey God's truth?

4) How might this parable speak to our culture, today?

REFLECTION

First, let's take a look at the *younger* son – 'the prodigal son'. This younger son is good at *subtraction*. According to the book of Deuteronomy, the *firstborn* son received 2/3 of the estate when his Father died (Deut. 21:15–17). But the prodigal is the *younger* son, so some quick subtraction tells him that:

$1 - 2/3 = 1/3$

So, as the younger son, he asks his Father for his share of the estate - 1/3. Now, ordinarily, getting your inheritance isn't a bad thing. But, what's the big deal with the son asking for it *now*? The deal is – you usually get an inheritance, *after* someone has died. His father is still *alive*! But the younger son wasn't just going to sit around and wait for his Father to die. He wanted his 1/3 *now*. By using subtraction, he's basically saying, "Dad, I don't really care about this home you've worked your whole life to build; In fact, I wish you *were dead*."

The younger son's treatment of his Father is so shocking! You can't help but reflect on how *evil* the younger son is to do this! But Jesus doesn't give us time to reflect. Instead, He continues the parable and says this, "the Father divided his property *between them*." Incredibly, the Father *honors* the younger son's request! He shames *Himself* by giving that son what he *doesn't* deserve. Even more incredible, is something you may not have noticed before - <u>BOTH</u> sons got their share *at that moment*.

The *younger* son gets his 1/3.

The *older* son gets his 2/3.

The Father has miscalculated; he has given away 3/3 of his estate - *All* of it! *Both* sons have benefited from their Father shaming himself! What's the deal, with these sons? Well, let's keep going and find out.

TABLE TALK

5) **Read Romans 5:1-11**. What might we have in common with the 'prodigal' son?

6) Reviewing the parable so far, what characteristics does the father portray?

REFLECTION

As you know—a fool and his money are soon parted. The younger son goes off and wastes his 1/3. He's flat broke and working for some foreigner on a pig farm. That's about as low as a Jew could go—working for a Gentile, with unclean pigs. Being paid so little he was starving. Not even allowed to eat the unclean pig's unclean food, because his employer considered the pigs *more valuable* than him.

Some simple subtraction shows the son, that:

$1/3 - 1/3 = 0$

So, he sets out for home, tail between his legs—rehearsing what he's going to say to his Father—planning to confess his sin and unworthiness – just begging for a job. '$1/3 - 1/3 = 0$'. And so, he heads home, to face the music.

TABLE TALK

7) **Read Luke 12:13-21**. What parallels are there between this parable and the 'prodigal' son's behavior?

8) Looking at Luke 12:13, why do you think Jesus reacts the way that He does to the man's question about inheritance?

9) In Luke 12:13, how is the man's question similar to the 'prodigal' son's behavior towards his father? What is this man wishing about his father?

10) Have you ever experienced a time when families were divided over inheritance? What was it like?

11) What plans do you have in place to ensure your inheritance won't divide your family?

12) Note: My great-grandparents were very wise. They put a clause in their will that stated, "Should any one in the family dispute their inheritance, verbally or through lawsuit, they hereby forfeit their inheritance, to be divided amongst their siblings. They are to receive $1 as part of forfeiture." Discuss the wisdom in that clause.

13) **Read Proverbs 13:22**. What is the author conveying about inheritance?

14) Does God *require* that parents leave an inheritance for their children? What is the only inheritance He requires?

15) Discuss this phrase: "It is easier to build strong children than to repair broken men."

16) What 'inheritance' are we unknowingly passing along to our children?

   a. Do we eat well?
   b. Exercise?
   c. Avoid gossiping about others?
   d. Tithe?
   e. Admit wrongdoing and ask for forgiveness?
   f. Be good stewards of our social media time?
   g. Make time to eat together as a family?
   h. Worship regularly?

REFLECTION

Meanwhile, there's the *older* son. He is good at *addition*. He stays at home and continues to work for his Father. Some simple math tells him, that he now has it *made*! Not only does he *already* have his 2/3, but dear old Dad is *still alive*, still *producing*, still *earning*. Before you know it, he will be back on his feet and contributing to his Roth IRA again! And the best part is, when he finally does die, the older son gets *everything*, this time. After all, his little brother is out of the picture for good. So, his addition tells him that:

2/3 + 3/3 = 5/3

This is *really* working out for the older son! All he has to do is keep his nose clean and work the land and he'll be set for life! Things are working out *beautifully* – until…

… 'Mr. Subtraction' decides to come home. He's carrying a sign, "Will work for food." He's not looking for a handout – he's just looking for a job. But his Father *isn't* hiring that day - he's only *forgiving*. While he is still a long way off, his Father sees him coming…

What's the deal?

How is it that the Father happens to see his long-lost son while he is still a long way off? That's only possible—if the Father's eyes have been scanning the horizon ever since His son left home, watching the road *every day*, searching for his return. Not the reaction you'd expect from someone who'd been *left for dead*! In the time between his son living 'high on the hog' and then having to feed them, the Father has been waiting for his son's return. But how could he possibly know that his son *would* come back?

The answer is so simple: Because the Father *knows His son*.

TABLE TALK

17) **Read Luke 12:22-34**. How well does your Father know you? What has He promised to you?

18) **Read Luke 20:13-15**. How has the Father allowed His Son to be treated by the world? To be treated by you?

REFLECTION

Now, we see something that no mature Middle Eastern man would *ever* do. The Father is *running* – running to His son! In those days, you couldn't run if you didn't hike up your robe, first. A dignified Father hiking up his robe to run, was a *shameful* act! Even the High Priest at the Temple wasn't allowed to lift up his robe to avoid getting it in the blood of the animal sacrifices as he walked. When you're an elder and a wealthy landowner in Jesus' day – people run to *you*, not the other way around! How *shameful* this Father is behaving!

But by now, the Father is probably used to that accusation, because the Father's 'poor use of math' has no doubt become the talk of the town: how *shameful* to give away the inheritance; how *shameful* to waste his days, sitting on his front porch, scanning the horizon for a worthless son; how *shameful* to run to his fallen son; how *shameful* to kiss him, to welcome him home!

The Father willingly *shames* Himself – embraces *shame* - <u>*before*</u> he embraces his son!

The Father loves him and has mercy on him *before* the prodigal son can even blurt out his well-rehearsed confession!

This gives us great insight into the heart of the Father and the power of the Gospel. God the Father loved us *before* we repented, and He forgave us *before* we realized we were sinners! The Gospel is not: "<u>If</u> you repent, God will <u>then</u> forgive you."

NO!

The Gospel is: 'while we were *still* sinners, Christ died for us.' (Rom. 5:8)

Did you notice that the Father in this story totally *ignores* the prodigal's confession of sins? He's so busy running, hugging, kissing, dressing His son, and preparing a celebration that He gives no response *whatsoever* to His son's 'big speech'. God's not interested in your *testimony* of your bad life.

He already knows the whole story. Because He knows you.

However you got here today, all that matters is - He's just glad *you're home*.

The question is not, "Is my repentance good enough?" The question is: "Do I believe my Father will forgive me?" If you don't believe your Father will forgive you, then it doesn't matter *how much* you repent. It doesn't matter how *awesome* your 'rehearsed testimony' sounds. If you think your *repentance* bought God's love for you -

you've got it backwards. God's *love* for you bought your *repentance*. And it cost Him '*more* than the farm'. But wait - that's the *rest* of the story. Jesus hasn't finished teaching us in this parable.

TABLE TALK

19) Discuss the difference between these two statements:
    a. "If you repent, God will forgive you."
    b. "God has already forgiven you; do you believe this?"

20) Discuss: In this parable, the father gives his son a ring. It's a signet ring, a symbol of family heritage, which was basically the credit card of the day. When purchases were made, wax was dripped on to the paper that contained the debt to be paid. The person wearing the ring would press their signet into the wax, as a visible sign the debt was to be paid by the household. What is the father telling his son by giving him this ring?

REFLECTION

There's still the matter of the *older* son. His math has *totally* backfired! He's gone from 'addition' to 'subtraction' in the blink of an eye! No more 5/3 in his financial portfolio. He was out 1/3 before and now that 'Mr. Subtraction' is home again, he's out *another* 1/3 – if not *more*! The Father is treating that *little punk* like he's his *firstborn* son! So, with his 'bad math' worked out, the *older* son complains to his Father, "You never even gave me a young goat to celebrate with my friends!"

But I imagine there were *lots* of young goats in his 2/3 inheritance, that he had the right to do whatever he wanted with, don't you think?

You see, whether you live by addition or by subtraction, when it comes to the Grace of God - math gets you *nowhere*.

This is the deal with the sons – and this is the *real* deal with you and me.

TABLE TALK

21) **Read Matthew 20:1-16**. How does this parable help us understand the parable of the prodigal son?

22) Have you ever felt like God 'owed' you something? When life happens, do you resent God for hard times, since 'you've been a good person'?

23) **Read 1 John 3:1-2**. What has God given to us? What does that make us?

24) What, then, does God call upon us, as His children, to do in this world?

BRINGING IT HOME

Whether you figure God by addition or by subtraction - it will *never* be enough for you. If you try to get out of God what you *think* you have coming to you, by addition or by subtraction – you either end up *begging* the Father for a job so you can try to earn your way back in to His good Graces...

...or you end up *accusing* Him of being stingy and neglectful, despite all the many good things you've received from Him.

The real loss in this parable, was *not* that the younger son left home with an inheritance, just as if his Father were dead. The real loss was that it was the *son* who was dead, because he had lost his greatest treasure – *his Father*.

And he didn't even realize it until after his Father had welcomed him home again.

The *older* son is so shocked by the grace and mercy of his Father that he forgets to take an account of all the wealth his Father had lavished on him *the entire time*. Think of how much easier the older son had things by 'staying on the farm'! Think of the peace, the security, the love he had received.

He was being jealous of something that he had *always* had.

His Father tells him so: 'Son, you are *always* with me, and *all* that is mine is *yours*.' (Luke 15:31)

The Good News of this parable is – your Heavenly Father *doesn't* do math! He embraces the shame *we* deserve. He waits and watches for us and then runs to forgive us and shower us with an inheritance as sons and daughters. And before we even have a chance to bargain for His love, it's already a done deal *in Christ*. We find ourselves wearing a son's robe and a ring that belongs to a prince. Whatever it was that we were going to say or do to talk our way out of trouble, either through lame excuses or a well-rehearsed testimony - doesn't matter anymore.

Because the feast is ready.

It's ready, because of *our* 'big brother', Jesus – the *author* of this parable.

The One Who gives us everything and more, through the power of His Cross.

If you've been a 'good son', working on the farm for your Father your whole life, think for a moment, how much *better* your life has been, by 'staying on the farm'. Think of the peace, the security, the love you've received!

You're being jealous of something that you *always* had.

Because of our brother, Jesus, the Father can say to us, "All that is mine is *yours*." Because of Jesus' forgiveness, He can say to ALL of us, Who work in His vineyard and who've been welcomed home, "I am with you always, even unto the end of the age." (Matt. 28:20)

A gracious Father, Who doesn't do *math*.

He does *Grace*, instead.

For you and me!

God's own child, I gladly say it:
I am baptized into Christ!
He, because I could not pay it,
gave my full redemption price.
Do I need earth's treasures many?
I have one worth more than any
That brought me salvation free, Lasting to eternity!

Sin, disturb my soul no longer:
I am baptized into Christ!
I have comfort even stronger: Jesus' cleansing sacrifice.
Should a guilty conscience seize me,
since my baptism did release me
In a dear forgiving flood, sprinkling me with Jesus' blood?

Satan, hear this proclamation:
I am baptized into Christ!
Drop your ugly accusation; I am not so soon enticed.
Now that to the font I've traveled,
all your might has come unraveled,
And, against your tyranny, God, my Lord, unites with me!

Death, you cannot end my gladness:
I am baptized into Christ!
When I die, I leave all sadness to inherit paradise!
Though I lie in dust and ashes
faith's assurance brightly flashes:
Baptism has the strength divine to make life immortal mine.

> There is nothing worth comparing
> to this lifelong comfort sure!
> Open-eyed my grave is staring:
> Even there I'll sleep secure.
> Though my flesh awaits its raising,
> still my soul continues praising:
> I am baptized into Christ; I'm a child of paradise!
>
> **—Lutheran Service Book**
> *594, copyright Robert E. Voelker, used by permission*

Closing Prayer: *Lord God, I see a lot of myself in the prodigal son. I've walked away from You so many times, I've lost count. How thankful I am that You continually welcome me, embrace me and forgive me through Your Only Son. I've also behaved a lot like the older son, thinking I'm somehow getting a 'raw deal' in this life. Even going so far as to be jealous when another person repents, rather than rejoicing that another 'son' has come home to You. By Your Holy Spirit, help me to live in Your Grace – a Grace I don't deserve. Help me to know that no matter what comes to me in this life, all You have to give is mine – right down to the last drop of Your Son's blood, as He hung on my cross. An eternal inheritance, given to me, that will never fade. An inheritance that calls upon me to welcome others – as You have welcomed me. Amen*

CONCLUSION
Welcome Home

John 14:1-6
"Let not your hearts be troubled. Believe in God; believe also in me. In my Father's house are many rooms. If it were not so, would I have told you that I go to prepare a place for you? And if I go and prepare a place for you, I will come again and will take you to myself, that where I am you may be also. And you know the way to where I am going." Thomas said to him, "Lord, we do not know where you are going. How can we know the way?" Jesus said to him, "I am the way, and the truth, and the life. No one comes to the Father except through me."

1 Corinthians 3:6
"I planted, Apollos watered, but God gave the growth."

Revelation 21:1-4
"Then I saw a new heaven and a new earth, for the first heaven and the first earth had passed away, and the sea was no more. And I saw the holy city, new Jerusalem,

coming down out of heaven from God, prepared as a bride
adorned for her husband. And I heard a loud voice
from the throne saying, "Behold, the dwelling place of God
is with man. He will dwell with them, and they will be his
people, and God himself will be with them as their God.
He will wipe away every tear from their eyes,
and death shall be no more, neither shall there be
mourning, nor crying, nor pain anymore,
for the former things have passed away."

THREE HOMECOMINGS

If you ever get the chance, take a road trip some time and visit the quiet little town of Altenburg, MO. It's there, among the rolling green hills and fertile clay soil, that the Lutheran Church—Missouri Synod had its beginnings. Back in 1837, the Anglo-Saxon Lutherans, escaping religious persecution from Germany, landed on the banks of the Mississippi River in Perry County, MO, to begin a new town, called, "Wittenberg". Wittenberg was originally named for the town in Germany where, on October 31st, 1517, Martin Luther nailed his 95 Theses (or statements) to the Wittenberg church doors. In these statements, Luther staked his claim on faith in Christ, alone, by the Grace of God alone, given through Holy Scripture alone. These statements stood in stark contrast against the claims of Rome that salvation from purgatory could be purchased through the sale of indulgences—beginning the avalanche that would later be called The Reformation. The Anglo-Saxons hoped the name of their new settlement in Missouri would honor Luther's bold claim of salvation by Grace through faith in Christ in the German town of Wittenberg. A beautiful gesture.

What the Anglo-Saxon Lutherans neglected to do, however, was survey the flood plain.

Staking their claim just a stone's throw from the mighty Mississippi, these pioneering Lutherans dug some twenty feet down to begin construction of a church. Lutheran churches, at the time, had seating where the last pew was at ground level, then proceeding downward in amphitheater style, the first pew would be at the bottom, where the altar was also located. This architectural design would not bode well, when the rains came. At every thunderstorm, the river would swell, and the church would quickly turn in to a swimming pool. Which meant that any time the skies darkened, the Anglo-Saxons would unbolt the altar and pews and haul them up to ground level, to get ahead of the for-certain floods from the Mississippi and avoid ruining the sacred items of the church.

Eventually, the leaders of Wittenberg suggested they looked for an alternate site for their town. And so, Wittenberg was abandoned for an 'alternative town'—literally, "Altenburg"—just a few miles up the road, where the flood plain was at a safer distance. Altenburg would serve to be the cradle for the future Lutheran Church—Missouri Synod, along with the first seminary for training her pastors, which was erected in 1839.

The rich history of Altenburg has equally rich cemeteries, one of which is located on the grounds of Immanuel Lutheran Church. As you scan the markers and tombstones, you see just how hard life must have been for those early settlers. Not many dates mark someone living beyond sixty years. Most died in their thirties. One passed away, when they were just ten days old.

The first time I roamed that cemetery, I was struck by all of the headstones, that in some way, shape or form, pointed to the Anglo-Saxon Lutherans' faith in Jesus. Many tombstones bear a phrase etched in the marble, *"Heir ruht in Gott"*, German for "Here rest in God." Others have elaborate reliefs cut into the stone, of Jesus returning in Glory on the Last Day. Some headstones quote Scripture from Psalm 91:16 "With long life I will satisfy him and show him my salvation." Over time, as the English language was being embraced by the German immigrants following World War I, *Heir ruht in Gott* remained, along with the English phrase below it, *"Called Higher."*

What is most striking of all, on that hallowed ground, is that no spouses are buried *beside* each other.

They are buried *across* from one another.

The first time I noticed this, I asked a groundskeeper why this was the case. Was it a holdover from a bygone era, when men worshipped in separate sections from women and therefore, were not laid to rest beside one another, as well? The answer, I would find, was far more beautiful than I could have imagined.

Back then, the Anglo-Saxon husbands and wives would purposely arrange their final resting places to be across from one another. When they died, they would be laid to rest on their backs, feet facing one another. This way, it would ensure that at the Resurrection of the Dead, when Jesus returned in Glory, the first faces they would see—would be the Resurrected face of their husband or wife.

These early faith-filled Lutherans lived and died in a wholehearted welcome of the Gospel—from birth, to death and beyond—looking forward to the Day when they would be welcomed by their Savior and welcome one another—together—forever!

Their graves lay as their testament to that truth, to this day.

***

Robby Robins was an Air Force pilot during the first Iraq war. After his 300th mission, he was surprised to be given permission to immediately pull his crew together and fly his plane home. They flew across the ocean to Massachusetts and then had a long drive to western Pennsylvania. They drove all night, and when his buddies dropped him off at his driveway just after sun-up, there was a big banner across the garage—"Welcome Home Dad!"

How did they *know* he was home? No one had called, and the crew themselves hadn't expected to leave so quickly. Robins said,

"When I walked into the house, the kids, about half dressed for school, screamed, 'Daddy!' Susan came running down the hall—she looked terrific—hair fixed, make-up on, and a crisp yellow dress. 'How did you know?' I asked.

'I didn't,' she answered through tears of joy. 'Once we knew the war was over, we knew you'd be home one of these days. We knew you'd try to surprise us, so we were ready *every day*.'"[110]

***

When I was young, *The Phantom of the Opera* was hands-down, my most favorite musical: the star-crossed love triangle between the soprano Christine, her dashing beau, Raoul, and the tragic figure of the Phantom. As I age, I've found that my favorite musical is a tie between *Phantom* and *Les Misérables*. The novel, by Victor Hugo, opens with a vagabond curled up on a stone bench on a desolate French street corner. His disheveled appearance makes him seem dangerous and causes the townspeople, from whom he sought food and shelter, to snub him. Finally, he slumps over in dejection—until a passerby points to a place where he can find refuge.

He goes to the door and knocks. The homeowner, the town's bishop, is startled by the late-night visitation but invites him in and listens to his story. The vagabond's name is Jean Valjean, and he reveals that he is a recently released convict, marked by the authorities as dangerous. Even so, the bishop welcomes him into his home and serves him dinner.

Later, in the middle of the night, despite the bishop's kindness—Valjean double-crosses him. Valjean remembers the sparkling silver spoon he used to eat his soup at dinner and sneaks to the dining room to steal the bishop's valuable silverware. The clanking of metal arouses the bishop, who rises to inspect the clattering below. When they meet face to face, Valjean strikes the bishop, leaving him unconscious, and escapes with a heavy knapsack of silver.

The following morning the bishop's servant laments the loss of her silver, but the bishop seems unbothered, telling the servant, "So we'll use wooden spoons. I don't want to hear anything more about it."

Moments later, authorities appear at the bishop's manor with the stolen silver and Valjean handcuffed.

Looking deeply into the thief's eyes, the bishop says, "I'm very angry with you, Jean Valjean." Turning toward the authorities, he asks, "Didn't he tell you he was our guest?"

"Oh, yes," replies the chief authority, "after we searched his knapsack and found all this silver. He claimed that you gave it to him."

Stooping in shame, Valjean expects the bishop to indict him. A new prison sentence surely awaits him.

But the bishop says, "Yes. Of course, I gave him the silverware." Then, looking intently at Valjean he asks, "But why didn't you take the candlesticks? That was very foolish. They're worth at least 2,000 francs. Why did you leave them? Did you forget to take them?"

The bishop orders his servant to hurry and fetch the candlesticks.

The authorities stand dumbfounded. They ask, "Are you saying he told us the *truth*?"

The bishop replies, "Of course. Thank you for bringing him back. I'm very relieved."

The authorities immediately release Valjean, who is shocked by the turn of events, and the bishop places the retrieved candlesticks into Valjean's knapsack.

Once the authorities leave, the bishop drops the heavy bag of silver at Valjean's feet. After drawing back Valjean's hood—which was cloaking his guilty face—the bishop sternly looks him in the eyes and orders Valjean, "Don't forget - don't ever forget you've promised to become a new man."

Valjean, trembling, makes the promise and with utter humility asks, "Why are you doing this?"

The bishop places a hand on Valjean's shoulders, making the sign of the cross over him as an act of blessing. The world-famous musical

of the same name, puts the bishop's words to Valjean this way:
> *"But remember this, my brother*
> *See in this some higher plan*
> *You must use this precious silver*
> *To become an honest man*
> *By the witness of the martyrs*
> *By the Passion and the Blood*
> *God has raised you out of darkness*
> *I have bought your soul for God!"*

***

What do the three stories above have in common?

They all reflect the *wholehearted hospitality of God.*

A God Who welcomes us as sinners – buying us back with the ransom of His Son's blood. A God Who readies a homecoming for you, one day. A God Who is preparing the greatest wholehearted welcome of all time – at the Resurrection of the Dead and the Life of the World to come. A Glorious Day when, as J.R.R. Tolkien once wrote, "Everything sad will become un-true."[iii]

As we've traveled the road of welcome together, one word besides 'welcome' that I hope you'll remember is: *relationships*. Relationships and welcome are some of the most central parts of the Bible - in particular, restoring relationships through Jesus. In the Garden of Eden, we hear that most tragic question of God to Adam and Eve, 'Where are you?' Jesus is the answer to God's question—He will be the One Who seeks, Who finds, Who restores, Who welcomes us—ultimately restoring mankind through His own suffering, death and resurrection.

As we've seen, the Early Church community, built on Christ, was living out relationships and welcome better than any other community on earth. The key difference for them was life was more than just the Early Church *being together*—the difference was in how they related life to *each other* and to their *world* – living out a welcome of deep relationships *centered* in Christ.

This restored relationship in Jesus changed how the Early Church saw people around them — not as a means to an end, like the Romans often viewed people, or how the Jewish communities viewed Gentile people, as a people to be avoided or separate from. The Early Church saw people—*everyone*—as someone for whom their *Savior died*. They embraced *everyone*. No agendas. No hidden motives. Just a humble welcome from an open heart, trusting the Holy Spirit to add to their numbers, when and how He saw fit.

That kind of deep welcome, with God leading the way, exploded into a worldwide movement that would live to see the mighty Roman Empire itself crumble into dust.

This movement of wholehearted welcome would later call on God's people to build hospitals (which, not coincidentally, is the root word for 'hospitality'), provide assistance for the poor, care for the widow, the orphan and the unborn, formalize education, topple dictatorships without firing a shot, advance equality for all races and welcome anyone and everyone into the homes and lives of the faithful.

This kind of wholehearted welcome, filled with the love and grace of Jesus, created environments that were so compelling that as a result, '…the Lord added to their number day by day those who were being saved.' (Acts 2:47) Hospitality, as God alone can give it, has little to do with *entertaining* and everything to do with a *state of being*—God's people resting in Him and in turn, offering that same rest to others.

What incredible change might take place among God's people today, if we 'got back to basics' as His redeemed? What if we carried the Gospel torch passed to us from the Early Church—and saw everyone we encountered as if we were looking at *Jesus*? How many 'Jean Valjeans' do we encounter every day—who need a glimpse of God's Grace through His People?

God's Word offers something better amid our disconnected and distracted lives—a simple, yet radical life-giving vehicle to wholeheartedly welcome others—to point them to the fullness of life in Christ, by welcoming them into our *lives*.

I got a great reminder of that, once.

I had called up a member of my congregation to schedule a home visit with her. She told me, "Pastor, whenever it's convenient for you, just come on by." When I shared that I didn't want to inconvenience her, she insisted any time was fine to see her. I jokingly replied, "Well, I at least wanted to give you a heads up so you could make the living room just the way you like it before I come over." The faithful saint replied, "If you want to see *me* – you're welcome any time. If you want to see *my house* – make an appointment."

That, my friends, is a lady who knows the heart of God and what a wholehearted welcome is all about.

It's easier to wholeheartedly welcome *others*—when we realize just how much *we've* been welcomed by God. I pray this book has helped in that realization. We know that God has kept His promises through His Son, and so we trust that He will keep His promise to one Day return in Glory. "For all the promises of God find their Yes in Him. That is why it is through Him that we utter our Amen to God for His glory." (2 Corinthians 1:20)

And what a homecoming—what a *wholehearted welcome*—it will be, in Glory!

But until then, God has called us to welcome others, as He has welcomed us. "For we are his workmanship, created in Christ Jesus for good works, which God prepared beforehand, that we should walk in them." (Ephesians 2:10)

In that realization, we will celebrate a homecoming unlike anything we've imagined—and live a wholehearted welcome for others that we never thought possible.

Some years ago, I came across a quote by Madeleine L'Engle, whose words will always remain with me: "We do not draw people to Christ by loudly discrediting what they believe, by telling them how wrong they are and how right we are, but by showing them a light that is so lovely that they want with all their hearts to know the source of it."[112]

One verse of Scripture that has continually jumped out at me, over the years is: "I planted, Apollos watered, but God gave the increase." (1 Corinthians 3:6) I can trust God's plan that He has a firm grip on the timeline of eternity. He has placed you on this earth for such a time as this, to be His *demonstrator of the Gospel*, through listening to people, welcoming them, showing mercy and loving them as He loves. God, in His own time, through the power of the Holy Spirit will lead those He calls to His side in Christ.

Let Him do the saving.

Let us do the welcoming.

God may call you to engage one person for a period of time only to plant the seed of His Gospel through works of mercy and service. He might then call another to take your place and to water that seed. And in His perfect timing, He may grant the increase through another person. As His forgiven child, we are incredibly freed to know our commission is simply to *love*, to *welcome* and to *relate* to those He places in our path.

No agendas.

No 'notches in the Jesus belt'.

Just mercy and grace, sharing wholehearted hospitality with people in a brokenhearted world.

A hospitality that looks and sounds - *a lot like Jesus*.

And that calls on you and me to cast aside the world's notions of 'entertaining' and embrace God's heart for welcome.

First, in our families—then, in our world.

My prayer is that our lives would be a *testament to welcome*—a welcome that God gives us in Christ. Welcoming one another in our families, our neighborhoods and in our church families.

A *unique welcome* that echoes the words and deeds of the saints who have gone on before us.

A *deeper welcome*, where God's people entrust themselves to the great welcome to come, in our Savior.

May that be our hope, as "Here, we rest in God", until Jesus *wholeheartedly welcomes* you and me—one Day, in Glory—forever and ever!

Until that great Day…

Welcome to the adventure - of *welcome*!

Soli Deo Gloria! Amen!

> For all the saints who from their labors rest,
> Who Thee by faith before the world confess,
> Thy name, O Jesus, be forever blest,
> Alleluia! Alleluia!
>
> Thou wast their Rock, their Fortress, and their Might;
> Thou, Lord, their Captain in the well-fought fight;
> Thou, in the darkness drear, their one true Light.
> Alleluia! Alleluia!
>
> Oh, may Thy soldiers, faithful, true and bold,
> Fight as the saints who nobly fought of old
> And win with them the victor's crown of gold.
> Alleluia! Alleluia!
>
> O blest communion, fellowship divine,
> We feebly struggle, they in glory shine;

Yet all are one in Thee, for all are Thine.
Alleluia! Alleluia!

And when the fight is fierce, the warfare long,
Steals on the ear the distant triumph song,
And hearts are brave again, and arms are strong.
Alleluia! Alleluia!

But, lo, there breaks a yet more glorious day;
The saints triumphant rise in bright array;
The King of Glory passes on His way.
Alleluia! Alleluia!

From earth's wide bounds, from ocean's farthest coast,
Through gates of pearl streams in the countless host,
Singing to Father, Son, and Holy Ghost,
Alleluia! Alleluia!

The golden evening brightens in the west;
Soon, soon, to faithful warriors cometh rest.
Sweet is the calm of Paradise the blest.
Alleluia! Alleluia!

—Lutheran Service Book
677, public domain

Closing Prayer: *Lord, as we look back over our lives, we find Your constant welcome to us – first in Yourself and then in Your Son. Give us a heart of welcome, that echoes Your heart for us. Help us to keep that Gospel truth in front of us, as we look even further in faith, to the Great Day when we will find our eternal rest and welcome in You. Amen*

NOTES
Discussion Starters

WHOLEHEARTED WELCOME

WHOLEHEARTED WELCOME

ENDNOTES

CHAPTER 1

1 S. Lock, "Revenue of the U.S. Hotel Industry 2001–2018," Statista, October 25, 2019, https://www.statista.com/statistics/245841/total-revenue-of-the-us-hotel-industry.

2 Biography.com editors, "Martha Stewart Biography," Biography, April 16, 2019, https://www.biography.com/people/martha-stewart-9542234.

3 Martha Stewart, "Entertaining," November 2019, https://www.marthastewart.com/1505862/entertaining.

4 Martha Stewart, Entertaining (New York: Clarkson Potter, 1982), 15.

5 Martin Luther, *Luther's Small Catechism, with Explanation* (St. Louis: Concordia, 2017), 133.

CHAPTER 3

6 S Rev. Dr. Scott Rische, "Mission Built on a Movement" (paper presented at The Pastoral Leadership Institute, Omaha, NE, April 12, 2013).

7 Robert Kolb and Timothy J. Wengert, eds, *The Book of Concord: The Confessions of the Evangelical Lutheran Church* (Minneapolis, MN: Fortress, 2000), 277–78.

8 Gen. 1:31a "And God saw everything that he had made, and behold, it was very good."

9 John 1:1 "In the beginning was the Word, and the Word was with God, and the Word was God."

10 Gen. 2:15 "The LORD God took the man and put him in the Garden of Eden to work it and keep it."

11 Gen. 2:21–22 "So the LORD God caused a deep sleep to fall upon the man, and while he slept took one of his ribs and closed up its place with flesh. And the rib that the LORD God had taken from the man he made into a woman and brought her to the man."

12 For further reading, see the communal relationship of God to mankind through the Holy Trinity and the Incarnation in Luke 3:21–22, John 1:14, John 14:16–17, Eph. 4:4–6 and Col. 1:15–17, to name a few.

13 Gen. 3:6–8 "So when the woman saw that the tree was good for food, and that it was a delight to the eyes, and that the tree was to be desired to make one wise, she took of its fruit and ate, and she also gave some to her husband who was with her, and he ate. Then the eyes of both were opened, and they knew that they were naked. And they sewed fig leaves together and made themselves loincloths."

14 Gen. 3:9 "But the LORD God called to the man and said to him, 'Where are you?'"

15 Gen. 3:12–13; 16–17.

16 Rom. 5:8 "but God shows his love for us in that while we were still sinners, Christ died for us."

17 One of many examples reflecting this narrative is found in Deut. 7:7–8 "It was not because you were more in number than any other people that the LORD set his love on you and chose you, for you were the fewest of all peoples, but it is because the LORD loves you and is keeping the oath that he swore to your fathers, that the LORD has brought you out with a mighty hand and redeemed you from the house of slavery, from the hand of Pharaoh king of Egypt."

18 Micah 5:2–5 "But you, O Bethlehem Ephrathah, who are too little to be among the clans of Judah, from you shall come forth for me one who is to be ruler in Israel, whose coming forth is from of old, from ancient days. Therefore, he shall give them up until the time when she who is in labor has given birth; then the rest of his brothers shall return to the people of Israel. And he shall stand and shepherd his flock in the strength of the LORD, in the majesty of the name of the LORD his God. And they shall dwell secure, for now he shall be great to the ends of the earth. And he shall be their peace."

19 Acts 2:42–47.

20 Gen. 12:1–3.

21 Exod. 19:4–6, emphasis mine.

22 Lev. 19:34, emphasis mine.

23 Deut. 10:19, emphasis mine.

24 1 Kings 8:41–43.

25 Acts 21:27–32 "The Court of the Gentiles was the outermost court in the Jerusalem Temple during the time of Jesus. No Gentile could proceed any further into the inner Temple areas, and even Roman citizenship did not protect a Gentile who broke this law. It was for this alleged crime that St. Paul was attacked and nearly beaten to death by an angry crowd during his last visit to Jerusalem."

26 Isa. 56:3–8, emphasis mine.

27 Isa. 19:23–25, emphasis mine.

28 Zech. 8:20–23, emphasis mine.

29 Luke 2:10–11,15, emphasis mine.

30 Chad Ashby, "Hospitality is War," (Feb 28, 2017). Biblestudytools.com

CHAPTER 5

31 Keven O'Gorman, "Modern Hospitality: Lessons from the Past," Journal of Hospitality and

Tourism Management 12, no. 2 (August 2005): 1–11.

32 Luke 10:25–37.

33 On a recent trip to Israel, we mapped out the terrain of where the setting for this parable would likely have taken place. The path the typical traveler would have taken could be traced from Jerusalem to Jericho, leading along the edge of a steep cliff where outcroppings could hide bandits all along the path. When Jesus taught this parable, very likely the hearers knew and understood the dangers that the lone traveler faced. While travelers depended upon the hospitality of others– in this case, what makes the parable so scandalous was that hospitality is offered by a Samaritan enemy of the Israelites. Rance Settle, May 2015, Personal Notes from Israel, Israeli Museum, Haifa, Israel.

34 Gen. 19:8.

35 John 2:1–12.

36 Rance Settle, Personal Notes from Israel, May 2015.

37 Matt. 10:11; Mark 6:10; Luke 9:4; Luke 10:7–8 all have similar instructions by Jesus to the disciples not only to enter the homes of a person who welcomes them but also to stay for days if allowed.

38 Matt. 22:1–10; Luke 14:15–24.

39 Luke 15:22–32.

40 Luke 22:24–30, especially vs. 27.

41 Rev. 19:6–9.

42 Luke 7:1–10 and 7:36–50 serve as bookends of hospitality to the neighbor, in particular, of a Centurion and a 'sinful woman', both outcasts in the eyes of the Jews, who are welcomed by Jesus into the kingdom.

43 Luke 7:44–47.

44 Luke 10:38–42.

45 Acts 16:14–15, 40.

46 Heb. 13:2.

47 Gen. 19:1–3.

48 Rev. 3:20.

49 Matt. 19:19.

50 1 John 4:19.

51 Bonhoeffer, *Life Together*, 21.

52 Eric Metaxas, *Bonhoeffer: Pastor, Martyr, Prophet, Spy,* (Nashville: Thomas Nelson, 2011), 246–78.

53 Bonhoeffer, *Life Together*, 21.

54 "Then where the ministry of listening, active helpfulness, and bearing with others is faithfully performed, the ultimate and highest service can also be rendered, namely, the ministry of the Word of God." Bonhoeffer, Life Together, 108.

55 Matt. 9: 37–38 "Then he said to his disciples, 'The harvest is plentiful, but the laborers are few; therefore pray earnestly to the Lord of the harvest to send out laborers into his harvest.'" See also 1 Cor. 3:6–8 "I planted, Apollos watered, but God gave the growth. So neither he who plants nor he who waters is anything, but only God who gives the growth. He who plants and he who waters are one, and each will receive his wages according to his labor."

CHAPTER 7

56 Andrew E. Arterbury, Entertaining Angels: *Early Christian Hospitality in Its Mediterranean Setting*. (Sheffield: Sheffield Phoenix), 2005, 183–84.

57 Arterbury, *Entertaining Angels,* 183.

58 Arterbury, *Entertaining Angels,* 184.

59 Arterbury, *Entertaining Angels,* 185–86.

60 Andrew E. Arterbury, "Entertaining Angels: Hospitality in Luke and Acts," *Christian Reflection,* The Center for Christian Ethics at Baylor University, Hospitality (2007): 21.

61 Matthew Lee Anderson, Earthen Vessels: *Why Our Bodies Matter to Our Faith* (Minneapolis: Bethany House, 2011), 185.

62 Christine D. Pohl, *Making Room: Recovering Hospitality as a Christian Tradition.* (Grand Rapids, MI: Eerdmans, 1999), 28.

63 W.C. Firebaugh, *The Inns of Greece and Rome: And a History of Hospitality from the Dawn of Time to the Middle Ages* (New York: Literary Licensing, 2012), 29–30.

64 Arterbury, *Entertaining Angels,* 184.

65 Joel Elowsky, "Mercy in the Early Church," *The Lutheran Witness,* (February 2019): 7.

66 Pohl, *Making Room,* 33.

67 Pohl, *Making Room,* 29–30.

68 Elowsky, "Mercy in the Early Church," 7.

69 Elowsky, "Mercy in the Early Church," 7.

70 Elowsky, "Mercy in the Early Church," 7.

71 Darren L. Slider, ed. "Tertullian, Apology 39" Accessed December 28, 2019. http://www.logoslibrary.org/tertullian/apology/39.html.

72 David Kinnaman, and Gabe Lyons. *Unchristian: What a New Generation Really Thinks About Christianity...and Why It Matters.* (Grand Rapids, MI: Baker, 2012).

73 Kinnaman, *Unchristian,* 68–69.

74 Kinnaman, *Unchristian,* 69.

CHAPTER 9

75 Elizabeth Diffin, "Still Blessing His Name," Today's-Christian.com and http://www.youtube.com/watch?v=AplQXJqJmAs&feature=related

76 C.S. Lewis, *The Problem of Pain.*

CHAPTER 10

77 https://twitter.com/rguezcheca/status/746054238355210240

78 Leonard Sweet, *From Tablet to Table: Where Community Is Found and Identity Is Formed.* (Colorado Springs: NavPress, 2014), 9–10.

79 Stanley Hauerwas and William H. Willimon, *Resident Aliens: A Provocative Christian Assessment of Culture and Ministry for People Who Know Something Is Wrong,* Expanded 25th Anniversary Edition (Nashville: Abingdon, 2014), 14.

80 Hauerwas. Resident Aliens, 15.

81 Rebecca L. Spang, *The Invention of the Restaurant: Paris and Modern Gastronomic Cultures.* (Cambridge: Harvard University, 2000). 13.

82 Spang. *The Invention of the Restaurant,* 13.

83 Spang. *The Invention of the Restaurant,* 13.

84 Joanne Finkelstein, *Fashioning Appetite: Restaurants and the Making of Modern Identity* (New York: Columbia University, 2014), 2.

85 Andrew P. Haley, *Turning Tables: Restaurants and the Rise of the American Middle Class, 1880–1920* (Chapel Hill: The University of North Carolina, 2011), 6.

86 Haley, *Turning Tables,* 6.

87 Haley, *Turning Tables,* 6.

88 Michael Symons, "The Rise of the Restaurant and the Fate of Hospitality," *International Journal of Contemporary Hospitality Management 25,* no 2 (2013): 247.

89 Barna Group. *Households of Faith.* Barna Group Publishing, 2019.

CHAPTER 13

90 Caroline A. Westerhoff, "Boundary and Hospitality". Center for Christian Ethics, Baylor University, 2007.

91 Westerhoff, 84.

CHAPTER 15

92 Kevin G. Harney, Seismic Shifts (Zondervan, 2005), p. 200; submitted by Marshall Shelley, Wheaton, Illinois.

CHAPTER 17

93 Jean Twenge. "Does Online Social Media Lead to Social Connection or Social Disconnection?" *Journal of College and Character* 14, no. 1 (Feb 8, 2013): 12.

94 Richard J. Foster, *Celebration of Discipline: The Path to Spiritual Growth*, Special ed. (New York: Harper One, 2018), 1.

95 Matthew Behrens. "The Other Half of Hospitality." *Life on Mission*. Accessed January 16, 2019. https://mailchi.mp/535ea1579e46/the-other-half-of-hospitality?fbclid=I-wAR3qLED2THM2PwPiJctPaAUxLqFgEpi0tmR26-z22VdapUrjWM9MB2750A8.

96 Martin Luther, *Lectures on Genesis: Chapters 15–20,* name of editor of individual volume, vol. 3, *Luther's Works,* ed. Jaroslav Jan Pelikan, Hilton C. Oswald, and Helmut T. Lehmann, (St. Louis, MO: Concordia, 1999), 178.

97 William H. Lazareth, *Luther On The Christian Home: An Application Of The Social Ethics Of The Reformation* (Philadelphia: Literary Licensing, LLC, 2011), 221.

98 Lazareth. *Luther On the Christian Home,* 221.

99 Rudolf K. Markwald and Marilyn Morris Markwald, *Katharina von Bora: A Reformation Life* (St. Louis, MO: Concordia Publishing House, 2002), 129.

100 Markwald. *Katharina von Bora,* 129.

101 Markwald. *Katharina von Bora,* 89.

102 *LW,* volume 3, 178.

103 William Lazareth, *Luther on the Christian Home,* 136.

104 Lazareth. *Luther on the Christian Home,* 90.

105 *LW,* volume 3, 177.

106 Joachim Jeremias, *Jerusalem in the Time of Jesus* (Philadelphia: Fortress, 1969), 311–12.

107 R. Kent Hughes. John: *That You May Believe. Preaching the Word* (Wheaton, Crossway, 1999), 331.

108 C. S. Lewis, *Mere Christianity: A Revised and Amplified Edition, with a New Introduction, of the Three Books, Broadcast Talks, Christian Behaviour, and Beyond Personality,* harpercollins ed. (San Francisco: Harper, 2001), 132.

109 *The Lutheran Book of Prayer.* rev. 5th ed. (St. Louis, MO: Concordia, 2005), 263.

CONCLUSION

110 Lee Eclov, in the sermon "Heaven," PreachingToday.com

111 J.R.R. Tolkien, *Return of the King.*

112 Madeleine L'Engle, *Walking On Water: Reflections On Faith and Art* (New York: Convergent Books, 2016), 122.

Made in the USA
San Bernardino, CA
08 July 2020